A Day of Gladness

A Day of Gladness

The Sabbath among Jews
and Christians in Antiquity

Herold Weiss

University of South Carolina Press

© 2003 University of South Carolina

Published in Columbia, South Carolina, by the
University of South Carolina Press

Manufactured in the United States of America

07 06 05 04 03   5 4 3 2 1

Library of Congress Cataloging-in-Publication Data

Weiss, Herold, 1934–
    A day of gladness : the Sabbath among Jews and Christians
in antiquity / Herold Weiss.
        p. cm.
Includes bibliographical references (p.   ) and index.
    ISBN 1-57003-468-0
1. Sabbath—History. I. Title.
    BV111.3 .W45 2003
    263'.1—dc21   2002013379

Earlier versions of some of these chapters have appeared as:

Herold Weiss, "Paul and the Judging of Days," *Zeitschrift fur die neutestamentliche Wissenschaft und die Kunde der alteren Kirche* 86 (1995): 137–53;
Weiss, "Philo on the Sabbath," in *Heirs of the Septruaging: Philo, Hellenistic
Judaism and Early Christianity,* ed. D. Runia, D. Hay, and D. Winston, Studia
Philonica Annual 3 (Atlanta: Scholars Press, 1991), 83–105; Weiss, "The Sab-
bath among the Samaritans," *Journal for the Study of Judaism* 25 (1994):
252–73; Weiss, "The Sabbath in the Fourth Gospel," *Journal of Biblical Litera-
ture* 110 (1991): 311–21; "The Sabbath in the Pauline Corpus," in *Wisdom and
Logos: Studies in Jewish Thought in Honor of David Winston,* ed. D. Runia and G.
Sterling, Studia Philonica Annual 9 (Atlanta: Scholars Press, 1997), 287–315;
Weiss, "The Sabbath in the Synoptic Gospels," *Journal for the Study of the New
Testament* 38 (1990): 13–27; reprinted in *New Testament Backgrounds: A
Sheffield Reader,* ed. Craig A. Evans and Stanley E. Porter (Sheffield: Sheffield
Academic Press, 1997), 109–23; Weiss, "The Sabbath in the Writings of Jose-
phus," *Journal for the Study of Judaism* 29 (1998): 363–90; Weiss, "*Sabbatismos*
in the Epistle to the Hebrews," *Catholic Biblical Quarterly* 58 (1996): 674–89.

They are used here with permission.

To Aida
in celebration of our fortieth
wedding anniversary

Contents

Preface

This book traces its origin to a request by a friend, Laurence Geraty, to present a paper at a regional meeting of the Society of Biblical Literature. He suggested that I read a paper on the Sabbath in the New Testament. He thought the subject had been neglected for some time. I thought his request was motivated by the fact that he was chairman of the planning committee and there had not been many proposals coming in. After thinking about it for a week or so, I agreed to present a paper with a more narrow focus. I would read on the Sabbath in the Synoptic Gospels. Doing the research for my presentation, it became clear to me that the topic had been handled primarily in terms of other agendas and that it was worthy of careful study. The evidence needed to be viewed with a more transparent methodology. Thus, my research began to branch out to other literature from the first century C.E. Along the way, several friends made suggestions as to which areas were worthy of my attention; for example, they suggested the Samaritans. Little by little the results were presented at national meetings of SBL and eventually published in scholarly journals. When I agreed to do that first presentation, I did not envision that a few years later I would have published eight articles on the Sabbath. By then it was clear that what was needed was a book that would give a clear overview of attitudes toward the Sabbath on the part of Christians and Jews for what they indicate concerning the Sabbath and what they indicate concerning the relationship of Jews and Christians during the time of their traumatic separation. I am delighted, therefore, that what started as a rather serendipitous request is culminating in the publication of this book.

Of course, this felicitous outcome owes much to the support and encouragement of many. In the first instance, I would like to thank my first department chairperson, mentor, colleague, and friend, Earle Hilgert. He has been my most faithful critic and supporter. He read early drafts of almost all these pages and offered insightful observations and much applause. Next I need to single out my colleague at Saint Mary's, Terence

Martin. He also read most of these pages and then served as an enlightening conversation partner over many memorable lunches, which usually extended well over the noon hour. Even though his field of research is not biblical studies, he is the judicious reader with the curiosity and the critical sharpness that prevented me from falling into weak arguments, and he saw implications into what I had written that had escaped me. My son Carlos also read the earliest versions of these pages. I owe to him many improvements in English usage. Besides these supporters, I wish to thank all my colleagues in the Department of Religious Studies at Saint Mary's who offered criticisms and suggestions at three of our departmental colloquia in which one or another of the chapters of this book was the topic at hand. I cannot fail to add that I was the beneficiary of two sabbaticals from Saint Mary's College, which afforded me the time to do research in the Philonic corpus, to rewrite the previously published articles, and to write the chapter on halakic Judaism together with the introduction. Of course, I am very grateful to the journals in which some of the arguments offered here first appeared for their gracious permission to reproduce them.

The good offices of wonderful colleagues and family may not have prevented the total disappearance of errors or inconsistencies. These, I am afraid, must be credited to my failures in judgment or industry. Moreover, my aim has been for my presentation to be comprehensive, if not exhaustive. A list could easily be made of materials not mentioned in this book. I would also like to express my regret that the significant monograph by Lutz Doering, *Schabbat,* came to me when my manuscript was already in the hands of editors. I can well imagine that my presentation of Sabbath halakah would have been richer had I had the opportunity to enter into conversation with Doering's work. Among other things, he presents evidence from Aramaic ostraca which, while corresponding with that of the Elephantine papyri, is quite interesting.

Finally, I would like to thank in a special way my editor at the University of South Carolina Press, Barry Blose, who saw the value of this project and conducted the tortuous process of transforming a manuscript into a book with the elegance and professionalism that one always hopes for. The book is dedicated to my wife, Aida, to whom I owe much more than this dedication can possibly convey.

A Day of Gladness

Introduction

Mythologically, the Sabbath is the capstone of creation. It consecrates the previous creative acts and integrates them as God's rest. By resting on the Sabbath and sanctifying it, God provided a window into the divine mode of being. In turn, by resting on the Sabbath humans repeat what God did in primordial time, and this reenactment places humans in touch with reality. The Sabbath rest of humans gives to their lives a significance that ordinary time cannot provide. In this way the myth anchors human existence on a transcendent plane and gives it meaning. In traditional societies, whether humans hunted, fought, sowed, harvested, ate, sang, danced, married, or died, they ritualized these activities as repetitions of what the gods had done at creation. Acts done extemporaneously, without a divine model, vanished with time. As Mircea Eliade[1] eloquently demonstrated, in traditional societies the repetition of divine archetypes is the only human activity that transcends the impermanent world of time. It is what gives social life a center. Seen within this context, the Sabbath rest, as the reenactment of a divine act, provides Jews with a cosmic center.

In their account of creation the priestly authors of the Pentateuch gave to the Sabbath the position occupied by the temple of Esagila in the *Enuma Elish,* the Babylonian creation myth. As a temple in time the Sabbath is a cosmic center where connections both with the gods above and the gods of the netherworld are possible. Sabbath observance centers the lives of Jews within a meaningful symbolic universe.[2] It is to this aspect of the Sabbath that it is possible to make a contribution by exploring the ways in which ancient Jews and Christians constructed their world of meaning. This involves an examination of the theological explanations given to its admitted significance. Ultimately it requires constructing a spectrum of views on the Sabbath that highlights the different ways it was observed and the symbolic worlds its observance reflected. In this way early Christianity and the complexities of Jewish-Christian relations in antiquity can be illumined.

That Jews did no work on the Sabbath was common knowledge in classical Rome.[3] Whether they belonged to the type of Judaism that eventually produced the Mishnah, to the Judaism that identified itself with the aristocracy that was primarily concerned with the celebrations taking place at the Jerusalem temple, to the Judaism that set itself apart as the elite who had entered into a renewed covenant with God and produced what are now known as the Dead Sea Scrolls, to the Judaism that considered itself more faithful to Moses and the traditions associated with Mount Gerizim and whose members were called Samaritans, to the hellenized Judaism of the synagogues whose exegesis found full expression in the works of the Alexandrine Aristobulos and Philo, or to the prophetic Judaism that Josephus wished to represent, all Jews centered their religious life on the Sabbath. But, even if the Sabbath was a universal distinguishing marker that set Jews apart, there was neither a theological consensus nor a unified code of Sabbath conduct among them. How to observe it and where precisely its significance resided were widely debated issues.

Jewish scholars looking at evidence about the Sabbath in the first century have been primarily concerned to show how it relates to the rabbinic halakah. These prescriptions for its observance in the Mishnah and later in the Talmud have served as the norm by which to evaluate Sabbath attitudes and conduct in evidence in first-century documents. Most researchers who have looked at the Sabbath in Philo, Josephus, the Dead Sea Scrolls, or the Gospels have taken this approach.[4] It is somewhat refreshing, therefore, to see that Robert Goldenberg's discussion of the Sabbath in Roman times considers it anachronistic to posit a "normative" Judaism for the first century, to which particular Jews may be compared. He demonstrates that time and place were significant factors in determining how Jews kept the Sabbath. Thus, he concludes that what characterized Sabbath observance in the Roman Empire was its diversity.[5]

Given the universal recognition of the Sabbath among Jews, it would seem only natural for Christians who were formed and nurtured in the Jewish religious matrix to share the same reverence for the Sabbath. Over the centuries, however, Christians have endeavored to obscure the Jewish roots of their faith and have shown some animosity toward the Sabbath. It has not been uncommon for Christians to leave the impression that Jesus and his disciples were not Jews. Christians have portrayed them as outsiders who denounced Judaism for its perverted misrepresentation of

God's will. Accordingly, they have argued that Jesus and his disciples from the very beginning had left the Jewish Sabbath behind. Ironically, at the same time they have claimed to be the true heirs to the promises made to Israel.

As a generalization, it may be said that when addressing this issue Christians have not been primarily concerned about the Sabbath. Their agenda has been to establish the origin and the significance of the Day of the Lord, Sunday. Studies of this question have been concerned with establishing on which day contemporary Christians should worship and whether or not the Sabbath rest should be part of it. Through the centuries, there has been a running debate between those who insist that the only day that can properly be called a Sabbath is the seventh day of the week, Saturday, and those who insist that the Christian Sabbath is Sunday, the first day of the week, the day of the resurrection of the Lord. These debates have been guided by the presupposition that whatever is reconstructed as the teaching of the New Testament should determine Christian faith and practice.

Those who wish to show that the sanctity of the Sabbath has not been transferred to Sunday and those who insist that it has build their arguments on the supposed silence the New Testament keeps about this question. Since the New Testament does not order the change, it is unwarranted, say the Saturday Sabbatarians. Those who give Sunday the quality of sabbatical rest counter that since the New Testament does not endorse the Jewish Sabbath, the church felt free to rescue the "spiritual" values of the Sabbath by transferring them to the Lord's Day. These debates have appealed to Jesus' intentions in his Sabbath healings as crucial evidence. Then, the question becomes whether or not, by means of his healings, Jesus had abolished the Jewish Sabbath. The present work seeks not to get drawn into these fruitless arguments. The focus here is on the Sabbath, not Sunday or the Lord's Day. The explicit aim of this study is to take a fresh look at the evidence and to reconstruct a more reliable picture of the way in which Christians in particular related to the Sabbath. In this effort, of course, the relations between Jews and Christians come prominently into view.

The landmark study on the question of the Christian day of worship has been Willi Rordorf's *Sunday*. His is the first study to use tradition criticism in order to trace the development of Sunday worship within early

Christianity.[6] His findings have been succinctly summarized with a catch phrase that, while doing an injustice to his full study, manages to signal in the right direction. According to it, while in the Old Testament the Sabbath came in as a day of rest and in time became a day of worship, in the New Testament Sunday began as a day of worship and in time became a day of rest. Rordorf sees Jesus' Sabbath activities as intentional provocations by means of which he challenged not only the legalistic strictures of the oral law but the validity of the written law itself. His disregard for the law was based on his messianic self-consciousness. Thus, his Sabbath violations reveal his messianic self-consciousness.

Jesus' radical abolition of the Sabbath law was one of the factors creating violent opposition to his ministry. Since this was not part of the charges made against him at his trial, however, Rordorf thinks that on this issue he must have been able to explain himself to the satisfaction of the authorities. Still, his provocative law-breaking left the early Christian church with a major problem because the Palestinian church was essentially Jewish. Providentially, especially under the influence of Paul, the early church read correctly Jesus' Sabbath provocations and gave them the messianic significance Jesus had intended. In this way, while Sunday gatherings to break bread together were initially commemorations of the resurrection, eventually the significance of the Sabbath rest was assigned to them once it was fully recognized that the Risen Lord was Lord of the Sabbath. Early church tradition thus built on the Jesus tradition that saw his Sabbath activities as messianic pronouncements. In other words, the Christian observance of Sunday has its origin in the messianic self-consciousness of Jesus, even if later it transformed itself into a day of rest under Jewish Christian pressures.

Rordorf's reconstruction has been challenged. For example, Samuele Bacchiocchi argues that Jesus did not abolish the Sabbath, which after all is embedded in the Ten Commandments. Besides, there is no evidence suggesting that Christians were meeting for worship on Sundays. On the contrary, Bacchiocchi insists, Jesus gave the Sabbath even greater significance than that accorded it by his contemporaries, and the authors of the New Testament follow his lead.[7] This study, however, is seriously flawed by its uncritical methodology. Bacchiocchi's agenda guides his positivistic reading of the Gospels. He claims that the new quest of the historical Jesus has reinvested the Gospels with the historical value that form and redaction criticism had taken away from them. This, however, is not the case. A serious reading of the gospel pericopes cannot avoid taking into account what source, form, and redaction criticism have contributed to our understanding of the Jesus traditions. In reference to Bacchiocchi's second point, even if it is true that in 1 Corinthians 11 Paul does not link the celebration of the Lord's Supper with the Lord's Day, and in Acts 20:7 the author does not identify the congregational meal eaten on the first day of the week as the Lord's Supper, one cannot ignore that Acts 20:7 does say that the disciples had "come together" to "break bread." It is rather disingenuous to argue that this was a social farewell party for Paul that had nothing to do with regular Sunday gatherings to break bread together. The same is true of the Pauline instruction to set aside monies for the poor in Jerusalem on Sundays (1 Cor 16:1), so that when he came by to pick up the collection the fund-raising had already been done. There is no hint that this activity was to be performed independently and privately by each Christian at home.

There has also been a reaction against Rordorf by those who wish to see Christian beginnings in terms of a clearly visible progression guided by divine providence according to a dispensationalist scheme. The contributors to *From Sabbath to Lord's Day*, wishing to defend the legitimacy of the Lord's Day, are engaged in a polemic against Bacchiocchi.[8] In agreement with Bacchiocchi, however, they also disagree with Rordorf's claim that Jesus abolished the Jewish Sabbath and declared it obsolete. According to Donald A. Carson, Jesus and his disciples did not break the Mosaic Sabbath legislation, which only enjoined the cessation from habitual daily work. Rather, their conduct highlighted the original divine intentions in the giving of the law and the covenant. The characterization of Sunday as a day of rest, then, did not come, as Rordorf argued, as the result of conservative pressures applied by Jewish Christians. Rather, it came about according to the divine scheme of things. When reconstructing this history one has to be careful to follow closely the dynamic continuities and discontinuities in the covenantal divine structure. The problem with Saturday Sabbatarianism and the ancient rabbis who produced the halakah, according to these authors, is that both detach the concepts of covenant and law from their historical bases and transform Scripture into a timeless code book. That some of the early Christians may have observed the Sabbath is accounted for by the fact that given the "veiled nature of Jesus' ministry" it took some time before they worked out the full implications of Jesus' introduction of the new age.[9] Ultimately, it must be recognized that Sunday is not a "holy" day, neither is it a "feast" day. There was no "transferal" of sabbatical qualities from Saturday to Sunday. What needs to be taken into account are the covenantal discontinuities.

Both Bacchiocchi and the contributors to *From Sabbath to Lord's Day* agree that the main problem at the time of Jesus was the way in which the Jews had perverted the divine gift of the Sabbath with their legalistic casuistry. They had been building a hedge about the Sabbath that was not part of God's original intention. How these authors came to know God's original intentions, of course, they do not reveal. The difference between them resides in their understanding of God's original intentions. Bacchiocchi argues for a more spiritual and "Christ-centered" observance of the seventh day. The contributors to *From Sabbath to Lord's Day* argue for the observance of the Lord's Day as the Christian day of worship. Rest contributes to, but is not constitutive of, the worship to be conducted in it. According to them, Christians experience a redemptive, humanitarian, liberating rest every day of their lives. It is not particularly a Sunday experience.

Worthy of note in this connection is the recent pastoral letter of John Paul II which asks of Catholics a more faithful observance of the Lord's Day. Unlike previous official statements, which appealed to the authority of the church to transfer the sanctity of the seventh day to the first day of the week, in *Dies domini* the pope bases his argument squarely on Christ's resurrection on Sunday. Early Christians instituted it as their distinctive day of worship as a weekly Easter. The pope goes on to point out, however, that to have a "deeper understanding" of the significance of Sunday one must take into account the "Plan of God" in a "theology of the Sabbath" found in the Old Testament. Rather than to see discontinuity, as the contributors to Carson's volume do, the pope sees an essential continuity in a Sunday theology of rest. Christian Sunday observance, according to him, must be sabbatical.

What these recent presentations of the Sabbath among the early Christians have in common is that they base their case on appeals to Jesus' messianic self-consciousness or God's intentions as evident in God's plan, to which, of course, there are no references in the ancient documents. It is not possible to deduce from the stories of healings or the walk by a wheat field what Jesus' theology of the Sabbath may have been. This would be so even if one were certain that the stories are essentially historical. The evidence, however, points out that the stories are essentially traditional and that the dialogues in them were created in order to have something relevant to say in the context of later debates.

Gospel studies that critically examine the evidence have demonstrated the difficulties encountered by anyone seeking to understand Jesus within a historical horizon. They have shown that Jesus was a good Jew who was involved in internal religious reform among his people. This means that as he called for a more radical obedience he was not standing against the law. Just as it is impossible to say exactly what instructions, if any, he gave concerning the Sabbath, it is also impossible to picture him as one who declared the Sabbath commandment obsolete. Most scholars today would agree with Paula Fredriksen to the effect that during his lifetime Jesus did not publicly teach against the law.[10] In the words of Gerd Theissen, "As for the Sabbath conflicts, . . . he remains within the framework of Jewish discussion of the Sabbath."[11] Taking this insight seriously, the present study does not seek to reconstruct Jesus' position on the Sabbath. Neither does it appeal to his self-consciousness or to God's intentions as clues to an inquiry of this question. It concentrates on careful readings of the relevant texts in order to understand what they have to say about the Sabbath.

It is not difficult to see why the early Christians eventually gave to their Sunday the sanctity that belonged to the Sabbath. This transference fits a well-known cultural pattern repeatedly observed by archaeologists. More or less consistently, new rulers do not build their sanctuaries on virgin soil. Rather, they build them on top of well-recognized holy ground. In Spain, for example, it is not uncommon to find Christian churches built on top of Roman temples, Islamic mosques on top of Christian churches, and newer Christian churches inside former mosques. In the Christian calendar, pagan festivals were absorbed and only superficially transformed. The Sabbath, the most obvious holy spot, could not just be ignored and left behind. It was Christianized. On this account, over the centuries sectarian movements have repeatedly staked their claims to a purer version of Christianity on their proper regard for the Sabbath whether kept on Saturday or on Sunday.

Methodologically, it is worth following a lead suggested by Raymond E. Brown.[12] In twentieth-century scholarship, reconstructions of early Christianity have traced a line of development that is marked by geographic, linguistic, and ethnic transitions. According to this standard procedure, it is assumed that Christianity began as a Palestinian, Aramaic-speaking, Jewish phenomenon. In time Greek-speaking Jews in Palestine joined the movement. Eventually the movement became a Jewish Diaspora movement, and finally it turned into a Gentile movement. Rordorf faithfully adheres to this developmental paradigm. The experience and the theology of the early Church, which took shape in this process, informs the gospel narratives. On this account, it is difficult to determine the historical contours of the life of Jesus. The consistent application of criteria of authenticity becomes critical. This, however, is rather problematic. Rordorf, like all those trying to reconstruct the historical Jesus, stumbles trying to keep separate theory from practice, and the social from the religious significance of the Sabbath. His basic problem, however, is his strict adherence to a model of Christian development along linguistic, geographic, and religious lines. His claim that Gentile Christianity never observed the Sabbath is open to serious questions. Rordorf resorts to unconvincing conjectures in order to account for the fact that at the end of the second century there were Sabbath-keeping Gentiles. Brown's alternative grid for mapping early Christianity seems a helpful corrective. In Brown's estimation the differentiation between Jews and Gentiles, or between Palestinian Aramaic-speaking and Diaspora Greek-speaking Jews within early Christianity is not as telling as the attitude these Christians had toward four basic Jewish markers:

- Did they insist on full compliance with the Mosaic law, including circumcision?

- Did they follow some Mosaic observances, but did not insist on circumcision?

- Did they voluntarily participate in temple rituals, but not require any legal observances?

- Did they consider both the law and the temple of no abiding significance?

Unaccountably, Brown does not give the Sabbath a role as a marker in his grid. Leaving it as an undifferentiated item of the Mosaic law does not do justice to its prominence. It is time to rectify this relegation of the

Sabbath to a minor role. As already argued, the Sabbath is central to the religious life of Jews, and as such it was also a most significant feature of the early Christian symbolic universe.

Brown's insight that Gentile converts to Christianity may have been more strongly committed to Jewish institutions than some Jews who were born into the faith is quite valid. Greek-speaking Christians of Gentile origin may have been more traditionally attached to Sabbath observance than some Jewish Christians from Palestine. On the other hand, Palestinian Aramaic-speaking Jews may have had a rather spiritual or eschatological understanding of the Sabbath. This has important methodological implications. A text with a positive view of the Sabbath need not be considered the product of a Judaizing author. Not prejudging the time and authorship of a text leaves it open to more possibilities. As a result, one may end up with a more faithful reconstruction of the first-century Christian landscape, enabling one to paint a spectrum of both Jewish and early Christian views on the Sabbath truer to the various views held.

Not all early Christians shared a common symbolic universe. Apocalypticism, for example, was a rather widely held worldview among Jews and Christians of the first century. But there was not much agreement among them in the details of their apocalyptic conceptions. That is one of the reasons that modern scholars studying apocalypticism in the biblical materials have had considerable difficulties defining the term. Since views of the Sabbath are inextricably linked to cosmology, a study of these views proves quite helpful in the differentiation of nuanced cosmological variations in the symbolic universes that framed the social context for life. Thus, attention to the Sabbath in Paul, the Epistle to the Hebrews, and Barnabas makes it possible to understand better the significant variations in their apocalyptic worlds. Moreover, discovering the universes informing the pictures of Jesus in the Gospels reveals cosmological visions that are quite distinct. Thus, a clearer delineation of views on the Sabbath held by the early Christians proves helpful in understanding their symbolic universes.

1

The Sabbath in Early Judaism

The origins of the Sabbath are unavailable to us due to the lack of adequate sources. The Babylonian creation myth, the *Enuma Elish,* already divides the lunar month into four seven-day periods, and in the *Atra-Hasis Epic* the god Enki, who can cleanse everything, says: "On the first, seventh, and fifteenth day of the month I will make a purifying bath."[1] *Sappatu* or *sabbatu* (the Akkadian sign may be transliterated either as *p* or *b*) is the day when human beings are created as the servants of the gods by means of a divine sacrifice. The relationship of the Babylonian *sabbatu* to the biblical Sabbath has been a matter of some debate, but the connection that both days have to the creation of human beings is widely recognized. Therefore, it has been suggested that the introduction of a day of rest at the end of every week had to do with humane considerations toward animals and laborers. Already at the time of the monarchy there were popular celebrations involving the cessation from agricultural labor.[2] This is evident in the earlier version of the fourth commandment, which offers as a rationale for the cessation from work the liberating power of God at the Exodus, rather than God's rest at the completion of creation. Deuteronomy 5 admonishes to remember that the Israelites had been in Egypt, where as slaves they had done harsh labor. When enjoying rest in the land of Canaan, they should allow their workers to enjoy rest too. With the destruction of the first temple, the Jews gave the Sabbath religious significance during the Babylonian exile in the sixth century B.C.E. At this time it became a central covenantal sign marking them as God's chosen people.[3] This was one of the most significant contributions to the development of the religion of Israel made by the prophet Ezekiel and the priestly authors and editors of the Pentateuch.

A Jewish settlement in a small island on the Nile not too distant from the first cataract, whose origins may be related to the exile, has left evidence of Sabbath observance from the fifth century B.C.E. Ostraca from Elephantine record Sabbath concerns in reference to the shipping and the delivery of goods. Particularly convincing is the threat issued by an enterprising shipper to Islah, apparently a woman business agent. He threatens her with death if she fails to meet the boat carrying fresh vegetables, which will arrive on the Sabbath. It would appear that the threat was aimed at overcoming the scruples Islah may have had against the performance of such a task on the Sabbath day.[4] Of interest also is the appearance of a new name for Jewish boys, *Sabbathai*. It became one of the most popular in Persian times.[5] The name also appears in papyri found at Elephantine.[6] The appearance of the name and its popularity until the first century B.C.E. may represent the desire of parents to proclaim their identity in terms of an institution that served as a sociological marker. Once that allegiance no longer needed to be paraded, the name rapidly lost its popularity.

By Hasmonean and Roman times, the Sabbath had acquired a central position in the self-consciousness of Jews everywhere in the Diaspora. It was also one of the few things about the Jews that Gentiles knew.[7] As such, it had become a clear marker in the boundary line that separated Jews and Gentiles. Among Jews it was understood that the process of assimilation into the stronger surrounding cultures would begin with neglect of some aspect of Sabbath observance. They seem to have had their own domino theory. The collapse of the nation would begin with forgetfulness of the Sabbath.[8] On the other hand, there was the notion that Israel needed to keep all the commandments as a condition for the Messiah to come. It became accepted, however, that "the observance of the Sabbath outweighs all the commandments of the Torah."[9] Therefore, when all of Israel would "remember" the Sabbath as it should, the Messiah would come and Israel would be redeemed immediately.[10] Thus, Rabbi Levi said, "If Israel kept the Sabbath properly even for one day, the Son of David would come. Why? Because it is equivalent to all the commandments."[11] This notion is also affirmed in the following dialogue between God and Israel: "O my people, behold, you have annulled all the Ten Commandments. Nevertheless, if you kept one Commandment . . . I would have forgiven you. And which Commandment is this? It is the Commandment concerning the Sabbath day."[12] It would appear, then, that perfect observance of the Sabbath commandment on the part of Israel would result in all sins being forgiven and, therefore, in the coming of the Messiah. On the other hand, if an individual would just keep one Sabbath properly, "it is counted to him as if he had observed all the Sabbaths from the day that God created

His world to the time of the resurrection of the dead."[13] These sayings demonstrate recognition both of the great importance of the Sabbath commandment and of the difficulty of observing it.

In his book *The Sabbath,*[14] Abraham Heschel retells a number of anecdotes about the way in which ancient rabbis emphasized the joy associated with the Sabbath day. Some of the anecdotes recorded by Heschel tell of rabbis who anticipated the coming of the Sabbath with the same expectations a bride has when entering the nuptial chamber. In preparation, of course, she anoints, adorns, and dresses herself appropriately. This meant that the Sabbath was the occasion when God and his bride, Israel, enjoyed intimacy. At times the metaphor was shifted to make the Sabbath Israel's bride, most worthy of devotion and faithfulness. If the Sabbath was the people's bride, of course, the bridegroom had to groom himself properly and be ready to entertain her as she deserved. This metaphor was extended to point out that Gentiles who kept the Sabbath were in fact interlopers in the bridal chamber. As Sabbath keepers they were adulterers, and should be put to death.[15] The Sabbath had been given by God to Israel within a discrete covenantal arrangement. As such it was Israel's sign of unique identity. It marked the nation as God's chosen possession.[16] The *Damascus Document,* first found in the Cairo Geniza at the turn of the twentieth century and then among the Dead Sea Scrolls, teaches that on the Sabbath Jews should not be found even in the vicinity of Gentiles.[17] In this way the Sabbath is a most effective instrument for separating insiders from outsiders.

Not all Jews in antiquity shared this point of view. The Alexandrine Aristobulus, a precursor of Philo, saw observance of the Sabbath on the part of Gentiles as a sign of its universal significance.[18] In this matter, both Philo and Josephus followed his lead.[19] They argued that Gentile observance of the Sabbath, which according to them was already widely in evidence, was a powerful argument for the superiority of the revelation received by the mediation of Moses, the greatest lawgiver among human beings.

Since the two records of the commandment in the Pentateuch do not agree on the terminology calling attention to the Sabbath, the discrepancy gave the rabbis the opportunity to expand on its significance. While Exodus 20:8 reads "remember," Deuteronomy 5:12 says "observe." The rabbis explained that the two words "were pronounced in a single utterance—an utterance which the mouth cannot utter, nor the ear hear."[20] In this way the very giving of the commandment was shrouded in impenetrable mystery, and the commandment itself gained in sacredness. As it became more and more central to the life of Judaism, the Sabbath acquired the holiness conferred in previous times only to the temple. This demanded a more self-conscious and explicit delineation of proper Sabbath conduct.

The biblical references to the Sabbath do not provide clear instructions as to how to "remember" or "observe" the Sabbath. Biblical semisilence about an issue that demanded serious attention could not be left alone. The scarcity of biblical guidance was welcomed by some who felt that the Scriptures' silence left them room in which to be comfortable on the Sabbath. Others felt that Sabbath conduct should be guided by the Torah in every possible way. To satisfy this felt need, the rabbis composed the Sabbath halakah, prescriptions for its observance. Sometime after the second Roman/Jewish war (132–135 C.E.), Rabbi Meir began to compile the existing halakah according to topics. As more of these prescriptions came to be recognized as part of the evolving oral law, they were added to Rabbi Meir's collection. Around the beginning of the third century, Rabbi Judah the Prince collated the material into what is now known as the Mishnah. It consists of 63 tractates, among which the one on the Sabbath is the largest. The rabbis were aware that their extensive Sabbath legislation was out of proportion to the biblical instructions on it. According to *Hagigah* 1:5, the laws of the Sabbath are like a mountain suspended by a hair.

The codification of this prescriptive material in the Mishnah usually does not include information as to the time or place in which the rulings were issued. Sometimes the authorial ascriptions are traditional rather than historical. It is difficult, therefore, to trace the development of Sabbath halakah among Jews from the second century B.C.E. to the second century C.E. We are on a more sure footing when reading *Jubilees* or the Qumran materials. They certainly belong to a time B.C.E.[21] Students of these materials regard the Qumran scrolls as products of people who broke with the urban elites in order to remain true to the covenant. As such, they saw themselves as the ones with whom God had established a new covenant.[22] The traditions informing their reading of the Scriptures and their intention to apply it to the details of everyday life may be traced to the same roots that nourished the Pharisaic efforts in the same direction. The Pharisees, however, remained in the city and were active in politics. It has, therefore, been argued that the covenanters' social isolation in the Judean desert, which detached them from the continuous stream of evolving halakah, may have halted the development of their views about proper Sabbath observance at a relatively early stage.[23]

Whether the Sabbath halakah found in the *Damascus Document* and in *Jubilees* represents a sectarian counterposition or a truncated stage in the development of what became the mainstream depends, to a large degree, on how one views Judaism in the second and first centuries B.C.E.[24] For there to have been sectarian opposing views, there must have been an established normative mainstream. There is no evidence to support the view that such was the case at that time. On the other hand, if there was a great variety of views it is problematic to see how one of them represents a truncated early stage of what eventually became the normative view. It would seem best, therefore, to view the situation as representing the free development of diverse halakic trajectories, even if it is to be recognized that some of them were truncated at an early stage. All these trajectories share their understanding that the Sabbath commandment is to be obeyed in the details of everyday life.

The adoption by the high priest in Jerusalem of a calendar that was popular within the Hellenistic world may have been one of the factors eventually determining what would become mainstream. This lunisolar-solar calendar had 354 days in a year, plus intercalary months as deemed necessary. It was introduced at the Jerusalem temple at the time of the Maccabean war in 167 B.C.E. The Jewish religious calendar had twelve months of thirty days plus four intercalary days, one every three months. This calendar gave the year 364 days, not quite the astronomical year of 365 days and a quarter but better than the 354-day year. It had the added advantage that with 364 days the year had exactly 52 weeks. As a result, every day of every month fell every year on the same day of the week. The yearly festivals did not wander through the days of the week, and the Sabbath did not wander through the days of the month.

The solar calendar had been in use in the early Second Temple period, as suggested by the priestly materials in the Pentateuch. Its use in cultic matters is also attested by Daniel 7:25, 2 Maccabees 6:7, and 1 Maccabees

1:59. When, after the war, the Maccabees regained control of the temple and eventually secured religious freedom, the traditionalists expected a return to the solar religious calendar. Jonathan's reaffirmation of the lunisolar-solar calendar in 150 B.C.E. drove many of them away from the temple and its feasts. According to them, the feasts were being held on the wrong day. Shemaryahu Talmon and James VanderKam think that this problem was the main reason for the withdrawal of the covenanters of Qumran to the Judean desert.[25] Philip R. Davies considers this only one of several reasons for their abandonment of Jerusalem and its temple.[26] In any case, the question of the calendar created a very serious debate as to whether the Sabbath was being observed at the right time. According to Talmon, the covenanters had two problems with the Sabbath celebrations at the temple. One was that they took place on the wrong dates since they were determined by a calendar whose origin was not in the Torah. The other was that the covenanters understood the day to begin at sunrise on Saturday and to end at sunrise on Sunday. At the temple the day started at sundown on Friday and ended at sundown on Saturday. These differences in the chronological identification of the Sabbath made it difficult for some Jews to live within the orbit of the temple at Jerusalem. This shows that among Jews controversies developed concerning the time at which the Sabbath is to be kept.

In general terms it may be said that the prescriptions of the *Damascus Document* are stricter than the extant rabbinic ones.[27] It is, therefore, striking that this text takes a most audacious stand against the death penalty, which both Exodus 35:2 and Numbers 15:35 impose on anyone who desecrates the Sabbath. By contrast *Jubilees* repeatedly points out that death is the inevitable consequence of disregarding one or another of its Sabbath prescriptions. Even Philo, who on most counts is to be considered rather open-minded, offers no objections or allegorical interpretations to the death penalty for Sabbath infractions. For their part, the Gospels accuse some Jews of wishing to kill Jesus for his Sabbath misconduct, but in the Passion stories there are no accusations of Sabbath breaking at his trial.[28]

In fact, in the extant literature there is no report of the application of capital punishment for Sabbath offenses. Later, rabbis sought to excuse the nonapplication of the law by explaining that in order for the law to apply the act of desecration had to be intentional.[29] Tractate *Shabbat* in *Mekilta* offers opposing views as to when the law applied. Some insisted that the law was to be enforced only in cases where the act had been fully completed. Others countered that "if he profanes it even for one moment he shall be put to death." In view of the continuing debate and the reiteration of the biblically mandated maximum penalty, the explicit rejection of it by the covenanters of Qumran is most admirable. Their text also provides a rationale for the nonapplication of the death penalty. The transgressor must be given a chance to make amends. This certainly does not support the notion that the Jews at Qumran were sectarian extremists.[30] On other issues, just as with this one, the Tannaitic rabbis were stricter than the covenanters.

It is difficult, however, to understand the rationale for the debates concerning the applicability of the death sentence. If the penalty was never carried out, were these purely academic exercises that had no practical significance?[31] The rabbinic sources elaborated distinctions both in reference to the act and in reference to the punishment in order to liberalize the rather harsh punishment prescribed in Scripture. Eventually three levels of punishment were recognized: a) death, b) extirpation, and c) liability for a sin offering.[32] The biblical expression "that soul shall be cut off from among his people" is rather ambiguous. It came to be understood to mean extirpation. At times it is difficult to determine what was intended by this sentence. Apparently it could mean either social ostracism or death. In the latter case, it is difficult to determine the difference between it and "that soul shall die." Social death and biological death, however, were sometimes considered synonymous. The rabbis eventually made the difference reside in the agent of death. Whereas the death penalty was applied by human authorities, extirpation was left to an act of God. They also established that the Bible prescribed extirpation for thirty-six activities.[33] How God would carry the sentence out was left unspecified. As for the liability for a sin offering, after the destruction of the temple it is difficult to determine how it could be discharged. Thus, all punishments became a bit academic. Legally, by introducing conditions to be met before the maximum penalty could be applied, there seems to have been somewhat of a crusade on the part of some rabbis for a more humane application of the law. The act of transgression had to have been intended, had to have been completed, and had to have been carried out in spite of warnings against it.[34] Even a deliberate Sabbath infraction that had not been witnessed by others could not be punished by death.[35]

Another indication that with the passage of time the rabbis endeavored to ameliorate the rather broad but also restrictive demands of the law was their elaboration of the notion of *erub*. At the time of the compilation of the Mishnah, *Erubim* is a rather sizable tractate. While *Shabbat* 14b traces the origin of the notion of *erub* to Solomon,[36] it seems to have arisen in the first century C.E. It seeks to humanize the observance of the commandment by setting limits to its power.[37] Typical examples are the arrangements that could be made in order to travel further or to have the benefits of a fire on the Sabbath.

Efforts to liberalize the scriptural text and make possible some movement on the Sabbath seem to have been the object of considerable debate among Jews. Origen, in a polemical thrust against the Jews, charges the Old Testament with demanding the performance of what is humanly impossible. Among these "impossibilities" he lists the command to stay at one's place on the Sabbath (Exod 16:29). He then reports that different Jews deal with this command differently. If it is taken literally in the strictest sense, to observe the commandment one would have to refrain from all movement. Origen names a prominent Samaritan teacher who understood the commandment in just this way.[38]

Quite early, however, there were efforts to make possible some movement, even if exactly how much was not universally agreed upon. Citing the doublet in Exodus 16:29, the rabbis said: "'Remain every man in his place.' That is, within four cubits. 'Let no man go out of his place.' That is, beyond two thousand cubits."[39] The two measurements represent efforts to establish basic limits for Sabbath movements. The four cubits have to do with the limits of one's residence when one finds himself outside the city on a Sabbath, in other words his private domain.[40] The two thousand cubits refers to the distance one could travel outside the city in the public domain. The number was extrapolated from the grants of pasture lands to the Levitical cities of refuge in Numbers 35:5, "And you shall measure, outside the city, for the east side two thousand cubits, and for the south side two thousand cubits, and for the west side two thousand cubits, and for the north side two thousand cubits, the city being in the middle." The text in Numbers, however, is confusing. Verse 4 reads, "The pasture lands of the cities, which you shall give to the Levites, shall reach from the wall of the city outward a thousand cubits all around." This gave rise to different allowable-travel-distances on the Sabbath for different Jews.

Most Jews came to agree that a Sabbath's day journey could not exceed two thousand cubits.[41] The *Damascus Document,* however, limits it to one thousand cubits. This text makes a distinction between traveling out of the city and taking an animal to pasture outside the city. The manuscripts from the Cairo Geniza and 4Q268 give one thousand cubits as the maximum distance allowed for either of these activities. 4Q270, however, does not make reference to either distance. Instead, it comments, "His holy Sabbaths are glorious festivals." 4Q265, *The Damascus Rule,* offers a more liberal ruling. This text allows the owner of an animal to take it to pasture two thousand cubits from the city. It also contradicts what the other manuscripts say in reference to helping a fellow human being who had fallen into a body of water and was in danger of drowning. Other Qumran manuscripts say that no one should try to rescue the one in jeopardy by means of a rope, a ladder, or any other instrument.[42] *The Damascus Rule* commands the passerby to throw the drowning person the end of his robe in order to pull him out by means of it.

Erubim were primarily concerned with the liberalization of Sabbath restrictions. For example, establishing a place of residence with a four cubit radius from where a person stood allowed for traveling to and from it a radius of two thousand cubits. Since the place where one had one's own food constituted one's place of residence, leaving food at proper intervals from each other would facilitate traveling longer distances on the Sabbath. Under different circumstances, a traveler caught on a Sabbath evening still some distance from home, recognizing a tree at a distance, could say, "Let my Sabbath resting place be at its root." This would make it possible for him to travel two thousand cubits to the tree and two thousand cubits from the tree, thus being able to reach home even after dark.[43]

Another way to facilitate movement was to establish a larger perimeter for one's dwelling. This could be done by means of a *shittuf,* or a partnership. In this case dwellings facing a common courtyard could become common ground for free movement by all the members of the contiguous households if each contributed something to a common dish of food placed at the center of the courtyard. This practice was particularly helpful in reference to the restrictions of carrying anything more than four cubits from one's dwelling. As it has been noted by others, what makes the halakic rules from Qumran particularly noticeable is that they seem to ignore the notion of *erub.*[44] This indicates that this halakic tool was not available at the time when *Jubilees* and the *Damascus Document* were composed, between 75–25 B.C.E. In the Judaism that emerges after the destruction of the Jerusalem temple, the Friday afternoon question "Have you prepared the *erub*?" became a weekly refrain.

In reference to the Sabbath, the rabbis are most recognized for their efforts to define what was work and, therefore, could not be done. Rather than to look at work in modern scientific or technological terms, they were interested in practical advice that could be understood and applied readily. Their interest was not in technical definitions. They valued listings. In this matter, as already stated, the Scriptures are rather laconic. Exodus 35:3 says that Moses specified, "you shall kindle no fire in all your habitations." In Exodus 16:29 he expressed the same idea both positively and negatively, "remain every man of you in his place, let no man go out of his place." Jeremiah, for his part, exhorted the people, "Do not bear a burden . . . or bring it in by the gates of Jerusalem," nor "carry a burden out of your houses" (17:19–21). Nehemiah 13:19–21 records that after the return from exile Jeremiah's exhortation was being ignored and that Nehemiah took measures not only to prevent the introduction of merchandise into the city by closing the gates on the Sabbath, but also to stop merchants from setting up shop in the vicinity outside the city gates. What is particularly significant about the texts in Jeremiah and Nehemiah, which are obviously related, is that they expand the specificity of the commandment as found in Deuteronomy and claim Sinaitic authority for their words.[45] Still, the refrain in Scripture is that on the Sabbath no work should be done. This is too broad a statement to serve as a guideline for conduct, and the activities just listed could not be understood as exhaustive, but could be quite restrictive if taken literally.

We already noted how the command to stay in one's place was liberalized. Jeremiah's injunction on the import or export of burdens into the city also created problems. It would seem that from the start it was not limited to merchandise to be sold. Thus, crossing a threshold from the private to the public domain, or vice versa, on a Sabbath required very careful considerations. The *Damascus Document* declares that one should not carry perfume on one's person while coming in or going out. A particularly important burden to be carried is an infant who is unable to walk. An infant, on the other hand, is not just a burden but a human being. The question then became who can carry the infant while crossing a threshold, the nurse?

the father?[46] In *Shabbat* 1.1 a detailed procedure is described by means of which two men may lawfully take in or out a burden on the Sabbath. In general terms, then, it may be said that the halakah demonstrates the efforts of the rabbis to find ways by which to allow the performance of activities that literalists wished to proscribe. As Robert M. Johnston observes, "The Rabbinic multiplication of rules was largely intended to make the law easier to obey, to spell out exceptions, to explain contraventions."[47]

The determination of what was work, and therefore not to be done on the Sabbath, received final rabbinic form by an appeal to the context in which the Sabbath commandment is given a more casuistic expression in Exodus 35:1–3. Here the commandment includes the judgment to fall on the offender and the prohibition to kindle a fire. Immediately following, Exodus 35:4–39:43 gives a detailed account of how the tabernacle was made according to "what the Lord had commanded" (35:4, 39:43). The description gives details of materials, measurements, and the skills needed to accomplish this task, as well as the names of the master craftsmen. From the passage the rabbis determined that there were thirty-nine types of work required for the completion of the project. Thus, they arrived at a list of the things that could not be done on the Sabbath.[48] These thirty-nine, however, came to be understood as paradigmatic, so that activities not mentioned in the biblical text eventually came to be understood as falling under one or another of those on the list. Most debates about the Sabbath involved the determination of whether or not an activity was to be included in one of the thirty-nine categories on the list. In these endeavors one of the prevailing principles was that personal benefit could not be derived from any Sabbath activity. Disagreements arose about whether one could take advantage of what in the natural or the normal course of events happens on a Sabbath. Thus, while it was recognized that one could not pluck a fruit to eat it, whether one could eat a fruit that had fallen to the ground on a Sabbath was not so clear. The same was the case with the egg a hen had laid on a Sabbath.[49]

To ensure proper observance of the Sabbath, just like the *Damascus Document* commands that Jews should not be found even near a Gentile, the rabbis made a list of things that should not be touched on the Sabbath, even when no labor was involved. These were *muktzeh.* Among them was money. The idea behind the prohibition was to avoid even the appearance of transgression. *Betzah* 5:2 gives a different list of *shebuth,* things which even though not technically "work" came to be considered as detracting from the Sabbath's sanctity. Among them are climbing a tree, swimming, clapping, and official acts such as marriage, betrothal, judging, etc. Other sources insist, however, that while human affairs are not to be conducted on the Sabbath, the affairs of heaven are quite permissible. This allowed for betrothals, or the arrangements necessary for the education of a child.[50]

Since the Scriptures also command the performance of discrete activities at specified times, conflicts inevitably arose between two scriptural commands. Typical examples were the rituals to be performed at the temple on the Sabbath, as well as the performance of circumcision on the eighth day of birth, which occasionally would fall on the Sabbath. An early tradition now found in the Gospel of John (7:19–23) appeals to the well-established rule that circumcision takes precedence over the Sabbath. This caused Rabbi Jose the Galilean to say: "Great is circumcision, for it sets aside the Sabbath, which is very important and the profanation of which is punishable by extinction."[51] Still, this did not quite settle the issue. Rabbi Eliezer and Rabbi Akiba understood differently what could be done on the Sabbath and what should be prepared before the Sabbath.[52] Given the differences, it is important to recognize, however, that the words of both prescriptions given by them were considered to be the words of God.[53]

Similarly the rabbis established, even after the temple had been destroyed, that "the offerings of the congregation override the Sabbath ... but the offerings of the individual" do not.[54] To this general rule, however, exceptions had to be made for some offerings that a priest had to offer on specified days for himself. In relation to the activities and the sacred objects in the temple, the Gospels bring up the conduct of David and his men when they were hungry and ate the bread of the presence, thus placing in tension the sacredness of the temple and the urgent need of hungry men. The example of David became useful to Christians who wished to defend certain Sabbath activities. Josephus records that while defending the temple from the Romans, John of Giscala and his men used the oil and the wine of the temple. John obviously thought that the emergency justified his action. Josephus leaves no doubt that he thought of it as a sacrilege. This desecration of the temple made Jerusalem liable to the fate of Sodom and Gomorrah.[55]

Tension between scriptural commands also surfaced in other areas. One of the unlikely candidates, among others, was sexual intercourse. On the one hand, the Lord commands that the Sabbath should be a delight (Isa 58:13), but, on the other, those engaging in intercourse could not be at rest. Besides, touching semen renders both participants impure (Lev 15:19), and, while encamped at Sinai on the occasion of the giving of the law, God commanded "come not near a woman" (Exod 19:15). Eventually, rabbinic halakah established that the bliss of conjugal ecstasy was not just permitted but almost required as part of Sabbath observance.[56] But the issue was not easily resolved and remained a matter of debate for centuries. *Jubilees* 50:8 explicitly forbids it.

Also in reference to making the Sabbath a delight, the notion developed that Sabbath meals should be specially bountiful and should include delicacies. It became specifically forbidden to mourn or to be sad on the Sabbath, and this rule applied not only to the living but also to the dead. Not even in Gehenna are crying and lamentations to be heard. As the Sabbath begins, the angel Dumah commands to those in Sheol, "Come out of Gehenna," and when it is over he orders, "Come to the house of the shadow of death and chaos."[57] In this way nowhere in the universe is mourning taking place on the Sabbath. This is beautifully illustrated also by the legend of Judith, a heroine whose exploits took place at the time of the Assyrian supremacy but gained popularity in the second century B.C.E. While mourning the death of her husband, Judith set up a tent on top of her house where she wore the garments of her widowhood and fasted in mourning. On Sabbaths, however, she stayed at home where she clothed herself splendidly and ate joyfully (Jdt 8:5–6). The Sabbath above all days is to be a day of delight. Sabbath fasting is explicitly forbidden in the *Damascus Document*, "Let no man fast voluntarily on the Sabbath" (11:4–5). *Jubilees* both prohibits fasting under penalty of death and prescribes, "They must eat and drink and enjoy themselves on this feast day" (50:12).

The rabbis also insisted that the Sabbath could not be a fast day.[58] This, of course, created tensions when the Sabbath and the Day of Atonement fell on the same day. As a day of judgment and fasting, the Day of Atonement could hardly be a delight. The rabbis used all their rhetorical skills in order to synchronize the two. But total agreements were not the norm.[59] What these debates really tried to establish was the relative importance of different realms of life. In other words, which realm had priority over another. Does the Sabbath have priority over circumcision or vice versa? Does it have priority over the activities at the temple? Is the Sabbath's delight to have precedence over the fasting required by the Day of Atonement, or the mourning required by a death in the family?

Attempts to resolve these dilemmas ensured the development of different halakic traditions within Judaism. These traditions have many things in common and many disagreements, but no recognizable strand consistently disagrees with another. The agreements and the disagreements are quite idiosyncratic. In the Mishnah the names of Hillel and Shammai became the tags with which the two main strands of tradition within rabbinic Judaism came to be identified. A baraita from the more liberalized later times says, "The Law is in accordance with Beth Hillel, but he who wishes to follow Beth Shammai may."[60] Of course, differences of opinion existed even among those who belonged to the same school or strand of thought. The Samaritans had their own way of applying the law, which in many ways was similar to the one found in the Mishnah. The same may be said of the rulings found in *Jubilees* and the *Damascus Document*. The Samaritans and the covenanters of Qumran sometimes agree between themselves and also with the Mishnah, but other times they exhibit idiosyncratic rulings. Besides these discrepancies, they also had internal differences. The Gospels make clear that within the early Christian communities there was no unified strand of halakic rulings concerning what could and what could not be done on the Sabbath, or when it had to be kept. In other words, exegesis of the few biblical texts was not under control, and the listing of the thirty-nine works that came to be understood as prohibited by the commandment did not settle the details of proper observance, particularly once they became paradigmatic abstractions.

The law is not expansive in its instructions for Sabbath rituals at the temple. For example the beginning and the end of the day was to be marked by the sound of trumpets. Whereas daily one sheep was offered at the morning and then another at the evening sacrifice, the number was doubled on the Sabbath. The temple liturgies also included singing by the Levites, and there are indications that Psalms were assigned to Sabbath worship.[61] As long as the temple functioned, however, it seems that the synagogues were not considered a substitute, an alternative, or a supplement to temple worship on the Sabbath.

New Testament scholars have more or less consistently assumed that the synagogues were places of worship before the destruction of the temple.[62] The words of Edward P. Sanders may be considered characteristic.

Speculating on the factors that contributed to the creation of synagogues, he writes,

> The practice of weekly gatherings might have begun among people who were not physically, but rather spiritually cut off from the temple—those who wanted a more informal and easily accessible form of public worship.[63]

Then, describing what public worship involved, he continues,

> In 1 Cor. 14 Paul also refers to hymns and lessons. Since his views of group worship was almost certainly influenced by the synagogue services he had attended, we may add singing to prayers and the reading and exposition of Scripture as possible synagogal activities.[64]

Particularly to be noticed is the way in which Sanders hedges his description with the words "might have begun," "almost certainly," and "possible." By making the synagogues provide a "more informal and easily accessible form of worship," Sanders suggests the synagogues did for the Jews what the mystery cults were doing for the pagans. The suggestion, however, seems gratuitous. Besides, there is no indication whatever that in 1 Corinthians 14 Paul is giving instructions for Sabbath worship.

The origins of the synagogue have proved most difficult to determine.[65] Also problematic is to know when the word refers to a group of people and when it refers to the building in which these people carried out some activities. Philo,[66] Josephus,[67] and New Testament[68] and pagan[69] authors sometimes called the synagogue "a prayer house." This function, however, was not in any way related to the Sabbath. The synagogues were such every day of the week.[70] It may have been the case that when Jews went to the synagogue on the Sabbath in order to study the law, prayers were said in connection with it. Philo and Josephus, however, describe the Sabbath gatherings as school sessions with no worship involved. This is also the purpose of the synagogue in the Theodotus Inscription, paleographically dated to before 70 C.E. In it Theodotus, the grandson and the son of rulers of the synagogue who is himself also one of the rulers, dedicates the building begun by his ancestors but completed by himself "for the reading of the Law and the teaching of the commandments."[71] He specifies that the building included an inn for those traveling from abroad, as well as an abundant water supply. It would seem quite unusual, if the synagogue were a building in which Sabbath worship was conducted, for Theodotus to have failed to point this out.

After the destruction of the temple, of course, the synagogues assumed a new role. It would seem that the formalization of the Eighteen Prayers (or Benedictions) at the turn of the first century reflects the beginnings of a shift in the Sabbath gatherings at the synagogue from rather lively discussions of points of law and community affairs toward a worship liturgy. The first indications of a liturgy that included singing as congregational worship comes from the middle of the second century.[72] The description of synagogal Sabbath services, which include the Shema, the Tepillah, and the Aaronic blessing, now found in the Mishnah,[73] reflects what had been established by the middle of the second century. It cannot be used to describe what took place on Sabbaths at the synagogues that Jesus or Paul attended.

The Dead Sea Scrolls and *Jubilees* also give evidence that the Sabbath served eschatological aspirations from very early times. Among the scrolls from Qumran are found the *Songs for the Sabbath Sacrifices,* which have been dated paleographically to the late Hasmonean or early Herodian period, 75–25 B.C.E. Their designation for Sabbath worship is in itself quite significant. Of course, in relationship to the temple the covenanters were a "break away" movement. It is also to be noted that in 11QPs there is a colophon listing the accomplishments of David, the psalmist.

> And David, son of Jesse, was wise, a torch whose light was like the sun's, learned, knowledgeable, and perfect in all his ways before God and men. And Yahveh gave him a wise and enlightened spirit. And he wrote three thousand six hundred psalms, and three hundred sixty four songs to be sung before the altar on the daily perpetual offering for every day of the year, and fifty two songs for the Sabbath offerings, and thirty songs for the offering of the new moons and the festivals and the Day of Atonement. (26:2–8)

Here, again, the Sabbath songs are explicitly mentioned on account of their unique role in the life of the covenanters of Qumran. The specific attribution of 364 songs for the daily offerings and of 52 songs for the Sabbath offerings is an explicit attempt to conform David's proverbial prowess as a songwriter with the solar calendar in use at Qumran. In this calendar the number of Sabbaths in a year was constant and, as stated above, they always occurred on the same days of the month. In the lunisolar-solar calendar used at the Jerusalem temple the number of Sabbaths in a given year would depend on the day of the week in which the year began. The reference, therefore, is polemically charged.

The *Songs for the Sabbath Sacrifices* are meant to be sung in unison by a choir in which the human voices join angelic ones in the praise of the Creator. These *Songs* exalt the power of God and proclaim his goodness in the triumph over evil. They were liturgical vehicles that made possible both communion with the angels and participation in their Sabbath celebrations at the heavenly temple.[74] According to *Jubilees* the angels in heaven kept the Sabbath before it was made known to any flesh that observance of Sabbath rest was a requirement (2:30). God together with the angels of presence and of sanctification rejoice every weekly Sabbath (2:17–18). In this way Sabbath worship makes possible for human and divine beings to participate in a common activity. As such, it anticipates the eschatological age when the evil that now separates human from divine beings shall be no more. If salvation is envisioned as life with God, that is to say in basically sociological terms, the Sabbath becomes a foretaste of that eschatological social reality.

At the time when the priests at the Jerusalem temple were sacrificing the two lambs of the Sabbath sacrifice, the covenanters accomplished the removal of sin by singing in unison with the angels. They did not see the sacrifices performed at the temple at the center of their worship. Their *Songs* testify to an alternative symbolic universe in which participation in the heavenly choir of angels was better than approaching the altar on Mount Zion. That the rituals at the temple also had eschatological significance is evident from the fact that Psalm 92, one of the Psalms sung in connection with the sacrifices, was declared by the rabbis to be "a song for the time that is to come, for the day that shall be all Sabbath and rest in the life everlasting."[75] This Psalm proclaims the triumph over one's enemies and the abundant blessings of the righteous, the universal eschatological hope.

While *Jubilees* and the Qumran materials give to the Sabbath eschatological significance as a time in which cosmic limits are broken and social intercourse with divine beings is possible in a world in which God's goodness and power are clearly in evidence, other texts see the Sabbath's eschatological message as referring exclusively to the future. Usually this is done by incorporating the Sabbath into a cosmic week. This schema was given its pithiest expression by Irenaeus, the Christian apologist of the second century: "For in as many days as this world was made, in so many thousand years shall it be concluded."[76]

The idea of a cosmic week is much earlier and appears in many forms, some identifying the seventh millennium as Sabbath and some not.[77] The Talmud records the following dialogue and its conclusion:

> Rabbi Kattina said: "Six thousand years shall the world exist, and one [thousand, the seventh] it shall be desolate, as it is written, 'And the Lord alone shall be exalted in that day' [Isa 2:2]. Abaye said: "It shall be desolate two [thousand], as it is said: 'After two days will he revive us: in the third day, he will raise us up, and we shall live in his sight' [Hos 6:2]. It has been taught in accordance with R. Kattina: Just as the seventh year is one year of release in seven, so is the world: one thousand years out of seven shall be fallow, as it is written, 'And the Lord above shall be exalted in that day,' and it is further said, 'A Psalm and Song for the Sabbath day' [Ps 92:1], meaning the day that is altogether Sabbath—and it is also said, 'For a thousand years in Thy sight are but yesterday when it is past' [Ps 90:4]."[78]

This text links the year of the jubilee with the Sabbath and argues that in this day the Lord alone is exalted. In other words, it affirms the idea that the Sabbath is God's not humanity's possession. This idea is found in other rabbinic texts,[79] Philo,[80] the Epistle to the Hebrews,[81] and Barnabas.[82] The text then appeals to Psalms 90:4 in order to show how a day for God is like a thousand years, thus providing the rationale for the world week. What is also interesting in this text is that since in the seventh year the land lies fallow, the seventh thousand years are to be desolate.

Sanhedrin 97ab offers another schema in which the Sabbath plays no role:[83]

> The Tanna debe Eliyyahu teaches: The world is to exist six thousand years. In the first two thousand there was desolation. Two thousand years the Torah flourished, and the next two thousand years is the Messianic era, but through our many iniquities all these years have been lost.

Here the desolation is not assigned to the last one or two thousand years but to the first two thousand, the time from Adam to the call of Abraham. From the time Abraham became a Jew to 172 years after the destruction of the temple the Torah flourished and, therefore, at the beginning of the third double-millennium the Messiah should have come. The delay of the Messiah's coming and the losing of the time since the ending of the second double-millennium has been caused by Israel's sins. Eliyyahu reduces the history of the world to six thousand years, and introduces the Messianic age after only four thousand. This gives him two thousand years for Israel to get serious in its obedience of the commandments. In this schema also, the flourishing of the Torah is what is important. It would seem that here obedience to the Sabbath does not make up for failings in the observance of the others. Therefore, the Sabbath does not become a seventh millennium. Still, again one sees how the Sabbath plays a pivotal role in the construction of the symbolic universe.[84]

The linking of the Sabbath to eschatological hopes is also traceable in the descriptions of primordial existence before sin found in the midrashim of Genesis that informed synagogue worship after the destruction of the temple. According to a late midrash, when the Israelites asked God to show them "the likeness of the world to come. He showed them the Sabbath."[85] Theodore Friedman argues somewhat persuasively that the multiplication of halakic prescription, which I said above were called for by the sanctity ascribed to the Sabbath and the wish to sanctify human life, are based on the haggadic, mythological exegesis of Genesis as life in paradise to be experienced again in the world to come, but of which the Sabbath is now a part.[86] To make his argument, Friedman seeks for the rationale that informs some rather strange prescriptions. For example, "Beth Shammai says: 'One does not kill a moth on the Sabbath.' Beth Hillel permits."[87] One of Shammai's most distinguished followers, Rabbi Eliezer b. Hyrcanus, expands on this saying, "He who kills a vermin on the Sabbath is as if he slew a camel."[88] What could possibly account for this way of justifying not killing a moth or a vermin on the Sabbath? Friedman argues that the justification appeals to the image of harmony and peace in the animal kingdom before the fall, which of course will also exist in the age to come, and which the rabbis understood should obtain already now on the Sabbath. The same seems to be the case in a rather unconnected list of things which one should not do on the Sabbath.

Beth Shammai says: "Contributions for the poor are not alloted [*sic*] on the Sabbath in the synagogue, even a dowry to marry an orphan young man to an orphan young woman. Quarrels between husband and wife are not adjudicated and one does not pray for the sick on the Sabbath." Beth Hillel permits these activities.[89]

What can possibly be the common denominator informing this list of proscribed activities? Most everyone would have some trouble understanding why praying for the sick is not allowed. The rationale for the prohibition, according to Friedman, is that none of these activities will be performed in the world to come, and therefore they should not be performed on the Sabbath, which is "the anticipation, the foretaste, the paradigm of life in the world to come." This, again, reveals the significance of the symbolic universe for the adoption of halakic prescriptions.

The kindling of the Sabbath lights provides the clearest instance of a haggadic, mythological reading of Genesis in an *Urzeit/Endzeit* pattern, according to which at the end God will reestablish what was before the fall. Even though there has been much research done in order to establish the origins of this practice, the results have been inconclusive since the midrashic assignation of it to Moses cannot be biblically verified.[90] Even Maimonides had to admit that it does not have a basis either in the Bible or in the rabbinical prescriptions.[91] The Mishnah presupposes its existence and prescribes its ritualization. A midrash on Genesis explains, however, that out of consideration for the Sabbath, God did not order the sun to become less bright after Eve and Adam's fall on Friday of creation week. Rather, he allowed the sun to shine on through the Sabbath, but at its conclusion its brightness diminished. Thus, when Genesis 2 says, "And God blessed the seventh day," it refers to the blessing of light which, under the circumstances, would not otherwise have been there. Then the midrash asserts, "The light of a man's countenance all the days of the week is not to be compared to the light that his countenance reflects on the Sabbath." The midrash then ends by linking the kindling of the Sabbath lights with life in the Messianic age:

If you observe the kindling of the Sabbath lights, I will show you the lights of Zion . . . as it is said, "The sun shall no more be light for you by days, nor shall the brightness of the moon shine for you, but the Lord shall be your everlasting light."[92]

The reference is to the superior light that lighted that first Sabbath in Eden and lights every Sabbath since. The kindling of the Sabbath lights are therefore repetitions of that archetypal act of God that kept the light of the not-yet-fallen creation willfully shining on that first primordial Sabbath and, of course, will restore that supernal light in the age to come. In this way every Sabbath was a slice of life in the Messianic age, "one sixtieth of the world to come."[93] As an anticipation of the world to come, the Sabbath gives humans the opportunity to be different, to live by a different, superior light. Later in medieval times the Kabbalah greatly enhanced this notion and developed the concept of the Sabbath soul which allows the Jew to participate more fully in the divine world.[94]

Sabbath rest was more than the mere cessation of labor.[95] It meant release from the troubles of the world. The rest that God enjoys since the completion of creation was thus envisioned as the rest into which God's people shall enter. The terminology is found in the promise of Moses in Deuteronomy and God's contravention of it in Psalms 95:11 (94:11 in Hebrew). The linking of Genesis 2:2 with Psalm 95, of God's rest with the people's rest, seems to have been part of a common exegetical tradition.[96]

The eschatological future as a perpetual Sabbath, as the destination reached by the soul when it finally arrives home, appears in the literature in various shapes and forms. Philo of Alexandria worked extensively with it, and Christian writers gave the concept wide currency. Among many Christians it developed in terms of a realized eschatology. Others tried to keep present existence in a perennial Sabbath in tension with a future bodily resurrection. Centuries later, Saint Augustine, the consummate rhetorician, framed this conception in its most memorable epigram: "Thou hast made us for Thyself and our souls are restless till they rest in Thee."[97]

Jewish conceptions of the eschatological significance of the Sabbath were central to the symbolic universe in which the Jews lived. Many of the prescriptions the rabbis promulgated for Sabbath observance were apparently directly related to the eschatological significance they recognized in it. The chronological anchorage on the seventh day was, on the one hand, very important, but on the other, according to some, not eternal. In these things, like in many others, there was no unanimity. In fact, it may be the case that the very variety of symbolic universes in which Jews built their social lives is one of the primary factors contributing to the vibrancy of their faith through the ages. A study of the views and attitudes toward the Sabbath reinforces the centrality of the Sabbath in the Jewish understanding of things. The rich variety of views on the Sabbath and the lively imagination that informs them demonstrate again that Judaism was not primarily a matter of doctrines, but of different ways of life shaped according to different understandings of the structure of the cosmos.

2

Philo on the Sabbath

In reference to the Sabbath, Philo proves himself to have been an observant Jew, even if his way of observing the day may not have been totally in accord with the rabbinic halakah now known to us. Eduard Lohse has correctly noticed that "Hellenistic Jews, like their brethren in Palestine, realized that they were pledged to obedience to the Torah and observance of the Sabbath."[1] Ronald Williamson is impressed because "Philo always speaks with great reverence for the Jewish Sabbath."[2] And Edwin R. Goodenough seems to show some pique when he writes, "Philo was a fastidious observer of the law."[3] Alan Mendelson thinks Philo considered it "a cornerstone of Jewish practice."[4] What seems unusual to modern readers is that Philo could uphold the necessity to take seriously the rather mundane details of Sabbath observance and also the responsibility to expand the significance of the Sabbath in ways that far exceeded those of any of his contemporaries. Goodenough observes that "it is of the highest importance that Philo finds the real meaning of the Sabbath and Festivals not in their commemoration of some events in Jewish history but in their mystic symbolism."[5] This claim may be correct in what it denies but needs to be reviewed in what it affirms. In comparison, Robert Goldenberg seems to overstate the case when he claims that for Philo the Sabbath is "a symbol of all the highest philosophical truths."[6] Unquestionably, for Philo the Sabbath had theological, cosmological, philosophical, religious, and social significance. Nevertheless, his comments about it seem to have primarily an apologetic tone.

On a first reading, Philo seems to say rather little about the Sabbath per se. He refers to it mostly when dealing with other subjects. Discussing the nature of inspiration and the foreknowledge and authority of Moses, or the different kinds of souls humans may possess, or the subjects worthy of conscientious study, or the complementarity of the body and the soul, or the necessity to transcend the senses and be guided by the dominant mind, he in passing may touch upon the Sabbath. Still, his concern for it is not secondary. He insists that "the law of the seventh day . . . we regard with most reverence and awe" (*Somn.* 2.123) and explains that "it should be observed in a reverent and religious manner" (*Decal.* 96). Often it is quite apparent that his comments about the Sabbath have an explicit reference to contemporary Sabbath observance (i.e., *Mos.* 2.216; *Hypoth.* 7.13).

Philo reports that he knows "some," whom Goodenough identifies as "philosophical spiritualists,"[7] who feel that the symbolic significance of the Sabbath extracts from the commandment all its practical import; thus, its actual observance is viewed as detracting from its importance.[8] These people judge "laws in their literal sense in the light of symbols of matters belonging to the intellect" and "are overpunctilious about the latter, while treating the former with easy-going neglect" (*Migr.* 89). What these people are doing is not wrong in itself. What is wrong, according to Philo, is its application to the Sabbath. Actually, Philo agrees with the symbolists on the meaning they give to the Sabbath. He writes, "It is quite true that the seventh day is meant to teach the power of the Unoriginate and the non-action of created beings" (*Migr.* 91), and "It is also true that the feast is a symbol of gladness of soul and of thankfulness to God" (*Migr.* 92). These two seem to be Philo's own primary concerns with the Sabbath. He has no problem, therefore, with the interpretation given to the Sabbath by the symbolists. His polemic with them is that they have "abrogated the laws laid down for its observance" (*Migr.* 91). As Peder Borgen points out, his "ideological argument serves as basis for exhorting them to keep the observances."[9] The rules for the proper observance of the Sabbath are, according to Philo, "the visible stewards without reproach" of "what is not visible" (*Migr.* 89).[10] Philo provides three main reasons why the laws giving the details of observance must be kept. In the first place, to contravene them is to go against "the customs fixed by divinely empowered men greater than those of our time" (*Migr.* 90). The identity of these men is left undetermined, but obviously the rules here considered are not being attributed to Moses. Philo is making a connection between biblical and traditional commandments, one which was commonplace among the rabbis.[11] Philo's first argument is, then, an argument from authority.

His second argument appeals to social reality and Scripture. All people live within a social setting, and Scripture teaches humans to guard their reputation. By desiring to "explore reality in its naked absoluteness," the symbolists "live as though they had become disembodied souls, and knew neither city nor village nor household nor any company of human beings at all" (*Migr.* 90). The social reality is that the symbolists live in Alexandria and their conduct has repercussions affecting the Jewish community. Nonobservant Jews, in Philo's estimation, bring about "the censure of the many and the charges they are sure to bring against us" (*Migr.* 93). In other words, Philo fears that on account of the extreme position taken by the symbolists those who, like himself, see the Sabbath in broad universalist terms will come under attack by those who see it in more nationalistic and covenantal terms. In this way, the symbolists are making life difficult for others in the Jewish community. In any case, Philo's argument is that actual observance of the Sabbath is a way of living as a Jew in society on good terms with all Jews.

His third argument is that if one is motivated by the desire to "gain a clear conception" of that reality of which the Sabbath is but a symbol, one must recognize that what makes for that clearer vision of reality is the discipline of actual observance (*Migr.* 93). Explaining the relation of meaning to practical observance as similar to that of the soul to the body, he writes,

> We should look on all these outward observances as resembling the body, and their inner meanings as resembling the soul. It follows that, exactly as we have to take thought for the body, because it is the abode of the soul, so we must pay heed to the letter of the laws. (*Migr.* 93)

It is impossible for the soul to live unrelated to a well-kept body. Attachment to the symbolic meaning of the Sabbath in terms of its essence, without the observance of the practical rules that give it social and religious shape, is equally impossible.

Philo gives a list of activities these symbolists were performing on the Sabbath, which he considered violations. It reads:

> light fires or till the ground or carry loads or institute proceedings in court or act as jurors or demand the restoration of deposits or recover loans, or do all else that we are permitted to do as well on days that are not festival seasons. (*Migr.* 91)

The injunctions against lighting fires and tilling the ground have their origin in the Pentateuch.[12] The others refer to town life and its more complicated legal and economic arrangements. Mendelson thinks that all of them have to do with "civic life," as distinct from personal or family life, but this does not seem to be the case.

At the opposite end of the spectrum, Philo comments on Jews who spent their Sabbath leisure in laughter, sports, or shows of dancers and mimes. He leaves no doubt that he also finds this way of spending the Sabbath objectionable (*Mos.* 2.211).

The importance Philo places on observance is clearly in evidence in his comments about the man who was caught gathering wood on the Sabbath, as told in Numbers 15:32–36. In this passage, *Mos.* 2.213–220 (and its shorter parallel in *Spec.* 2.250–251), Philo points out that "the echoes of the divine commands about the sacredness of the seventh day were ringing in his (the stick gatherer's) ears" (*Mos.* 2.213). Therefore, in going out to gather sticks "he only succeeded in showing his disobedience" (*Spec.* 2.250). He left the camp "knowing that all were resting in their tents" (*Mos.* 2.213). By contrast those who witnessed "the wicked deed" had gone "into the wilderness to pray in the quiet open solitude" (*Mos.* 2.214).[13] After they had witnessed "this lawless sight," only their desire not to become a lynch mob and not to pollute the sacredness of the Sabbath with blood (*Spec.* 2.251), prevented them from killing the man on sight (*Mos.* 2.214). Instead, they searched for Moses and found him teaching the priests and the multitude.[14] Informed of the crime and knowing "that the action deserved death," Moses had as his only purpose at the judgment of the offender to determine the method of execution (*Mos.* 2.217–218; *Spec.* 2.251).

Philo elaborates on the nature of the offense, which is "the perfection of wickedness, and covered practically all the prohibitions enacted for the honoring of the seventh day" (*Mos.* 2.218), in terms of the significance of fire:

> not only the mechanical but also the other arts and occupations, particularly those which are undertaken for profit and to get a livelihood, are carried on directly or indirectly by the instrumentality of fire. And, therefore, he [Moses] often forbids the lighting of a fire on the seventh day, regarding it as the cause which lay at the root of all and as the primary activity; and, if this ceased, he considered that other particular activities would naturally cease also. But sticks are the material of fire, so that by picking them up he committed a sin which was brother to and of the

same family as the sin of burning them. And his was a double crime; it lay first in the mere act of collecting, in defiance of the commandment to rest from work, secondly in the nature of what he collected, being materials for fire which is the basis of the arts.

Obviously, the Promethean myth is not far from his mind. But in Philo's view the commandment occupies a privileged position. The explicit scriptural prohibition is the lighting of a fire, Exodus 35:3. Philo connects this to the gathering of wood, but the Bible does not quite do so. Samuel Belkin finds in this clear evidence for Philo's knowledge of traditions later embedded in rabbinic halakah.[15] Still, while for Philo the basic sin was that of "gathering," for the rabbis it was "plucking."[16] It must be admitted, however, that in *De specialibus legibus* Philo appeals to this narrative to argue that humans should "be rich in ways of purifying things profane." Profanation of a holy thing, the Sabbath, is unquestioningly worthy of death. In chapter 1 some consideration was given to whether or not the death sentence was actually ever carried out.

Philo takes seriously the biblical admonition that the benefits of the Sabbath should also be enjoyed by the servants and the animals in the household. He even includes the plants.

> He [Moses] not only requires the free men to abstain from work on the Sabbath, but gives the same permission to manservants and handmaids, and sends them a message of security and almost of freedom after every six days, to teach both masters and men an admirable lesson. The masters must be accustomed to work themselves without waiting for the offices and attentions of their menials, and so in the event of times of difficulty such as occur through the vicissitudes of human affairs, they may not through unfamiliarity with personal service lose heart at the outset and despair of accomplishing the tasks set before them, but use the different parts of their body with more nimbleness and show a robust and easy activity; while on the other hand the servants are not to refuse to entertain still higher hopes, but should find in the relaxation allowed after six days an ember or spark of freedom, and look forward to their complete liberation if they continue to serve well and loyally. (*Spec.* 2.66–67)

This passage is quite unique, even if not completely clear. What is not clear is whether the task in question is considered permissible on the Sabbath or not and whether the servant in question is a Gentile or not. Is Philo saying that an action that would be considered impermissible "work" if performed by a servant, is not such when performed by a master on the Sabbath?[17] Or, is Philo saying that a Jew should not require that a Gentile servant be used to perform impermissible "work," something which the rabbis also specified. Belkin thinks that only permissible "work" is being considered, and that Philo is requiring the master to do it rather than having his servant do it for him, as the rabbis would have allowed.[18] In any case it is clear that Philo is concerned to make the Sabbath a day of freedom for servants, even if it means that the master has to perform some personal task himself.

Philo elaborates on the Sabbath's message of freedom, particularly for servants. For him the weekly Sabbath and the Sabbatical Year[19] are two expressions of the basic idea of freedom; therefore, on the Sabbath there are no servants. In this way the Sabbath is "an ember or spark of freedom." Philo is talking about actual physical labor on the Sabbath, as evident from what he considers to be the benefits this arrangement has for the masters. It will give them a chance to keep their muscle tone in good condition—something which, given the unpredictability of the future (cf. *Agr.* 174–180; *Somn.* 2.149), would serve them well if circumstances should deprive them of their servants. For masters the Sabbath is not a harbinger of freedom, but a reminder that the blessings of life are not to be taken for granted.[20]

From another perspective, the physical abstention from work on the Sabbath has to do with the complementarity of the body and the soul, and the need for both to work together. He writes:

> Since we consist of body and soul, he [Moses] assigned to the body its proper tasks and similarly to the soul what falls to its share, and his earnest desire was, that the two should be waiting to relieve each other. Thus while the body is working, the soul enjoys a respite, but when the body takes its rest, the soul resumes its work, and thus the best forms of life, the theoretical and the practical, take their turn in replacing each other. The practical life has six as its number allotted for ministering to the body. The theoretical has seven for knowledge and perfection of the mind. (*Spec.* 2.60)

This premise allows Philo to take away from the Sabbath any negativity associated with the prohibition to work.[21] On the contrary, the multitudes of Jews who on the Sabbath attend the synagogues, or schools, which were open "by the thousands in every city" (*Spec.* 2.62) demonstrate the Sabbath's positive aspects. Sabbath observance benefits both the practical and the contemplative life. To the body it brings relaxation and refreshing that allow it to regain the strength necessary to work another six days, something that even athletes need and appreciate (*Spec.* 2.60). To the soul it provides the opportunity to become knowledgeable of the truths and principles indispensable for the good life. These are best arranged under two main headings: the duty toward God displayed by piety and holiness, and the duty toward fellow human beings shown by love of humanity and justice (*Spec.* 2.63). In these schools Jews pursued "the study of wisdom with the ruler expounding and instructing the people what they should say and do, while they received edification and betterment in moral principles and conduct" (*Mos.* 2.215). According to Philo, the synagogues of his own day are nothing but "schools of prudence and courage and temperance and justice and also of piety, holiness and every virtue by which duties to God and men are discerned and rightly performed" (*Mos.* 2.216). He refers to such schools as present "throughout the cities" (*Mos.* 2.216), among the Therapeutai (*Contempl.* 30–32), and among the Essenes (*Prob.* 81).[22] These schools are indispensable because the knowledge of the laws is essential to the life of the wise. For Philo what takes place in these schools is intrinsic to the purpose of Sabbath observance (*Hypoth.* 7.10–15).[23]

What Philo considers the positive aspects of Sabbath observance today would be described as self-improvement. He writes that on the Sabbath, Jews give

> their time to the one sole object of philosophy with a view to the improvement of character and submission to the scrutiny of conscience. Conscience, established in the soul like a judge, is never abashed in administering reproofs, sometimes employing sharper threats, sometimes gentler admonitions; threats, where the wrongdoing appeared to be deliberate; admonitions, to guard against a like lapse in the future, when the misconduct seemed unintentional and the result of want or caution. (*Opif.* 128)

The Philonic prescription for Sabbath observance is that on the Sabbath the conscience do its work because on this day wisdom, like manna, falls from heaven in great abundance (*Mut.* 260). The connection of the Sabbath with manna is paradigmatic, even if no manna fell on the Sabbath. He elaborates further:

So he commanded that they should apply themselves to work for six days but rest on the seventh and turn to the study of wisdom, and that while they thus had leisure for the contemplation of the truths of nature they should also consider whether any offence against purity had been committed in the preceding days, and exact from themselves in the council-chamber of the soul, with the laws as their fellow-assessors and fellow-examiners, a strict account of what they had said or done in order to correct what had been neglected and to take precautions against repetition of any sin. (*Decal.* 98)

In this passage Philo does not employ the word "conscience." Still, the examination of one's actions of the previous week is not to be done at the schools where philosophy is studied, but privately in the courthouse of the soul. Philo also speaks of the Sabbath as a time when the mind "welcomes solitude and rejoices in its own society, feeling that it needs no other and is completely sufficient for itself" (*Abr.* 28–30).[24]

The examination of one's conduct is to be done not only to improve character. Its primary objective is to make possible the celebration of the Sabbath as a feast. Only the wise, those whose names are in the books of record, the righteous ones who follow nature and her ordinances (*Sacr.* 111; *Mos.* 2.211; *Spec.* 2.42), may truly celebrate a feast. By contrast, "none of the wicked keeps a feast, even for the shortest time, tormented as he is by consciousness of wrongdoing and depressed in soul, even though he simulates a smile with his face" (*Spec.* 2.49). In this way private introspection on the Sabbath not only enhances one's soul but enables one to honestly celebrate all feasts. In their ignorance, Gentiles have difficulty viewing the Day of Atonement as a feast since it requires fasting. Philo, however, defends Moses' wisdom in designating "the Fast a feast, the greatest of the feasts, in his native tongue a Sabbath of Sabbaths, or as the Greeks would say, a seven of sevens, a holier than the holy" (*Spec.* 2.194).[25] As the time for self-examination, weekly Sabbaths may be considered Days of Atonement in miniature.

Philo reports two incidents in which the Jews were tested by Roman officials in terms of their loyalty to the Sabbath commandment. The first of these tells that when handouts of grain were made to the populace in

Rome, it was not unusual for them to take place on Saturdays. When such was the case, the Jews did not go out to receive them. Philo points out that the emperor accommodated the Jews by making arrangements for them to receive their quotas on the following day (*Legat.* 155–158).

The other incident involved an unnamed Egyptian official who wished to bring about "a general backsliding" among the Jews.[26] According to his domino theory, to tip over the first piece in the set he would compel the Jews to work on the Sabbath. His efforts, however, not only failed but actually proved counterproductive. His decree brought about a general outcry of indignation comparable to what could be expected if "their native city [had been] sacked and razed, and its citizens [were] being sold into captivity" (*Somn.* 2.123–124). In a desperate attempt to bring about compliance with his wishes, the official confronted the Jews with the following argument:

> Suppose there was a sudden inroad of the enemy or an inundation caused by the river rising and breaking through the dam, or a blazing conflagration or a thunderbolt or famine, or plague or earthquake, or any other trouble either of human or divine agency, will you stay at home perfectly quiet? Or will you appear in public in your usual guise, with your right hand tucked inside and the left held close to the flank under the cloak lest you should even unconsciously do anything that might help to save you? And will you sit in your conventicles and assemble your regular company and read in security your holy books, expounding any obscure point and in leisurely comfort discussing at length your ancestral philosophy? No. You will throw all these off and gird yourselves up for the assistance of yourselves, your parents and your children, and the other persons who are nearest and dearest to you, and indeed also your chattels and wealth to save them too from annihilation. See then, I who stand before you am all the things I have named. I am the whirlwind, the war, the deluge, the lightning, the plague or famine or disease, the earthquake which shakes and confounds what was firm and stable: I am constraining destiny, not its name but its power, visible to your eyes and standing at your side. (*Somn.* 2.122–125)

Philo is interested in the example of human vainglory and folly here portrayed, so he does not tell the story's end. It may be safely inferred that the official's argument failed. Philo envisions his fellow Jews letting war and high water play havoc in town while they stayed quietly at home, walked to the synagogue in the prescribed manner, and sat there eager to bring light upon obscure points in their laws. Whether Philo knew that Jews may have taken part in "civic emergencies" (like dam repairs) on the Sabbath is impossible to determine. It is telling, however, that Philo should construct this story in such a way as to depict the breakdown of proper Sabbath observance as the sure way to destroy the Jewish community.

Students of Philo are well aware of his delight in the Pythagorean approach to numbers.[27] From this perspective, the number seven offers an inexhaustible supply of applications.[28] Philo revels in its possibilities as often as he has a chance, not infrequently repeating himself. *De opificio mundi* 90 starts with the words, "I doubt whether anyone could adequately celebrate the properties of the number seven, for they are beyond all words." In spite of his hesitancy, Philo launches on a display of his encyclopedic knowledge, thirty-six sections in length.[29] In paragraph 127, he writes:

> These and yet more than these are the statements and reflections of men on the number seven, showing the reasons for the very high honor which that number has attained in Nature, the honor in which it is held by the most approved investigators of the sciences of Mathematics and Astronomy among the Greeks and other peoples, and the special honor accorded to it by that lover of virtue, Moses. He inscribed its beauty on the most holy tables of the Law, and impressed it on the minds of all who were set under him, by bidding them at intervals of six days to keep a seventh day holy.

It would appear, then, that the presence of the Sabbath commandment in the law is not due to the fact that creation took place in seven days, but to the high honor seven enjoys in "Nature," independent of creation.[30] Due to its primordial place in nature, seven can be second to none because "nature determines precedence not by length of time, but by worth" (*Post.* 62). Philo explains:

> For this reason also the seventh day, although in order it is the number born after six, yet in value takes precedence of every number, nothing

differing from one. This will be made clear by the lawgiver himself, who in his epilogue to the narrative of the creation says: "And God rested on the seventh day from all His works which He had made, and God blessed the seventh day and hallowed it, because in it God rested from all his works which God had begun to make." After this he adds: "This is the book of the heaven and the earth." Now these things were created on the first day, so that the seventh day is referred back to one, the first and starting point of all. (*Post.* 64–65)

What modern scholarship understands to be the colophon of the priestly account of creation Philo takes as the indication that seven is prior, or at least equal, to one. The discovery of this is attributed to "the students of mathematics, who have investigated it with the utmost care and consideration." They are the ones who have characterized it as

the virgin among the numbers, the essentially motherless, the closest bound to the initial Unit, the "idea" of the planets, just as the Unit is of the spheres of the fixed stars, for from the Unit and Seven springs the incorporeal heaven which is the pattern of the visible. (*Decal.* 102)

On the basis of the preceding observations, Philo identifies two sevens: "the seven which includes the most creative of numbers, six, and that which does not include it but takes precedence of it and resembles the unit" (*Decal.* 159). The identification of seven with one makes possible for the soul that rests in God and toils no more at any mortal task, and has thus left behind the six, to "have its being ordered in accordance with the One and the Monad, the truly existent" (*Deus* 11–12). Thus Anna, the mother of the prophet Samuel, who "with endurance and courage persevered to the finish in the contest, where the prize is the acquisition of the Best, should bring forth the Monad which is of equal value with the Seven" (*Deus* 13). If seven is equal to the monad it is easy to think of the Sabbath in a very special relationship to God.

Philo also elaborated on the complementarities and contrasts between seven and six, which after all is also a perfect number (*Opif.* 89). Six is the one that gives its properties to the created world of mortal things (*Leg.* 1.4, 16). On this account it cannot claim supremacy, but must be content with second place (*Deus* 12). Even as the most creative of numbers, six is contained within seven (*Decal.* 159). Six and seven, together, provide the pattern for human life since the visible things created in six days follow the pattern of the invisible heavenly world, whereas seven is the perfect number.

Philo advises:

> But while God once for all made a final use of six days for the completion of the whole world and had no further need of time-periods, every man being a partaker of mortal nature and needing a vast multitude of things to supply the necessities of life ought never to the end of his life to slacken in providing what he requires, but should rest on the sacred seventh days. Have we not here a most admirable injunction full of power to urge us to every virtue and piety most of all? "Always follow God," it says, "find in that single six-day period in which, all-sufficient for His purpose, He created the world, a pattern of the time set apart to thee for activity. Find, too, in the seventh day the pattern of thy duty to study wisdom, that day in which we are told that he surveyed what he had wrought, and so learn to meditate thyself on the lessons of nature and all that in thy own life makes for happiness. (*Decal.* 99–100)

While seven and one are the primordial numbers of heaven, the pattern of created things, seven and six are the perfect numbers providing the pattern for life on earth. God's creative activity by means of six and seven exhibit the true model for "those who should live as citizens under this world-order" (*Decal.* 98). Philo is clear, however, that the pattern is for the benefit of humanity, not just the Jews.

In contrast to six, the number of mortal things, seven is the number of "the happy and blessed things" that are "more divine" (*Leg.* 1.4–5). On the seventh day God ceased molding the masses that are mortal and began to make that which is divine (*Leg.* 1.16), among them reason (*Leg.* 1.16) and the dominant mind (*Abr.* 30). These faculties get their exercise and training on the Sabbath.

While six/seven may serve to contrast mortal/divine, Philo also uses the pattern to contrast earth-born/differently-born. The priestly account of Moses' ascent to Mount Sinai to receive the law says: "The glory of the Lord settled on Mount Sinai, and the cloud covered it six days; on the seventh day he called Moses out of the midst of the cloud" (Exod 24:16). Philo explains that six has to do both with "the creation of the world and the election of the contemplative nation," in this way establishing that both were created for virtue. Having been brought forth according to six, both the world and the nation reflect the nature of God but were "mixed with a body and had corruptible parents." On the seventh day Moses was called to the top of the mountain, where he experienced a second birth far better than the first, making him "an unmixed and simple soul of the sovereign, being changed from a productive to an unproductive form, which has no mother but only a father, who is [the Father] of all." Having experienced "the divine birth" Moses became different from "the earth-born first molded man" (*QE* 2.46). It would appear, then, that those who approach God on the seventh day become differently-born, and in this way are disengaged from the world of six, the world of productive activity. Being born of seven, they now belong to the world of the masculine without the feminine, the world of the mind rather than the world of the senses.

Philo uses the contrast six/seven in order to contrast war and peace. He argues:

He [Moses] shows consistency, too, when he gives to the seventh day, which the Hebrews call Sabbath, the name of rest; not, as some think, because the multitude abstained after six days from their usual tasks, but because in truth the number seven, both in the world and in ourselves, is always free from factions, and war and quarreling and is of all numbers the most peaceful. (*Abr.* 28)

Since, in modern terms, seven is a prime number, Philo can see in its uncompoundedness a sign of peace. As such, it is ungenerated and incorruptible. Allegorically this is demonstrated by the six senses (the usual five plus speech), which "wage ceaseless and continuous war on land and sea," while the seventh faculty, the dominant mind, "after triumphing over the six and returning victorious through its superior strength . . . released from the cares and concerns of mortal kind gladly accepts a life of calmness and serenity" (*Abr.* 29–30). The student who with the aid of God, "Nature at its best," attains to the "completion of learning . . . enjoys the peace that never ends." The notions of learning and peace immediately bring to Philo's mind the notion of seven. "Peace and seven are identical according to the Legislator: for on the seventh day creation puts away its seeming activity and takes rest." Then, without explicit reference to the uncompounded nature of seven, he adds, "For the peace that is made by one city with another is mixed with and marred by intestine war; but the peace of the soul has no admixture of discord whatever" (*Fug.* 172–174).

As an uncompounded number, seven is both motherless and ever-virgin. The first because even though born it was "not carried in the womb," and the second because it is "neither bred from corruption nor doomed to suffer corruption" (*Mos.* 2.210).

Philo expounds the correlations between seven and six not only in the realm of being but also in the realm of knowledge. Seven is "the light of six. For seven reveals as completed what six has produced, and therefore it may be quite rightly entitled the birthday of the world, whereon the Father's perfect work compounded of perfect parts, was revealed as what it was" (*Spec.* 2.59). It is, therefore, on this basis that the famous Philonic designation of the Sabbath as "the birthday of the world" is to be understood.[31] It is connected to two related motifs: universality and revelation. These two characteristics of the Sabbath make it the only strictly "public" festival (*Opif.* 89). The Sabbath is not the festival of a single city, country, or people, but the festival of the universe (*Opif.* 89). In its celebration animals and plants join the human family. Thus, its universality is without parallel (*Spec.* 2.70; *Mos,* 2.22).

Appealing to common experience, Philo points out that although it is unheard of that one nation would adopt the institutions of another, many nations have adopted the Jewish Sabbath. Philo provides many examples of pagans who validly observe the Sabbath, even some who, incorrectly, observe it once a month (*Decal.* 96). By observing it they testify to the superiority of the Jewish institutions and the superiority of Moses as a lawgiver. This is also proof that eventually, when the political and economic fortunes of Israel are restored, all nations will adopt the Mosaic legislation (*Mos.* 2.17–25, 44). In this way the Sabbath observance of pagans is a proleptic fulfillment of the eschatological future which, undoubtedly, is universal in scope.[32]

According to Philo, since the Sabbath is the evidential sign of creation, its significance as revelation is clear and was made manifest by the miracle of manna in the desert. The gift of manna reproduced the miracle of creation on three counts: 1) it brought about plenty in the desert; 2) the air, rather than the earth, yielded this bounty; and 3) it came about without labor (*Mos.* 2.267). In this way the miracle confirmed that the first day on which the manna fell corresponds to the first day of creation and established the basis for a sure chronology of the universe.[33] The Sabbath, like the number seven, is an essential constitutive structure of the universe that belongs to the whole and cannot be appropriated as an exclusive property of one of the parts. What is true of the number is true of the day.[34] Quoting Genesis 2:4a, "When it came into being," Philo points out that the reference is not temporal since "the things that come into being under the hand of the First Cause come into being with no determining limit. There is an end, then, of the notion that the universe came into being in six days" (*Leg.* 1.19; cf. *Opif.* 13; *Leg.* 1.2).[35] Since the universe came to completion on the seventh day, its creation is limitless. In other passages he points out that the six-day time period is, as it were, a concession to what obtains within material reality and should not be applied in a strict sense to the God who created the world (*Leg.* 1.2–4; *Decal.* 101). On the other hand, Philo observes that Moses "considers the seventh day, called also in his records the birthday of the whole world, to be of equal value to eternity" (*Spec.* 1.170). This claim, of course, is unsupported by Scripture. Still, Philo's understanding of the seventh day as an intrusion of eternity in creation is what gives it the capacity to be the revelation of the uncreated.

By creating the world in terms of six and seven God provided the pattern for the best two kinds of lives: the practical and the theoretical (*Decal.* 97–102). Somehow, however, these patterns were lost with the passage of generations,[36] thus making it necessary for Moses to introduce the Sabbath to humankind. He did it by means of a special prophetic pronouncement and an accompanying miracle. It took place in connection with the gift of manna when Moses announced that on the Sabbath no manna would fall and that on Friday it would fall double and keep unspoiled for two days (*Mos.* 2.263–264). For Philo the observance of the Sabbath is based on the events surrounding the gift of manna. On the other hand, the reason for its existence is based on the special honor of the number seven (*Decal.* 97). This means that the fourth commandment in the Decalogue serves only to institutionalize what is in reality the case (*Decal.* 96).

Philo knows "some" who, in keeping with the uncompounded nature of the number seven, call the Sabbath "the Virgin," emphasizing its chastity. Those who identify it in this way are also prone to call it "the Motherless, begotten by the father of the universe alone, the ideal form of the male sex with nothing of the female." He also knows "some" others who call the Sabbath the *Kairoi* (Seasons), "judging its conceptual nature from its manifestation in the realm of sense." By doing so, Philo says, this group is interpreting the Sabbath in terms of the number six, which is the number of those things which belong to the created world, from the heavenly bodies down. "Moses from a higher point of view," however, did not call the Sabbath "Seasons." Instead, he called it "Contemplation and Full Perfection" (*Spec.* 2. 56–59). Clearly Philo agrees to the titles "Virgin" and "Motherless" but disallows "Seasons." Those who employ the latter fail to see that the Sabbath exists in the uncreated world, something that Moses took pains to point out. To fail to recognize this concept, therefore, is to fail to transcend the realm of sense, which is what wisdom empowers humans to do. It is worth noticing that while Philo disassociates himself from the symbolists and puts forth an argument in favor of actual observance, he does not do as much against the sensualists.[37]

Even if at its core the Sabbath commandment contains a prohibition, for Philo the Sabbath itself is not negative but positive. If abstention from work were its essence, as some seem to insist (*Abr.* 28), then its main function would be to teach self-control, making it possible for those trained in abstention to rule over their activity and inactivity (*Hypoth.* 7.11). That, however, is not the case. As Philo explains, the fourth commandment "is concerned with the number seven, the ever-virgin, the motherless. Its purpose is that creation, observing the inaction which it brings, should call to mind Him who does all things invisibly" (*Her.* 170).[38] The seventh day, then, gives humans the opportunity to contemplate the Creator, who "is not a mere artificer, but also Father of the things that are coming into being" (*Leg.* 1.18). As Philo explains, "even as it is the property of fire to burn and of snow to chill, so it is the property of God to make" (*Leg.* 1.5). The Sabbath reveals something essential in the nature of God. "The cause of all things is by its nature active; it never ceases to work all that is best and most beautiful. God's rest is rather a working with absolute ease, without toil and without suffering" (*Cher.* 87). The Sabbath rest, therefore, is to facilitate the contemplation of God's activity and to point out that the activity of God serves only to underline the passivity of creation (*Migr.* 91).

This means that God's rest is quite different from any and all human rest. Nevertheless, it must be remembered, the pattern for Sabbath rest is God's rest. Philo recognizes that it is impossible for "the sun and moon and the whole heaven and universe" not to experience movement, or activity, in other words, suffering (*Cher.* 88). Therefore, in the truest sense "there is but one thing in the universe which rests, that is God" (*Cher.* 87), and God's rest does not involve inactivity, but rather a different kind of activity. That is why the opposite of rest is not movement, but "unnatural movement" (*Abr.* 27). It is as activity without suffering that God's activity during creation week serves as a model for human activity. From the basic premise that only God truly rests, Philo draws two conclusions. On the one hand, only God truly celebrates festivals. On the other, all festivals, including the Sabbath, are God's "and pertain not to any man at all" (*Cher.* 90).

From his apologetic stance, Philo is eager that Sabbath observance not be taken as evidence of laziness.[39] As pointed out above, Sabbath observance means the change from practical to contemplative activity. This change brings peace and equality. Both teach indispensable lessons that counteract the human tendency of wishing to manufacture the future, or at least to build defenses against what the future might bring. Elaborating on these themes, Philo repeatedly refers to the vicissitudes of life and the human desire to avoid them by means of much "unnatural movement." The Sabbath and its rest teach humans the need to trust God. Philo equates the gift of manna, real food, with rest in God and peace (*Her.* 173–174). The heavenly food meant an ample supply of the good things, spontaneous and self-grown, "especially on the Sabbath" (*Mut.* 260).[40] Those who yearn to possess all things at once reveal lack of hope and lack of faith (*Leg.* 3.164). Philo likes to remind his readers that only God possesses and, therefore, only God enjoys (*Cher.* 83, 86; *Mut.* 22). The inequities of life may tempt some to think that those who have goods need not hope or trust. Those with this mind-set forget that tomorrow things may be turned upside down. Thus the Sabbath, which is an ember of freedom for the slave and training in manual work for the master, is a lesson in equality and faith for all (*Spec.* 2.68). Its purpose is "to teach the power of the Unoriginate and the non-action of created beings" (*Migr.* 91). The contemplation and introspection that is appropriate to its observance is "a symbol of gladness of soul and thankfulness of heart" (*Migr.* 92).

From the above discussion we can draw a few observations and conclusions. Philo knows "some" Jews who view the Sabbath exclusively as a symbol of eternal reality. As such, it transcends any and all cultural concretizations. Preoccupations with the determination of permissible Sabbath activities are looked upon as misguided by these Jews. They would deny that there is a divine commandment involved. He also knows "some" who consider the Sabbath a religious festival functioning within the structures of the created world. As such, it is a very concrete reality whose significance is purely immanent. Philo shows himself broad-minded enough to refrain from condemning either group. Still, he reminds the nonobservant symbolists that the Sabbath is, after all, a commandment that requires observance.

Philo is also quite aware of the need for the Jewish community to present a common front vis-à-vis the Gentile world. He sees the Sabbath as giving the Jews solidarity. Observance of the Sabbath by all Jews, according to him, is essential. Even in the face of civic emergencies and governmental threats, he would expect all Jews to remain loyal to the Sabbath commandment. He also expects governmental officials to respect Jewish institutions, such as the Sabbath.

Philo is not quite of one mind in his understanding of the relationship of the Sabbath to its observance. He insists that observance is a precondition for the proper appropriation of its meaning. The meaning and the observance are as inextricably related as the soul is to the body. This metaphor is somewhat confusing because Philo also insists that the soul's aim is to become free from the body. Thus, while he says that there is an organic relationship between the dweller and the dwelling, he also wishes to break this relationship. It would seem, then, that the tension between the body and the soul is also at play between the Sabbath and its observance. On the one hand, the proper care of the dwelling fosters the well-being of the dweller, while on the other the aim of the dweller (the soul) is extrication from the dwelling (the body).

This concept is also complicated by Philo's differentiation between the Sabbath and the laws governing its observance. In its essence the Sabbath is not law. Philo views the Sabbath not as an institution within creation that establishes the identity of its Creator, but as an eternal reality that precedes creation and makes possible for those within creation, who are caught by the body and its senses, to escape the created world. He distinguishes the Sabbath within creation, as the seven that follows six, from the Sabbath in eternity, as the seven that is equal to the one. Both of them are also to be distinguished from the Sabbath of the law given at Sinai much later. He also differentiates between the Sabbath commandment given by Moses and the rules for its observance given by other ancient worthies whose authority is also to be respected.

Philo, who consistently distances himself from covenantal theology, does not see the Sabbath as "the sign of the covenant" (Exod 31:13–17; Ezek 20:12, 20), but as "the birthday of the world." This designation makes two points: 1) the Sabbath does not belong exclusively to the Jews (*pace* Exod 16:29), and 2) it has revelatory functions. The universality of the Sabbath is grounded in the essence of the number seven in uncreated reality. From there, it extends to the whole created world. Its revelatory character is grounded in its bridging the distance between one and six. As the festival of the cosmos, the Sabbath makes possible within creation a more perfect contemplation of the being of God, a being whose nature is continually to create. The Sabbath creates the conditions for the contemplative life, which advances wisdom and leads to a life of virtue.

Philo is eager to take away from the Sabbath the negativity contained in the commandment. He does this by affirming that both the six days and the seventh day offer opportunities for creating. The seventh day's required abstention from making created things has the benefit of establishing space for the creative activity of the mind. For Philo, between the six days devoted to the development of the practical life and the seventh day devoted to the contemplative life, the difference is not that the seventh negates activity. Rather, the seventh day brings about a change of activities. It provides the soul with opportunities to exercise itself for growth in virtue and the contemplation of God by the study carried out in the schools and the self-examination done in solitude. Sabbath observance is not abstention from labor, but exercises in the contemplative life. Seven, peace, and learning belong together.

The sacredness of the Sabbath is such that Philo unflinchingly calls for the death penalty for those who profane it. Given the resourcefulness for allegorizing he abundantly displays in other contexts, it is noteworthy that he does not allegorize the biblical imposition of the death penalty on Sabbath offenders.

Philo's understanding of the universality and revelatory character of the Sabbath is fully appropriated by giving the Sabbath eschatological significance. Rather than being a sign of the covenant with Israel, the Sabbath is a sign of the universal future adoption of the Mosaic legislation by all nations. The fact that some pagans already keep the Sabbath reveals the workings of God's will for all.

Mary Douglas has observed that in order to survive, conventions must be given a foundation in nature. She writes, "even self-enforcing conventions, which everyone would like to see maintained, have little chance of survival unless they can be grounded in reason and nature."[41] In the case of the Sabbath, it would seem that the priestly writers were the ones who grounded the Sabbath in nature, but, as far as we can tell, it was left to Aristobulus, and more fully to Philo, to show that its place in nature was also a place in reason, and, therefore, it could serve as the grounds for argument. Philo does not argue the Sabbath. On the basis of the Sabbath he argues for the Jew's love of wisdom, peace, revelation, prophecy, etc. Philo's elaboration on the nature of the number seven makes clear that he thinks comprehension is not dependent on ecstatic experience but is within the realm of reason. Thus, while in its essence it belongs to the uncreated world, as part of the created world the Sabbath makes possible the contemplative life and fosters peace, freedom, equality, faith, and hope.

3

The Sabbath among the Samaritans

Any discussion of the Samaritans must begin with a definition of who they are.[1] Even if our knowledge of them is somewhat limited, modern studies have made clear that they cannot be considered a social grouping unconnected to what has been called "normative" Judaism.[2] The designation of sect or heresy, as applied in the context of Christian ecclesiology, would be misapplied if given to the Samaritans.[3] Frank M. Cross frames the issue properly when he writes:

> It is difficult to speak of the Samaritans as a fully separated sect, so long as direct Jewish influence shaped their doctrine and practice, so long as the Biblical text which they used was held in common with the Jews, so long as Jew and Samaritan used a common national style of script. In other terms, when do Samaritan and Jewish theology and discipline begin to separate, increasing diverging lines of development? When does the textual tradition of the Samaritan Pentateuch branch apart from the textual tradition established at Jerusalem? When does the Samaritan script begin to evolve in its distinct path?[4]

In the light of the extant evidence, the answer to Cross' questions is that, although political and economic tensions between the north and the south in Israel can be traced to pre-Davidic times and although religious concerns were connected to these tensions, the serious animosities that characterized Jew-Samaritan relations did not come to the forefront until Maccabean times and the destruction of the Samaritan temple on Mount Gerizim in 127 and of the city of Shechem in 109 B.C.E.[5] These traumatic events, however, did not quite bring about a total separation between the two communities. Samaritanism represents one of the many varieties of Judaism in evidence within Jewish society in Roman times. Even Josephus, whom J. A. Montgomery correctly characterized as no more than reflecting the contemporary Jewish biases against Samaritans, may be considered to be, "perhaps unconsciously and in spite of himself,"[6] an eloquent witness to their belonging within the Jewish equation.

Complicating understanding of the Samaritan phenomenon is the realization that neither halakically nor geographically can they be easily circumscribed. The picture of Samaritans as a small religious group confined to the valleys around Mount Gerizim, preoccupied with the survival of the religious claims of their ancestors and suffering from a siege mentality, is utterly inadequate. Archaeological evidence and the rereading of some ancient texts are showing the extent to which the Samaritans participated fully in the life of Hellenistic culture both in Palestine and in the Diaspora.[7] Modern scholarship has also demonstrated that Samaritanism was a multifaceted phenomenon. Tensions within the group are evident in Samaritan literature.[8]

In his *De Principiis,* Origen reports having had conversations with learned Jews.[9] Apparently these talks gave him some grasp of the different views held by Jews on several issues. According to him, Jews faced what he describes as "some impossibilities" in the law. In view of that, they had adopted different ways of resolving them. One of these impossibilities is the commandment "to sit in one's place on the Sabbath." Origen says that while some Jews have established that the law allows traveling two thousand cubits, "others, among whom is Dositheus the Samaritan, condemning an argument of such sort think that in whatever position someone is found on the Sabbath day, so he must remain until the evening."

This passage contains several interesting facts: (1) the presence of a Samaritan Diaspora in Alexandria at the beginning of the third century; (2) the Samaritan position is counted among Jewish answers to the question; (3) implicitly, Dositheus' ruling is one among others, not necessarily one with which all Samaritans agree; and (4) some other Jews agree with Dositheus.[10] The description by Origen of Dositheus' ruling is somewhat ambiguous. Its meaning depends on how the word *schema,* which translates as "position," is interpreted. Is it meant as the position in which a person's body is found, in which case it prescribes total immobility, or as the location in which the person is found, in which case one is not allowed to leave a room or a house? Another interpretation would read Origen's *schema* to mean "social condition," thus allowing for unlimited movement.

Some indication of Samaritan practices may be gained from Chronicle II, *Sepher ha-Yammim.*[11] According to the chronicler "at that time" (fourth century), the Roman overlords recognized Baba Rabbah as the leader of the whole of Palestine, and as a result the Samaritan community "enjoyed honour, glory, and abundant strength, that they would rejoice and be glad in the revelation of their faith." The foreigners were weak to the point of being unable to impose taxes on them. In order to shift the balance of power, the Romans sought the help of the Judeans, promising them permission to rebuild their temple on Mount Zion if they succeeded in killing Baba Rabbah.

Encouraged by Roman chicanery, the Judeans plotted Baba Rabbah's death. Knowing that he would be coming to the town of Nemarah to spend the Sabbath at the synagogue, they decided to ambush him there "while they were standing in prayer," because "at that time the Samaritan-Israelite community would be unable to take up arms" (16:3). The plan of the Judeans, however, was undone by the Lord who "in His wisdom disclosed their secret plot on the fifth day of the week." Aware of the plot, Baba Rabbah acted as if he knew nothing and on the eve of the Sabbath went to the synagogue dressed in his fine Sabbath linen garments (16:17) as if he intended to spend the whole Sabbath day at the synagogue (16:2). Later that Friday night, however, Baba Rabbah took off his Sabbath garments and, wearing regular clothing, slipped out of the synagogue unnoticed.

At sunrise a crowd of Judeans surrounded the synagogue, entered it, and unsuccessfully searched for Baba Rabbah. Frustrated, they then set fire to the synagogue. At that time Baba Rabbah and his men gave a great shout, putting the Judeans to flight. After pursuing them, Baba Rabbah's men captured the Judeans without using arms on the Sabbath, and held them overnight. The following day Baba Rabbah brought them out for judgment. Considering that they had sought to kill him "on the night of the holy Sabbath when we were standing in prayer, singing praises, magnifying and extolling the Lord our God and the God of our fathers" (16:29), the king-priest determined that they be executed and burned, "doing just as the Lord had commanded in His Holy Law, (as it says), 'And you shall do unto him as he had intended to do to his brother.' He also confiscated from the Judeans the hill opposite the tower. He slew the inhabitants of it" (16:30). It is clear that the execution of the Judeans was carried out as punishment for attempted murder and for the burning of the synagogue, and not for Sabbath breaking.[12]

This story reflects a strong Samaritan bias. It also has glaring inconsistencies. For example, at the plotting of the attack and at the judgment of the Judeans it is said that the attack was to take place on Friday evening, at the time of the prayers for the beginning of the Sabbath. The account of the attack itself, however, says that it took place at dawn on Saturday morning. Had the attack taken place as planned, it would have succeeded.

For our purpose, the story emphasizes that normally Samaritan men spent the whole Sabbath day at the synagogue, making every effort to reach it before sundown on Friday. This would seem to imply that Baba Rabbah did not allow even traveling to the synagogue on the Sabbath. No reference is made to eating on this day, which would agree with evidence indicating that some Samaritans at times fasted on the Sabbath.[13] The story also makes reference to the special clothes reserved for that day. Concerning the question of whether or not war could be conducted on the Sabbath, it says that while the Judeans planned an attack on this holy day with premeditation and set the synagogue on fire, Baba Rabbah chose to slip out of the synagogue without his Sabbath clothing instead of fighting.[14] To stop the attack, like Joshua and the Israelites at Jericho, all he had to do was to "cry out against them in a loud voice. All his men also cried out in unison" (16:20). Still, they gave chase and captured the attackers on the Sabbath without using arms. The postponement of their judgment and execution till the next day follows the pattern found in the story of the man caught gathering sticks on the Sabbath in Numbers 15:32–36.[15]

As noticed in chapter 1, the restriction to stay in one's place on the Sabbath was liberalized by means of the concept of a Sabbath day's journey. Some prescribed one thousand cubits, while most seem to have agreed to two thousand. The covenanters of Qumran assigned one thousand to the distance allowed to travel and two thousand to the distance one could take an animal to pasture. Some Samaritans, however, did not allow feeding an animal at all. Its food had to be set out on Friday. As already observed, Dositheus and others did not agree to the concept of a Sabbath day's journey.[16] The eleventh-century chronicle of Abu ʿl-Hasan aṣ-Ṣûri (1030–40 c.e.), *Kitâb aṭ-Ṭabbâḥ*, reports debates on the issue.[17] In order to resolve the question, the author appeals to the incident of the man found gathering firewood on the Sabbath. Those who found the lawbreaker were out in the field themselves and were not reprimanded by Moses. This means that it is permissible not only to go to the synagogue but also to leave the house for other permissible activities on the Sabbath. In contrast, the chronicle of Yûsuf b. Salama al ʿAskari (1042 c.e.), *Kitâb al-Kâfî,* makes the point that the prohibition to go out of one's place on the Sabbath (Exod 16:29) was given in order to prevent the gathering of manna, something that was to be done on regular working days. On the other hand, Exodus 33:7 says that "everyone who sought the Lord went out into the Tent of Meeting which was without the camp." Therefore, only going to the synagogue was permissible on the Sabbath.

Whether Samaritans made of the Sabbath a day of feasting, when special meals accompanied with good wine were enjoyed, or a day of fasting is somewhat unclear.[18] The issue became particularly important when the Day of Atonement fell on a Sabbath.[19] According to *Jubilees,* however, fasting on a Sabbath was punishable by death. Other evidence, besides the story of Baba Rabbah already mentioned, supports the notion that the Samaritans may have fasted at least on some Sabbaths.[20] Both the *Kitâb al-Kâfî* and the *Kitâb aṭ-Ṭabbâḫ* explicitly prohibit the drinking of wine on the Sabbath.[21] The rationale is the requirement to sanctify it. The ruling is based on the demand that priests and Nazarites abstain from wine before approaching the altar. Greek and Roman authors report the practice of Sabbath fasting among Jews. Usually this information is taken to indicate the authors' lack of intimate knowledge of Judaism, but, in fact, they may have been correct at least in reference to some Jews.[22]

Whereas on the question of fasting some Samaritans seem to have taken the opposite view to that found in *Jubilees,* on the question of marital relations on that day they were in complete accord (*Jub.* 50:8). This issue seems to have become a much debated one within Judaism in the eleventh century, the time of the Karaite controversy.[23] The *Kitâb aṭ-Ṭabbâḫ*[24] argues on the basis of the command given while the people were encamped at the foot of Mount Sinai, "come not near a woman" (Exod 19:15), and emphasizes the need for holiness. The *Kitâb al-Kâfî*[25] appeals also to another scriptural text, Leviticus 15:19, which declares a woman impure for seven days after menstruation. It also adds a heated polemic against the Jews who pollute the day in this way. Other Samaritans argued that sexual intercourse prevented the participants from remaining serene and quiet on the Sabbath.[26] It would appear, then, that when the Karaites made this an issue within talmudic Judaism, they were only bringing to center stage what had been in the wings for centuries.

Abu ᶜl-Fath reports that the followers of Dositheus eventually divided into eight groups.[27] Among these, the followers of Abiya and of Dosa distinguished themselves by attributing to Dositheus the total abolition of all religious laws.[28] In order to make their point they went out of their way to profane the Sabbath and to ignore purity regulations, especially those concerned with cemeteries. These reports of Abu ʿl-Fath, however, must be read with some caution because clearly he sees himself as anything but a Dosithean. He writes: "All these rules were established by Dusis. May God curse him."[29] Still, it is noteworthy that among Samaritans, who are considered to have been rigorists, there may also have been some antinomians.

A study of the halakic traditions about the Sabbath among Samaritans[30] is important not only for what it may point out concerning the idiosyncrasies of the Samaritans but also for the light it casts upon our understanding of Judaism in general. It is impossible to trace the way Samaritans and Jews in general influenced each other. The same can be said of relations between Jews and the covenanters of Qumran, who saw their existence cut short by the war with Rome. As stated in chapter 1, it is not accurate to describe Qumranites and Samaritans as heretical sects with rigorist views, and claim that "normative" Judaism developed along more humane lines. Even if it is true that the efforts of the rabbis were, in general, to adapt the observance of the law to the realities of daily life, the rabbis, especially before Hillel became the most influential, also held very rigorous views. Iain R. M. Boid sidesteps the issue of influences and developments, pointing out that "in the numerous instances of disagreements between one Samaritan tradition and another the overwhelming tendency is for at least one Samaritan tradition to agree with some Jews against other Samaritans, who very often agree with other Jews." He concludes, therefore, that "there is no uniquely Samaritan tradition of the halachah, unconnected with the Jewish one." He then summarizes his conclusions by stating: "*There is a halachic tradition common to all Israel, both Jews and Samaritans. There are some points on which there is variation within the tradition. Both in given individual instances and overall the variation is independent of the divisions between Samaritans and Jews.*"[31] From our review of the Sabbath rulings, it would appear that what Boid says about the halakah in general is particularly true in reference to the Sabbath.

A notable Samaritan document from the fourth century deals with the Sabbath in rather singular terms. It sings the praises of the Sabbath as one of the wonders of creation that only those who have wisdom may properly discern. It is the work of a Samaritan by the name of Marcus, which in Samaritan Aramaic was rendered Marqah. His "sayings" are called the *Memar Marqah*.[32] It has been characterized as "a homiletical exegesis of the Pentateuch."[33] This description, however, is too generous since the work does not aim to cover the five books of Moses. Commenting on the introduction to the Song of Moses in Exodus 15:1 ("Then Moses and the people of Israel sang this song to the Lord"), Marqah focuses on the first word as follows:

> At the beginning of the song is THEN, for TIT was made an extensive garden. The True One commanded it and Abraham made it—*and the Lord God planted* (Gen 2:8), the True One spoke; and Abraham planted a tamarisk tree (Gen 21:33), the True One wrote.
>
> Then Moses began and said in the sea; he composed his song a garden of praise; he said THEN to rear a fine garden with living trees, and also when he began to proclaim the word THEN Creation was renewed at that. THEN included Creation and Sabbath, Sabbath being an excellent pillar, all of it good, for God established it on the foundation of Creation; thus Moses began with mighty proclamation. THEN is the Beginning, the opening—wholly excellent! Sabbath is a city—wholly blessed! Beginning is an origin, wholly spiritual! Sabbath is a place, wholly sacred! . . . Beginning was created and Sabbath brought into being. The covenant with Abraham was manifest in the number ZAIN (= 7). (2.7, Macdonald, 56)

This language is, admittedly, a bit obscure.[34] Still, some observations are possible. The passage begins and ends linking creation to Abraham. Creation is a garden which, according to Moses, God and Abraham planted together. Within creation, the Sabbath is related to it as a pillar to its foundation. More importantly, as the pillar in the garden, the Sabbath stands for both the tree of life and the tree of the knowledge of good and evil. Creation itself established two things: the beginning and the Sabbath. The beginning, which the prologue of the Fourth Gospel links to the Logos, Marqah links instead to the Sabbath. This beginning, moreover, although wholly spiritual, has been created. The Sabbath, which rests on it, in turn, is wholly sacred. Thus, the Sabbath is conceived as a reality within creation.[35] As a sacred place it is a blessed city. This city is for the habitation of those who, being spiritual, live in the garden where creation is renewed.[36] It turns out that, rather than being in time, the Sabbath is in space.

Even if some of the language and the ethos of Marqah resonate with those of Philo,[37] Marqah goes out of his way to make the Sabbath the link between creation and the covenant with Abraham. Philo, on the other hand, ignores a theology of the covenant and never presents the Sabbath as a sign of the covenant. In fact, for him the Sabbath is embedded in eternal reality and as such belongs to humankind as a whole.[38] Marqah, as will become clear, keeps the Sabbath closely bound to Abraham and Israel.

Moses' victory over the Egyptians at the sea is viewed by Marqah in terms of the victory of God over the sea hinted at in Genesis 1:2. The song of Moses is his garden. Both the garden of creation and the garden of the song are enclosures where nature and words function in superlatively creative ways under the mastery of human agents. Singing this song at the sea, Moses brings about a spiritual creation, the garden of his song.[39] The image of the garden serves Marqah to show Abraham and Moses rather than, for example, hypostatic Wisdom (Prov 8) as the master workmen helping God at creation.

The linkage of Moses in the sea to creation is also expressed in the following exhortation:

> Let us return to the True One and believe in the Lord our Maker and Lord, and also in Moses our prophet and Saviour. If it had not been for Moses the world would not have been created and none of these wonders would have been manifested. (2.9, Macdonald, 73)

It was through the wonder at the sea that "the kingdom of Israel has now been created" (2.9). That Moses is not only the savior but also the agent of creation, as he sang the praises of God while standing in the sea, shows Marqah's purpose in his *Memar*. The work may justifiably be characterized as an eulogy to the magnificence of Moses.

Among things in the world, Marqah says, God set apart seven as divine: the light, the Sabbath, Mount Gerizim, Adam, the two stone tablets, the great prophet Moses, and Israel (2.10). To be noticed is that the Sabbath is set apart from the two stone tablets of the Decalogue and linked to the first day of creation and the light. For Marqah the Sabbath is not just law.[40]

At times it appears not to be a day. Even if created, it is a transcendent, sacred space. For him also, as for Aristobulus and Philo, the number seven is ontologically related to the Sabbath and the holy (4.1).

Like Philo, Marqah is fond of gematria and numerology. He also sees special significance in the number ten, giving several sets of tens that magnify the great prophet Moses:[41] the ten wonders at the Exodus, the ten parts of the form of Adam, the ten forces of the unseen, the ten ways of righteousness, the ten foundations of Genesis, and the ten elements of the Sabbath. These last are the covenant, holiness, blessing, rest, warning, observance, life, death, cessation from work, and prayer. Each one of them is based on a Sabbath reference in the Pentateuch. He sums them up as follows:

> All these are good foundations which magnify those who keep them. The covenant lasts for ever; holiness is never changed; The two of them belong to God! By them he honored Israel. Blessing is for those fully deserving reward for action: rest for those who keep it: warning against departing from its bounds: observance of it is the supplier of life: cessation from work because work is not fitting on Sabbath: prayer during it is acceptable, for it comprises four prayers that are acceptable and unchangeable. (4.1, Macdonald, 138)

The four prayers are those for healing, petition, grace, and entreaty. These are all included in the Sabbath prayer. The paragraph ends with Marqah's pronouncement: "Life to those who observe its commands and death to those who break its fences!" As it is for Philo, for Marqah obedience is of the essence.

According to Marqah, Sabbath observance is "the supplier of life." This claim seems to be unique. It is good Jewish theology to affirm that life is dependent on the Torah. Psalm 119, a synagogue psalm, makes life dependent on God's promise (119:50), mercy (119:77), and steadfast love (119:159). It also affirms that God's laws are the basis of hope (119:43) because they are the source of life. "I will never forget thy precepts; for by them thou hast given me life" (119:93). Qoheleth, for his part, concludes its ruminations with an unexpected twist. The second epilogue affirms that the solution to the human predicament is to "Fear God and keep his commandments; for this is everything to human beings" (12:13b). Marqah has drawn the circle much smaller and, on account of its special status within creation, singled out the Sabbath as the source of life. "Observance of it is the supplier of life." This should be seen in connection with the image of the pillar in the garden that stands for the trees that give and delimit life.[42]

From the song at the sea in Exodus 15, Marqah moves to the Song of Moses in Deuteronomy 32. Again enlarging on the song by free association, he writes:

See how it is in Genesis and number the letters—six—like the six days, for each one resembles the other; and the name which brought all created things into being sealed the whole. Therefore, he said, "God finished" (Gen 2:2). *Bereshith* was the starting point and *God finished.* Also the six days, Sabbath and holiness. Therefore the great prophet Moses proclaimed at the beginning *KI.* Since these things came *in the name....* Therefore he began by saying, "For in the name." (4.2, Macdonald, 139)

According to Marqah, Moses' song begins with the words: "For (*ki*) in the name of the Lord I will proclaim: 'Ascribe greatness to our God'"[43] Connecting the beginning of the song and the beginning of Genesis 1:1, Marqah desires to show how the ten foundations of creation magnify Moses. "God finished" (Gen 2:2) seems to have been called to mind by the introduction of the song in Deuteronomy 31:30: "Then Moses spoke the words of this song until they were finished." The conclusion of the song is therefore tied to the conclusion of creation with the Sabbath. The cluster of ideas has a logic of its own. Creation is perfected in the Sabbath and its holiness, and created things are sealed in the name that shares the holiness of the Sabbath and brought forth creation from beginning to end.

After this introduction, Marqah expands on the first two words of the actual song: "Ascribe greatness." This he does on the basis of gematria on the Aramaic WHBW GDL. W (6) stands for the six days of creation and everything created in them. H (the tetragrammaton?) is the "name" to which all creatures answer. B (2) is for the two worlds, this one and the next. W (6) is the end. On this Aramaic basis, Marqah writes, "He made known that the one is like the other, and he increased the speaking of wisdom." This cryptic remark seems to be elucidated with the exposition that follows:

When he said GDL (greatness) he sought to strengthen the words by holiness. When Creation and Sabbath were gathered to him, he magnified its

holiness with G and D and sealed it with L. This is a city wholly great, at
the entrance of which is written: *The Lord our God is one Lord* (Deut 6:4,
Targ.). Happy are they who dwell in it! He makes them all to be possessed
of the Favour. (4.2, Macdonald, 140)

It would seem that living in the city of the only Lord God is possible
in this world, and it is on account of this that the end of the world does
not bring drastic changes for those who find holiness and perfection in the
Sabbath. In this way both worlds are alike for those who posses wisdom.
As created things were sealed by the name, so now creation and the Sabbath have been sealed by Moses when he ascribed greatness to God at the
beginning of his song. The Sabbath within creation serves as a foretaste of
the world to come.[44] It is the sacred place, marked by a single pillar in the
garden of God. It is the city where those possessed of God's favor dwell in
safety. As an image it has become the navel of the world and has effectively
replaced the temple.

The image of the garden, not just the pillar within the garden of creation, also appears in Marqah in reference to life in heaven. The righteous,
who live in the garden, possess two things, shade and well-being.[45] One
affords "refreshing coolness" and the other "rest." He then exalts, "What a
splendid portion, the portion of righteousness! He who is humble will be
in great glory in this world and the next" (4. 12).

It is rather remarkable that the images of the city and the garden should
be used to illumine the concept of the Sabbath. On first impressions the
garden and the city seem to stand for the alternatives of nature and culture. But closer examination makes one question this facile dichotomy.
Even if the Yahwist in the primeval stories of Genesis 1–11 seems to contrast Eden and Babel, it would seem that later reconsiderations of the
human condition found in the garden and the city complementary images
with which to visualize utopia, as the book of Revelation makes clear. In
it eschatological existence takes place in the garden, where the river and
the tree of life are found . . . in the New Jerusalem, the city of God. The
precious stones which are characteristic of Eden now adorn the city with
streets of gold and gates of pearls. Where Revelation envisions the temple
and the throne, Marqah finds the Sabbath.

The garden and the city are also juxtaposed in the Song of Songs, where
they serve as dramatic backdrops for the longings, the frustrations, and the

encounters of the two lovers.[46] The Song also identifies the Beloved as a closed garden (4:12). In the poem now recorded in 4:12–5:1 the Beloved demonstrates the human ability to reexperience paradise through the arts of culture, poetry, personal sophistication, etc.[47] It is to the garden that is the Beloved that the Lover comes to feed among the lilies. The garden is nature perfected by culture, but also nature as the sustainer of cultural life. Paradise is not raw nature, but nature under the rational vision and the untiring labors of human beings. Already in the Persian satrapies, according to P. Briant,[48] the *paradeisoi* (gardens) were important ideological prototypes on account of their being both models of what can be and exceptions within the surrounding countryside. As such, they were *vitrines idéologiques*. These enclosures consisted of residences for the satraps or the king, gardens with kiosks, fountains, patterned paths, and woods where every known tree could be found.[49] The garden represents the return of culture to nature, but also the turning of nature into culture. The person of power and wisdom, King Solomon, goes to the garden to see the spring, but while in the garden, feeding among the lilies, he is beyond the surrounding world. His solitude cannot be disturbed. Gardens are spots where one can escape time and responsibilities and find oneself in touch with what is eternal. To return to Marqah, at the center of the garden is the tree of life, the pillar of the Sabbath. Sabbath observance is the supplier of life.

In the Song of Songs the Beloved also becomes, in the eyes of the Lover, a city with strong walls and towers where peace may be found (8:10). The city is the home of justice and security, where time is integrated, and past, present, and future are unified by human purposes. In the apocalyptic imagination there are two cities: Babylon and Jerusalem. They are the harlot and the virgin bride. In the Song of Songs, the daughters of Jerusalem constitute a sympathetic chorus, and the night watchmen support the one who longs for love.

The wisdom traditions that informed the composition of the Song of Songs and the apocalyptic literature continued to be elaborated in creative ways. The garden and the city where paradise is regained became powerful images of the full life. They emerge not only in apocalyptic visions, which following the *Urzeit/Endzeit* pattern call for a new heaven and a new earth, but also in a theology of the Sabbath that aims to give transcendence to the life of obedience in this world, as prescribed by the synagogue.

Descriptions of the Samaritans as sectarian extremists do not do them justice. The situation was undoubtedly quite fluid. The social and religious reality of the Jews in the Roman world was very complex, with competing, discrete points of view as to how to be a true Jew. It is clear that the Sabbath halakah of the Samaritans was not a deviant development that grew in isolation or represented a fallback to an earlier rigorism. Rather, the Samaritans throughout their history remained in full dialogue with the cacophony of halakic voices within Judaism. Moreover, their Sabbath views were not simply a matter of law and purity. They were also informed by a theologizing that was also *au courant* with the philosophical currents informing Hellenistic culture at large. In many ways their concerns about the Sabbath were similar to those found among Christians. Both groups were part of the larger religious phenomenon rooted in the Pentateuch.

4

The Sabbath in the Writings of Josephus

In reference to the Sabbath, modern scholarship has tended to tap Josephus' writings with one of two questions in mind. In the first place his works provide a rather impressive string of imperial, provincial, and municipal decrees granting the Jews significant religious privileges, including noninterference with their Sabbath observances.[1] The evidence Josephus marshals to sustain his apologetic effort is judged today as quite trustworthy.[2] That Jews could observe the Sabbath according to their religious laws within the Roman Empire is a historical datum standing on rather solid ground. It must be admitted, however, that the above-mentioned edicts were reissued or appealed to with some frequency, and this testifies to the unwillingness of some among whom the Jews lived to gracefully recognize the privileges granted by imperial authorities.[3]

Second, Josephus reports that in times of war, adversaries of the Jews took tactical advantage of their Sabbath observance. Furthermore, pagan authors scoffed at the Jews because, on account of their superstitious strict adherence to their law, they had lost their freedom. This charge concerned Sabbath practices directly. On this question, however, the evidence in Josephus is inconsistent. Thus, his claim that Jews had a widely accepted policy on Sabbath fighting stands on much softer ground.

Josephus' reports of Jews not fighting or fighting on the Sabbath have been interpreted differently by recent scholars. Max Radin dismisses the reports as untenable in light of previous biblical accounts of Jews engaged in warfare. The Bible does not say that during times of war hostilities ceased on the Sabbath. In the postexilic period, to our knowledge, no policy to this effect was developed. We know, however, that Jews were highly regarded mercenaries in foreign armies. Accordingly, Josephus' reports are not credible.[4] Alger F. Johns, on the other hand, gives full credence to some of Josephus' reports and postulates that Jerusalem was attacked on a Sabbath at the time of Nabuchadnezzar on account of an already existing nonfighting policy of the Jews.[5] Sidney Hoenig, for his part, argues that the apparently contradictory reports in Josephus can be understood in terms of the historical development of halakah.[6] Robert Goldenberg, without making direct reference to Josephus' reports, explains that there was no universal policy. According to him, on this matter Jews acted differently during different times in different regions.[7]

The two issues mentioned above are not the only ones about the Sabbath that interested Josephus.[8] After all, both as a polemicist and an apologist Josephus could not ignore the centrality of the Sabbath in his ancestral tradition. It was certainly one of the few things about Judaism of which Gentiles were well aware.[9] To gain a coherent picture of all his Sabbath references, however, it is necessary to recognize their function. He seems to have a particular dislike for anyone who would compromise in reference to the Sabbath. Thus, his accounts may tell us more about Josephus than about the person whose actions he describes.

The fourth commandment places an injunction against all work on the seventh day. Josephus does not tire from reminding his readers that on the seventh day Jews "abstain from labor" and "rest from all work."[10] It is doubtful, however, that Josephus may be called upon as a witness to the rabbinic definitions of what constitutes work since his descriptions are rather general.[11] The evidence he provides does not warrant a judgment on Josephus' position in internal halakic debates.[12]

In his treatise *Against Apion* Josephus quotes both Hecataeus and Agatharchides extensively, claiming that in this way the reader will gain an unbiased picture of the Jews. Before quoting Agatharchides, he further advises the reader that "he mentions us only to ridicule our folly, as he regards it" (*C. Ap.* 1.205). He then quotes:

> The people known as Jews, who inhabit the most strongly fortified of cities, called by the natives Jerusalem, have a custom of abstaining from work every seventh day; on these occasions they neither bear arms nor take any agricultural operations in hand, nor engage in any other form of public service, but pray with outstretched hands in the temples until the evening. (*C. Ap.* 1.209)[13]

Whether the three specific injunctions against the bearing of arms, agricultural work, and public service and the positive injunction to spend the day in prayer were to be found in Agatharchides' work or are introduced here by Josephus is difficult to determine. Neither the negative nor the positive descriptions of Sabbath activities appear in *Antiquities* 12.6, where Josephus also refers to the same passage from Agatharchides.[14] These injunctions seem to be programmatic in Josephus' own mind. His summary makes the point that even though it is true that the Sabbath may appear to be a day controlled by a negative command, "Do no work on it," in fact it is a day in which praying in the temples (ἐν τοῖσ ἱεϱοῖσ)[15] is done with more intensity than at any other time. In other words, the prohibition of work has a positive aim in view. It makes possible the intensification of the life of piety, which praying exemplifies.[16]

This theme is picked up in two other passages. In a speech before Agrippa on behalf of the Jews of Ionia, Nicholas of Damascus is credited by Josephus for having pointed out that "we give every seventh day over to the study of our customs and law, for we think it necessary to occupy ourselves with these which are capable of keeping us from sinning, as well as with other studies" (*A.J.* 16.43). His request is, simply put, 'ακωλύτωσ τὴν πάτϱιον ἐυσέβειαν διαφυλάττειν (*A.J.* 16.41). In order to be able to do this, however, two conditions are indispensable. First, outsiders must not interfere with the religious observances of the Jews, and second, Jews must have a thorough knowledge of the religion of their ancestors. Nicholas asserts that their customs and law are not only excellent but also ancient. This claim makes it very difficult for those who regard them as sacred to abruptly abandon them (*A.J.* 16.41–45).

In *Against Apion* Josephus exalts the wisdom of Moses in drafting the Jewish law, guided as he was by his view of God. In this, Moses was superior to all the Greek philosophers who "adopted these conceptions of God from principles with which Moses supplied them. . . . In fact, Pythagoras, Anaxagoras, Plato, the Stoics who succeeded him, and indeed nearly all the philosophers appear to have held similar views concerning the nature of God" (*C. Ap.* 2.168). Moses is superior to all philosophers, however, not only because he provided them with basic principles but also because, unlike those who limited their discourse to the likeminded elite and entertained their views in the realm of theory, he divulged his views to the masses[17] and gave to his views a footing in practice as well as theory. "By making practice square with precept, [Moses] not only convinced his own contemporaries, but so firmly implanted this belief concerning God in their descendants to all future generations that it cannot be moved" (*C. Ap.* 2.169). In the Mosaic legislation, Josephus points out, theory and practice are one and indivisible. Moses did not permit the letter of the Law to remain inoperative. Starting from the very beginning with the food of which we partake from infancy and the private life of the home, he left nothing, however insignificant, to the discretion and caprice of the individual. What meats a man should abstain from, what he may enjoy; with what persons he should associate; what period should be devoted respectively to strenuous labour and to rest—for all this our leader made the Law the standard and rule. . . . He appointed the Law to be the most excellent and necessary form of instruction, ordaining, not that it should be heard once for all or twice or on several occasions, but that every week men should desert their other occupations and assemble to listen to the Law and to obtain a thorough and accurate knowledge of it, a practice which all other legislators seem to have neglected. (*C. Ap.* 2.273–275)

In this way, Josephus points out, the law is the ὅϱον . . . καὶ κανόνα of the Jews who live under it ὥσπεϱ ὑπὸ πατϱὶ . . . καὶ δεσπότη (as under a father and hard master)(*C. Ap.* 2.174). "For ignorance he [Moses] left no pretext" (*C. Ap.* 2.175). This is the case only when the Sabbath fulfills its most essential positive functions.

The superiority of the Jewish way of life, therefore, is traceable not only to the superiority of the vision of God granted to Moses, on the basis of which Moses drafted the best laws of any human society, but also to his inclusion in the law of prescriptions addressing the details of everyday life. Among these, Josephus singles out the Sabbath rest. For Jews the law resides not only in the mind as precept, but also in living it out as practice. To ensure that this takes place, Moses established the Sabbath for the study of the law, since practice of the law is impossible without adequate knowledge of it. For Josephus the Sabbath plays a determining role in constituting the people as one in which memory is at work, obedience is natural, "transgression is a rarity, and evasion of punishment by excuses an impossibility" (*C. Ap.* 2.178).[18]

It would seem that Josephus does not fail to refer to any memorable Sabbath practice or event recorded in Scripture. For example, Leviticus 24:8 notes that the twelve loaves of the bread of the presence, which according to Exodus 25:30 were to be set "on the table before me always," were, in fact, to be replaced with new ones every Sabbath. This detail is noted twice by Josephus, in *Antiquites* 3.143 and 255. Likewise, Numbers 28:3–10 specifies that, whereas the "continual offering" consisted of the daily sacrifice of one lamb in the morning and another one in the evening, on the Sabbath two lambs were to be offered at each of the appointed times. Josephus also dutifully records this detail in *Antiquities* 3.237.

Josephus claims that Moses "invented" (εὗρε) a small silver cornet, of which he had two made. Their use was regulated so that the sounding of one meant that the captains of the tribes were being called for deliberations, and the sounding of both meant that all the people were being summoned. Following the instructions given in Numbers 10:1–10, Josephus specifies that, in addition, the trumpets were to be blown when the encampment was to be moved, as a "remembrance before your God" when burnt offerings and sacrifices were being offered, or when going out to war. He follows the passage in Numbers, which specifies that burnt offerings and sacrifices take place "on the day of your gladness ... and at your appointed feasts, and at the beginnings of your months" (10:10). Josephus then adds, "They also used these cornets when presenting their offerings in their temple services both on the Sabbaths and on the other [holy] days" (*A.J.* 3.294). The expression "the day of your gladness" may legitimately be understood to refer to "extraordinary public festivals," as suggested by H. St. J. Thackeray.[19] Thus, the biblical text may have prescribed the blowing of the trumpets at extraordinary festivals besides the yearly and the monthly regular festivals. This may be suggested also by the Septuagint's reading of the phrase in the plural, "the days of your gladness." On the other hand, the use of the plural Sabbaths in order to refer to a single Sabbath is well attested,[20] and the general designation of the festivals as yearly, monthly, and weekly is a commonplace. Josephus' interpretation of "day of your gladness" as Sabbath is, in any case, quite legitimate.[21]

In the two passages that describe the priestly ministrations, Josephus gives particular attention to the high priest.[22] Of special interest is that the earlier, shorter description is introduced with the following: "The high priest accompanied them, not on all occasions, but on the seventh days and new moons, and on any national festival or annual assemblage of all the people" (*B.J.* 5.230).[23] If this practice has to do with the "continual" offering that, as noted above, on Sabbaths consisted of two lambs rather than one, there is no other reference indicating that at these occasions the officiating priest was assisted by the high priest. Josephus' description of the high priest "accompanying" the priest on Sabbaths would seem to solemnize the procedures even more.

According to Josephus, some pagans also observed the Sabbath rest. In this he agrees with Aristobulus and Philo of Alexandria and disputes those who argued that it was impossible for a pagan to observe the Sabbath.[24] He writes that, not only were the Greek philosophers dependent on Moses for their views about God, but also "the masses have long since shown a keen desire to adopt our religious observances; and there is not one city, Greek or barbarian, not a single nation, to which our custom of abstaining from work on the seventh day has not spread" (*C. Ap.* 2.282). This claim is not only preposterous but contradicted by his own repeated defense of the Jewish observance of the Sabbath rest vis-à-vis those who ridiculed it. According to the pagan critics, by observing the Sabbath rest, Jews unnecessarily left themselves exposed to enemy armies who found them easy prey.

Josephus gives two accounts of Ptolemy's capture of Jerusalem, an event otherwise unknown to ancient sources. It had provided detractors of the Jews with the prime example of the inherent idiocy of the Sabbath law. In the *Antiquities* he writes,

> And this king seized Jerusalem by resorting to cunning and deceit. For he entered the city on the Sabbath as if to sacrifice, and, as the Jews did not oppose him—for they did not suspect any hostile act—and, because of their lack of suspicion and the nature of the day, were enjoying idleness and ease, he became master of the city without difficulty and ruled it harshly. This account is attested by Agatharchides of Cnidus, the historian of the Diadochi, who reproaches us for our superstition [δεισιδαιμονίαν], on account of which we lost our liberty, in these words, "There is a nation called Jews, who have a strong and great city called Jerusalem, which they allowed to fall into the hands of Ptolemy by refusing to take up arms and, instead, through their untimely superstition ['ακαιρὸν δεισιδαιμονίαν] submitted to having a hard master [δεσπότην]." (*A.J.* 12.4–6)

In *Against Apion* he quotes Agatharchides as having written,

The people known as Jews, who inhabit the most strongly fortified of cities, called by the natives Jerusalem, have a custom of abstaining from work every seventh day....[25] Consequently, because the inhabitants, instead of protecting their city, persevered in their folly ['ανοιάν], Ptolemy, son of Lagus, was allowed to enter with his army; the country was thus given over to a cruel master [δεσπότην πικρόν], and the defect of a practice enjoined by law was exposed. That experience has taught the whole world, except that nation, the lesson not to resort to dreams and traditional fancies about the law, until its difficulties are such as to baffle human reason. (*C. Ap.* 1.209–211)

According to Agatharchides the religious observance of the Sabbath rest on the part of Jews is an "untimely superstition" that caused the citadel of Jerusalem to lose its liberty. This event shows that the Jews are not ruled by reason but that they allow dreams and fancies to sustain a bad law. This way of life only gets them into difficulties which no self-respecting nation with reasonable laws ever needs to face. Josephus counters the argument squarely by agreeing that reason must prevail. He questions, however, whether reason supports the view that Sabbath observance is a "defective practice," sheer "folly," and that safety takes precedence over piety.

His argument is based on God's retributive justice. Piety must take precedence over safety because whether the city stands or falls is determined by divine providence and the Deity is going to be gracious to those who are pious. In this way, he argues, reason supports those who obey God and trust in the Deity, rather than those who prefer safety over piety. He writes: "Dispassionate critics will consider it a grand and highly meritorious fact that there are men who consistently care more for the observance of their laws and for their religion [ἐυσεβειάν] than for their own lives and their country's fate" (*C. Ap.* 1.212).

In the proem to the *Antiquities* he announces:

the main lesson to be learnt from this history by any who care to pursue it is that men who conform to the will of God and do not venture to transgress laws that have been excellently laid down, prosper in all things beyond belief, and for their reward are offered by God felicity; whereas, in proportion as they depart from the strict observance of these laws, things (else) practicable become impracticable, and whatever imaginary good thing they strive to do ends in irretrievable disasters. (*A.J.* 1.14)

Josephus recognizes the implication of the argument and, again, faces it squarely. Giving priority to the observance of the law over life and country may lead to martyrdom.[26] Thus he boasts, "There should be nothing astonishing in our facing death on behalf of our laws with a courage which no other nation can equal." In fact, Jews are willing to face death to uphold laws that others find intolerable, such as "personal service, simple diet, discipline which leaves no room for freak or individual caprice in matters of meat and drink, or in the sexual relations, or in extravagance, or again the abstention from work at rigidly fixed periods" (*C. Ap.* 2.234). The insertion of the word "again" [πάλιν] in the last phrase indicates that he had in mind the Sabbath all along. Especially on this point Josephus feels he must correct the distorted views propagated by those who ridicule the Jews, the Manethos, Chaeremons, Lysimachuses and Molons of this world (*C. Ap.* 2.236).

In his defense of the Jews, Josephus singles out Apion, "the grammarian, . . . a man of low character and a charlatan to the end of his days," whose writings, while "displaying the gross ignorance of their author," nevertheless "deserve serious refutation" (*C. Ap.* 2.1–3). One of the ideas demanding refutation is Apion's explanation for the origin of Jewish Sabbath observance. According to Josephus, in his narrative of the exodus Apion includes the following:

> After a six days' march they developed tumors in the groin, and that was why, after safely reaching the country now called Judaea, they rested on the seventh day, and called that day σάββατον, preserving the Egyptian terminology; for disease of the groin in Egypt is called σάββω. (*C. Ap.* 2.21)

Josephus' reaction to Apion's alleged etymology is predictable. "One knows not whether to laugh at the nonsense, or rather to be indignant at the impudence, of such language" (*C. Ap.* 2.22). He then proceeds first to ridicule Apion's account and then to point out the etymological error. "There is a wide difference between σάββω and σάββατον. Σάββατον in the Jew's language denotes cessation from all work, while σάββω among the Egyptians signifies, as he states, disease of the groin" (*C. Ap.* 2.27).[27] As was pointed out above, in Josephus' mind Sabbath means first and foremost "cessation from all work" ['ανάπαυσισ . . . 'απὸ παντὸσ ἔργον].

According to Josephus, the Jews did not discover until the time of the Maccabean War that the Sabbath commandment left them exposed to their enemies on that day.[28] In his telling, after the rebellion at Modain, the king's officers pursued the followers of Mattathias into the wilderness and found them hiding in caves. The officers then

> attacked them on the Sabbath day and burned them in their caves, just as they were, for not only did the Jews not resist, but they did not even close the entrances to the caves. And they forbore to resist because of the day, being unwilling to violate the dignity of the Sabbath even when in difficulties, for the law requires us to rest on that day. (*A.J.* 12.274)

As a consequence, one thousand men with their women and children died of suffocation in the caves.

Following the account in 1 Maccabees 2:29–41, Josephus reports that the survivors then appointed Mattathias as their leader, and he established a new policy concerning war on the Sabbath. According to Josephus, Mattathias

> instructed them to fight even on the Sabbath, saying that if for the sake of observing the law they failed to do so, they would be their own enemies, for their foes would attack them on that day, and unless they resisted, nothing would prevent them from all perishing without striking a blow. These words persuaded them, and to this day we continue the practice of fighting even on the Sabbath whenever it becomes necessary. (*A.J.* 12.276–277)

If Mattathias' decision to fight on the Sabbath was the accepted rule of conduct for all Jews in Josephus' day,[29] then Josephus could not have argued in his *Against Apion* that in order to observe the sanctity of the Sabbath Jews choose piety over safety, since martyrdom is preferable to disobedience of the law. According to both 1 Maccabees and Josephus, however, Mattathias argued precisely the opposite.[30] He makes the point that pagans who ridiculed Jews for not fighting on the Sabbath are credited with having already made: when life and limb are at stake, the Sabbath law becomes a bad law. How could Josephus overlook that Mattathias' ruling, which he accepts as valid to his own day, was against his panegyric of the Jews who would rather die than disobey the Sabbath law?[31]

Both in the *Jewish War* and in the *Antiquites* Josephus makes the point that Matthathias' ruling was further qualified.[32] This happens in his description of the capture of Jerusalem by Pompey in 63 B.C.E. In the *War* he writes,

> Indeed, the labors of the Romans would have been endless, had not Pompey taken advantage of the seventh day of the week, on which the Jews, from religious scruples (διὰ τὴν θρησκείαν), refrain from all manual work, and then proceeded to raise the earthworks, while forbidding his troops to engage in hostilities; for on the Sabbath the Jews fight only in self defense (ὑπὲρ μόνον γὰρ τοῦ σώματοσ 'αμύνονται τοῖσ σαββάτοισ). (*B.J.* 1.146)

In the *Antiquities* it reads,

> But if it were not our national custom to rest on the Sabbath day, the earthworks would not have been finished, because the Jews would have prevented this; for the Law permits us to defend ourselves against those who begin a battle and strike us, but it does not allow us to fight against an enemy that does anything else. (*A.J.* 14.63)

Since on the Sabbath the Romans were not physically attacking the Jews, they could not be prevented from building the earthworks that would allow them to position their catapults within striking distance for the eventual attack.[33]

According to Josephus, foreigners were aware of this interpretation of Matthathias' ruling that allowed Jews to defend themselves on the Sabbath. He writes,

> Of this fact the Romans were well aware, and on those days which we call the Sabbath, they did not shoot at the Jews or meet them in hand to hand combat, but instead they raised earthworks and towers, and brought up their siege-engines in order that these might be put to work the following day. (*A.J.* 14.64)

Among foreign generals, however, only Pompey when setting siege to Jerusalem planned with the knowledge that Jews would defend themselves on the Sabbath if attacked. Others deliberately postponed an attack until the Sabbath, with varying results.

After the death of Judas Maccabeus, Bacchides pursued Jonathan to the marshes of the Jordan. Then, "he waited for the Sabbath day and came against him, thinking that he would not fight on that day because of the Law" (*A.J.* 13.12). Jonathan, however, "exhorted his companions, telling them that their lives were in danger, . . . and after praying to God to grant them victory, he joined battle with the enemy" (*A.J.* 13.13). Eventually Jonathan and his men had to escape by swimming across the Jordan, where Bacchides did not pursue them. But Josephus ends the account recording that on that Sabbath Bacchides lost about two thousand men (*A.J.* 13.14). Since no losses of Jonathan are reported, it would seem that Josephus thought Jonathan gave good account of himself with God's blessing.[34] But why did Jonathan have to convince his troops to fight? Here it seems that, according to Josephus' own account, Jews were quite ignorant that self-defense was permissible on the Sabbath.

Before his attack on Jerusalem, while conquering Galilee, Ptolemy "made a sudden attack on Asochis on the Sabbath and, taking it by storm, captured about ten thousand persons and a great deal of booty" (*A.J.* 13.337). Does this mean that he had not yet been informed that, if attacked, Jews would defend themselves on the Sabbath? Or were the general military conditions so clearly in his favor that he took advantage of them? Apparently, while the capture of Asochis took place on a Sabbath, Ptolemy had not chosen the day with premeditation. Josephus says nothing as to whether the inhabitants bravely defended themselves or offered no resistance on account of the day.

When a Parthian general went out to stop Asinaeus and Anilaeus—two Jewish brothers who installed themselves as protectors of the poor but terrorized the countryside exacting heavy payments from the local land-owners and herders—he planned an ambush on the Sabbath. He assumed that the Jews would not fight and he would be able to capture them without a battle (*A.J.* 18.314–319). Josephus takes pains to explain that the Parthian used every precaution in order to catch the brothers by surprise, at ease on the Sabbath. It would seem that according to the interpretation of the rule of Mattathias, these Jews could have quite legitimately defended themselves. The Jewish scouts who reported the presence of the Parthian army, however, say, "We are caught in a trap like so many animals at pasture. There are all these horsemen approaching and our hands are tied because the commandment of our ancestral law orders us to do no work" (*A.J.* 18.322). Asinaeus thought otherwise. He took up arms and convinced his soldiers to do likewise. The outcome of his boldness was that the Jews "slaughtered them in great numbers . . . and put the rest to flight" (*A.J.* 18.324). What is remarkable in Josephus' account is that he makes clear the soldiers thought they should not fight and that by fighting Asinaeus was violating the law (παρανομεῖν) even though Josephus writes elsewhere that Jews had established a rationale allowing them to fight in self-defense on the Sabbath.[35]

The story of the two brothers is the well-known tale of those who climb from rags to riches by improper means and have a tragic end.[36] Anilaeus insulted Mithridates, the commander of a Parthian army, by plundering his villages. Mithridates, as expected, responded by selecting a prime cavalry force and camping in a village of Anilaeus', "where he rested with the intention of fighting on the following day, inasmuch as it would be the Sabbath, a day in which the Jews abstain from work" (*A.J.* 18.354). Thanks to a tip from a Gentile Syrian, Anilaeus was able to turn the tables on Mithridates and attack him by surprise on the fourth watch with much success, after having marched all night during Sabbath hours. Regarding this episode, one should recall that Josephus quotes Nicolas of Damascus to the effect that when John Hyrcanus aided Antiochus Sidetes in a campaign against Parthia, he requested and Antiochus granted that they not march for two days out of respect for a Jewish festival. Josephus comments, "Nor does he speak falsely in saying this; for the festival of Pentecost had come around, following the Sabbath, and we are not permitted to march either on the Sabbath or on a festival" (*A.J.* 13.252).[37] John Hyrchanus, however, is singled out by Josephus as a most virtuous prince who enjoyed unique favor with the Deity (*Ant.* 13.282, 284, 288, 299–300). Thus, in Josephus' mind, Anilaeus violated the Sabbath by marching during Sabbath hours.

Anilaeus and his brother had become brigands in "the service of lawlessness, into which they plunged in violation of the Jewish code at the bidding of lust and self-indulgence" (*A.J.* 18.340). Anilaeus' victory, therefore, was a Pyrrhic one. Even though Anilaeus, mindful that if he killed Mithridates Jews everywhere in Parthia would pay the consequences, had spared the commander's life that Sabbath day after they had marched all night,[38] eventually Mithridates caught him and killed him. Again, in this incident a pagan thought that the Jews would not fight on the Sabbath, but his calculations proved wrong. Josephus is no admirer of Mithridates, but neither is he of the two Jewish brothers who caused their kinsmen to fight on the Sabbath.[39]

From the evidence presented above, we clearly see the difficulty of taking all of Josephus' accounts at face value. If there had been a clear policy allowing fighting in self-defense, no Jew should have been charged of being a lawbreaker for doing it and there would have been no need to convince those with religious scruples to fight.[40] Also, it would seem that the enemies of the Jews would have known of the policy and acted accordingly, as only Pompey is said to have done. More likely, the issue of Sabbath fighting was never really settled, but remained forever an open question because, as Goldenberg says, "the refusal of some people to bear arms was more important than the willingness of others."[41]

In view of the impasse presented above, I would like to propose another way of reading the evidence in Josephus. Evidently Josephus had a great deal of reverence for the Sabbath, and considered abstention from work during its hours essential. He never tires of reminding his readers that Jews do no work on the Sabbath; he does this almost every time he puts the word on paper. Interestingly, when describing his own military activity during the Galilean phase of the war with Rome, he makes it a point to dramatize his own scrupulous Sabbath observance.

Both in the *Jewish War* and in *The Life* Josephus refers to an incident when the people of Tiberias rebelled against his leadership and hoped to align themselves with the advancing Romans. The situation became critical when a small contingent of Roman cavalry was sighted nearby and Josephus feared it might gain entrance into the city. He was at the moment in Tarichaeae with only seven soldiers. Both versions of the story establish that action could not be delayed until the next day because that was the Sabbath, and "it would have been impossible for them to bear arms on the morrow, such action being forbidden by our laws, however urgent the apparent necessity" (*Vita* 161). The *Jewish War* reads, "on the following day, moreover, he could take no action owning to the restrictions of the Sabbath" (*B.J.* 2.634). The accounts vary as to the reason why his army was not in Tarichaeae with him that Friday. According to one, "he had just sent all his soldiers on a foraging excursion" (*B.J.* 2.634). According to the other, "I had dismissed my soldiers from Tarichaeae to their homes because, the next day being the Sabbath, I desired that the Tarichaeans should be spared any annoyance from the presence of the military" (*Vita,* 159). Whether the soldiers were out securing provisions or had gone home on account of the Sabbath, Josephus finds himself confronting a dilemma.[42]

He must prevent the Roman cavalry from entering Tiberias, but he cannot have his army or engage the enemy until Sunday. He saves the day by making recourse to "a deception at sea," thereby taking care of the emergency and not breaking the Sabbath. In *The Life* he makes the further point that his piety extended to making the Sabbath observance of all the people of Tarichaeae more agreeable by the absence of soldiers. Thereby he proves himself both pious and resourceful.

In the account of an attempt on his life at the synagogue in Tiberias, where a few followers of John of Gischala tried to convince the people of Tiberias to repudiate Josephus and then tried to kill him, Josephus points out that the plot involved a Sabbath. Since on Friday John's lackeys had outdone themselves praising Josephus, "corroborating these assertions by the most awe-inspiring oaths known to us," Josephus left for Tarichaeae. Still he took precautions by leaving behind people who would inform him of what was said of him in his absence. The reader is left to understand that Josephus dutifully observed the Sabbath at his place. In the meantime, at Tiberias the synagogue meeting turned into a political rally that would have degenerated into a riot, "had not the arrival of the sixth hour, at which it is our custom on the Sabbath to take our midday meal, broken off the meeting" (*Vita* 279). It is clear that while he is a faithful Sabbath observer, those who wish him ill are not.

This pattern can be seen in the whole of the Josephan corpus. While the truly pious observe the Sabbath, those who are not demonstrate their impiety by breaking it. Josephus considers the Sabbath a barometer of piety and describes Sabbath observance as if it were a label with which to tag people.

We already referred to the Maccabean martyrs who on the Sabbath did not even defend themselves by closing the openings of the caves in which they had found refuge (*A.J.* 12.271–274) and also to the defenders of Jerusalem who did not attack the Romans who were building earthworks outside the walls of the city on the Sabbath (*A.J.* 14.63–68). Josephus takes pains to point out that in spite of the difficult situations in which those inside Jerusalem found themselves, the Sabbaths and the festivals were observed in the temple as if everything were normal. Eventually Pompey's troops entered the city on the Fast Day, on the third month of the hundred and seventy-ninth olympiad, in the consulship of Gaius Antonius and Marcus Tullius Cicero. The priests who were officiating at the temple, Josephus insists, none the less continued to perform the sacred ceremonies; nor were they compelled, either by fear for their lives or by the great number of those already slain, to run away, but thought it better to endure whatever they might have to suffer there beside the altars than to neglect any of the ordinances. And that this is not merely a story to set forth the praises of a fictitious piety, but the truth, is attested by all those who have narrated the exploits of Pompey, among them Strabo and Nicolas of Damascus and, in addition, Titus Livius, the author of a History of Rome. (*A.J.* 14.67–68)[43]

The Maccabean martyrs in 167 B.C.E., the priests in Jerusalem in 63 B.C.E., and he himself in 66 C.E. were, no doubt, pious observant Jews.

Josephus does not consider a Jew who fights on the Sabbath a good, pious Jew.[44] As we have pointed out already, Asinaeus and Anilaeus were not pious. In obvious contrast with the Jews who were in Jerusalem at the time of the attack by Pompey, the Jews in Jerusalem in 70 C.E., who were celebrating the Feast of Tabernacles,

> seeing the war approaching the capital, abandoned the feast and rushed to arms; and, with great confidence in their numbers, sprang in disorder and with loud cries into the fray, with no thought for the seventh day of rest, for it was the very Sabbath which they regarded with special reverence. But the same passion which shook them out of their piety brought them victory in the battle. (*B.J.* 2.517–518)

Josephus makes clear, however, that the triumph of these Jews, like the triumph of Anilaeus, only served to "fill the cup of irretrievable disaster" (*B.J.* 2.532). He did not consider those still in Jerusalem at this time to be good Jews. For Josephus, Sabbath breaking and being ruled by passion equally exhibit and reinforce lack of virtue.

Josephus sets up the above scene by recounting how the Jewish rebels had entered Jerusalem in the first place and killed the Roman garrison there. Metilius, the Roman commander, had offered to surrender their arms and all their belongings. In response Eleazar sent envoys to give the oaths that guaranteed the safety of the Romans as they took their leave. But when the Romans came out, once they had put down their arms, Eleazar had them all killed, with the exception of Metilius himself. This act of infamy made all the inhabitants of Jerusalem realize that war was now inevitable. Josephus says that such treachery aroused

dread of some visitation from heaven, if not of the vengeance of Rome. . . .
For, to add to its heinousness, the massacre took place on the Sabbath, a
day on which from religious scruples Jews abstain even from the most
innocent acts. (*B.J.* 2.455–456)

According to Josephus, in this case retributive justice, the most significant power in history,[45] brought about immediate reprisal: "The same day
and at the same hour, as it were by the hand of Providence, the inhabitants
of Caesarea massacred the Jews who resided in their city" (*B.J.* 2.457).
This, in turn, caused Jews everywhere to attack Gentiles, and other Gentiles to carry out preemptive strikes against Jews, creating a situation that
made the massive use of force appear to be the only solution. Among the
many things that Josephus says against the rebels who brought about the
war, their disregard for the Sabbath is quite salient.

Possibly, halakic development had established some guidelines for permissible Sabbath fighting by the time Josephus writes. It could have also
been the case that the debates about the conditions under which fighting
was allowed appealed to what was considered to be Maccabean precedent.
We cannot overlook, however, that after claiming that Mattathias declared
fighting in self-defense on the Sabbath permissible, and that his ruling
had been followed till his own day, Josephus does not report a single incident in which that rule informed the action of Jews under attack. The only
exception that could possibly be considered is Joanthan's fighting when
attacked by Bacchides on the banks of the Jordan (*A. J.* 13.12–14).

Other Josephan passages support our reading of the texts. In his description of Antiochus, the renegade who inflamed the city of Antioch against
the Jews at the time of Vespasian's arrival in the region, Josephus singles
out the two acts that thrust the Jews into a crisis. First, Antiochus falsely
accused them of plotting to burn down the whole city. Then, he suggested
that the Jews be compelled "to sacrifice after the manner of the Greeks."
When the Antiochenes applied this proposal, "a few submitted and the
recalcitrants were massacred." After that, Antiochus obtained troops from
the Roman general and with them ruled harshly over his fellow Jews

> not permitting them to repose on the seventh day, but compelling them
> to do everything exactly as on other days; and so strictly did he enforce

obedience that not only at Antioch was the weekly day of rest abolished, but the example having been started there spread for a short time to the other cities as well. (*B.J.* 7.50–52)

Significantly, after idolatry, which all Jews would agree is the most grievous of sins, Josephus singles out the breaking of the Sabbath as the one that most seriously threatens the Jewish community.[46]

Also noteworthy is that Josephus chooses to exhibit his dislike of the Samaritans by presenting them as Sabbath breakers who welcome other Sabbath breakers. In this he is certainly allowing his prejudices to slander them.[47] In contrast he pictures the Essenes as the model Sabbath keepers. This apposition of two Jewish groups who had separated from the established Judaism of the Jerusalem temple is probably the best example of how Josephus uses the Sabbath as a label according to his own biases.

Josephus' admiration of the Essenes is well known.[48] He has nothing but praise for the way in which they live, keeping themselves pure and righteous. One of their purity requirements relates to bowel movements. It necessitates digging a little hole in an isolated spot and refilling it over one's stool. From the perspective of the requirements of the Sabbath rest, it involves three problematic activities: traveling to an isolated spot, digging, and shoveling. In view of this, Josephus says that they are "stricter than all Jews in abstaining from work on the seventh day; for not only do they prepare their food on the day before, to avoid kindling a fire on that one, but they do not venture to remove any vessel or even to go to stool" (*B.J.* 2.147). It would appear that Josephus is not just reporting, but actually admiring their Sabbath observance.[49] He gives the Essenes his highest compliment. In their observance of the seventh day they are "the most excellent of all Jews" (διαφορώτατα Ἰουδαιῶν ἁπάντων).[50]

By contrast, the Samaritans are in Josephus' view non-Jews who pretend to be Jews.[51] His need to remind his readers constantly about this is in itself quite telling,[52] and his eagerness to characterize them as scoundrels and opportunists causes him to contradict himself.[53] Among the specific charges Josephus makes against the Samaritans, there is a rather heavy concentration on the Sabbath. Having learned that Alexander the Great had been kind to the Jews on his way to Egypt, the Samaritans met Alexander and asked him "to remit their tribute on the seventh year, saying that they did not sow therein" (*A.J.* 11.343). Josephus leaves no doubt that they are seeking advantage under false pretenses. He also charges that Samaria is inhabited by apostate Jews (*A.J.* 11.340) and, therefore, under Persian rule (when Ezra and Nehemiah enforced stricter observance in Judea) "anyone who was accused by the people of Jerusalem of eating unclean food or violating the Sabbath or committing any other such sin, he would flee to the Shechemites" (*A.J.* 11.346). (Josephus calls them this in reference to the Samaritan capital city, Shechem.) Finally, When Antiochus Epiphanes was enforcing Hellenistic ways in Judea, just before the revolt of Mattathias at Modain, Josephus reports that the Samaritans eagerly disassociated themselves from the suffering Jews by means of a letter to the king. They wrote, "Our forefathers because of certain droughts in their country, and following a certain ancient superstition (δεισιδαιμονίαν), made it a custom to observe the day which is called the Sabbath by the Jews" (*A.J.* 12.259). It is interesting, indeed, that Josephus should report that in their effort to distance themselves from the Jews the first thing the Samaritans had to explain was their Sabbath observance. This detail does not agree with his insistence that they did not observe it and that they welcomed those Jews who did not observe it, effectively revealing his own agenda.[54]

The Sabbath is also used by Josephus to draw a contrast between John of Gischala and Titus. Since John is a Jew and Titus a pagan, one could expect that the first would be concerned with the Sabbath while the second would disregard it. In fact, the reverse is the case. Finding himself vulnerable inside Gischala surrounded by Titus' forces, John refuses Titus' offers of peace, arguing that since it was a Sabbath they could neither resort to arms nor negotiate a peace treaty.[55] A peace settlement would, therefore, have to wait until the next day. Titus considered that it would be "a great gain in being spared any transgression of their national customs." Then Josephus comments,

> By such language John imposed on Titus; for he was concerned not so much for the seventh day as for his own safety, and, fearing that he would be caught the instant the city was taken, rested his hopes of life on darkness and flight. But after all it was by the act of God, who was preserving John to bring ruin upon Jerusalem, that Titus was . . . influenced by this pretext for delay. (*B.J.* 4.102–104)

In other words, Titus is not an innocent being deceived by John and John is not a clever fellow who wiggled his way out of a tight spot. Still, Josephus castigates John for having chosen safety and flight over obedience to the Sabbath commandment. John's impiety is further displayed by his escape from the city at night with his men and their families. Josephus depicts a tumultuous riot in which the women and children were trampled and abandoned by men who cared only for their own lives and were encouraged by John who proclaimed, "Save yourselves." In the meantime, Titus had demonstrated his piety by respecting the Sabbath (*B.J.* 4.111).

It is within this overall framework that one must read about Titus' visit to the Sabbatical river. When Titus was on his way back to Rome, marching triumphant through Syria, "exhibiting costly spectacles in all the cities," he saw a river that Josephus considers worthy of mention on account of its nature (θέαται . . . ποταμοῦ φύσιν 'αξίαν ἱστορηθῆναι). First, he establishes the location of the river. "It runs between Arcea, a town within Agrippa's realm, and Raphanea." Then, he describes the characteristic that makes it noteworthy.

> When it flows, it is a copious stream with a current far from sluggish; then all at once its sources fail and for the space of six days it presents the spectacle of a dry bed; again, as though no change had occurred, it pours forth on the seventh day just as before. And it has always been observed to keep strictly to this order; whence they have called it the Sabbatical river, so naming it after the sacred seventh day of the Jews. (*B.J.* 7.96–99)

Thackeray[56] refers to a Christian missionary who identified the river as the one now called *Neba el Fuar* and explained its peculiar flow as caused by "the draining of subterranean reservoirs of water, on the principle of the siphon." Most people will agree that Josephus' account is only a legend.

What is interesting, however, is that Pliny the Elder, whose curiosity about extraordinary natural phenomena brought about his death in 79 C.E. at Herculaneum, also knows about this river.[57] Pliny and Josephus, however, differ in describing the river's flow pattern. While Josephus says that it was a dry bed for six days and flowed mightily on the Sabbath, Pliny describes the reverse order. It flowed for six days and rested on the Sabbath. Thus, Thackeray judges that Pliny makes the river "strictly sabbatarian" while Josephus represents the river as a "sabbath-breaker."[58]

Rabbi Akiba,[59] for his part, agrees with Pliny and claims that the superiority of the Jewish Sabbath is proven by the river Sambation, which runs for six days and stops on the seventh. *Targum Pseudo-Jonathan* (Exod.

34:10) says that in his promise to Moses that his eternal covenant with the people of Israel would never be transferred to other people, God said that he would perform miracles for them by the rivers of Babylon when the Israelites were taken into captivity. He would make them come up from there and make them dwell in the region of the river Sambatyon.[60] Later, Rabbi Judah ben Simon (*Gen. Rab.* 73), on the other hand, names the river Sambation as the one crossed by the ten tribes in their deportation by Shalmaneser.[61] The traditional location for the settlement of the lost tribes, however, does not agree at all with the location given to the river by Josephus. Still, Josephus may be dependent on the tradition found in *Pseudo-Jonathan.* According to it, the Judean exiles would be rescued from Babylon to the region of the river Sambatyon "on that day." This, apparently, is "salvation geography."

Both Jewish and pagan sources agree against Josephus in reporting that the river ran for six days and rested on the Sabbath. The reversal of the pattern in the river's flow, therefore, is due either to a distinct tradition or to Josephus' own agenda. It would seem more probable, given the unanimity of the other accounts, that the latter is the case. According to Josephus, Titus' triumphal march takes him by the waters of salvation. While Syrian cities display expensive shows in his honor, nature joins with a display of life-giving waters of an eschatological order. It may be well to remember in this connection that Josephus in the proem to the *Antiquities* makes the point that those who wish to know the nature of God and of the laws that lead to a happy life (ἐυδαίμονα βίον) should "contemplate the works of God with the eye of reason" (*A.J.* 1.19–20). In his mind, the Sabbatical river exhibits God's work of justice (salvation) in a way that reason can appreciate.

From the evidence presented above, we can conclude that Josephus held the Sabbath in very high esteem and thought that its observance was of the utmost significance for the preservation of the nation. For him it was of the essence that on the Sabbath no work, not "even the most innocent of acts" (*B.J.* 2.456), or one considered most beneficial or essential, be done. Like Philo, who is more emphatic on this issue, Josephus also considers the Sabbath an opportunity to study the law.[62] In general, however, it cannot be said that he emphasizes its benefits in terms of the opportunities it provides for the development of the life of virtue by the acquisition of wisdom. Even though it seems that he cannot refer to the Sabbath without mentioning the requirement to do no work on it, he refers to its positive aspects by arguing for its reasonableness, identifying it as the day of gladness, and giving it eschatological significance within a sacred geography.

In his scheme of things, where retributive divine justice is at work in a rather immediate way, Jews who do not keep the Sabbath are punished and may be considered enemies of the Jewish people. Exactly how to keep the Sabbath, of course, is a matter on which Jews have never come to universal agreement. Halakic debates on Sabbath observance have been endemic to Judaism and to those who have their religious roots in the Hebrew Scriptures, like the Samaritans and the Christians. Thus, there would seem to be no reason to suppose that from the days of Mattathias to those of Josephus, all Jews agreed that it was permissible on the Sabbath to fight in self-defense. Clearly, that had been an open question and was still such in Josephus' own day. His descriptions of how Jews conducted themselves on the Sabbath while at war, therefore, reflect not the decision of individual Jews vis-à-vis a halakic rule, but Josephus' need to characterize the protagonists of his story according to his own views of piety. His narrative succumbs to his agenda, and therefore it is impossible to understand why he refers to Mattathias' policy at all. We may even say that his presentation suffers from internal contradictions. It is difficult to see how Josephus can admire martyrs and, at the same time, argue that the pax romana is the dawn of the eschatological age.

It is not at all the case, as some scholars have argued, that as a "religious devotee he is wanting,"[63] or that "it may be fairly inferred that Josephus . . . had little interest in religion for its own sake."[64] From what has been presented here it may be fairly inferred, rather, that he had a deep interest in the life of observance. Whether as a general in Galilee he had been a meticulous observer of the commandments, it is not for us to know. There is no reason to doubt, however, that he valued the observance of the Sabbath, wished to be known as an observant Jew, and envisioned an observant Jewish nation within the Roman Empire. The evidence suggests he was not cynical in his use of Sabbath observance as a barometer of piety.

5

The Sabbath in the Synoptic Gospels

There has been much debate among scholars concerning Jesus' attitude toward the Sabbath. Some years ago Raymond E. Brown wrote: "That Jesus violated the rules of the scribes for the observance of the Sabbath is one of the most certain of historical facts about his ministry."[1] Today, however, there is less certainty that in Jesus' times "the rules of the scribes" were as fixed as the quotation implies. It was also accepted opinion not long ago that Jesus had not only challenged the rules of the scribes, in other words the oral law, but actually declared the written law obsolete.[2] Characteristic of this earlier scholarship was the assessment of the Sabbath as part of the "Jewish Law" that Jesus had openly rejected. More-recent scholarship has questioned the credibility of such a portrayal of Jesus. Most scholars today would agree with Paula Fredriksen's assessment that Jesus was an observant Jew.[3] In other words, his Sabbath conduct was well within the Jewish matrix. Our concern here, however, is not with the conduct or the teachings of the historical Jesus, but with the records in the Synoptic Gospels.

An inquiry of the Synoptics requires that the methodology being employed be clearly in evidence. It would seem that the best way to proceed is by following the form-critical guidelines that link the oral traditions found in the Gospels to the social settings in which they took shape. Ever since Rudolf Bultmann classified the controversy dialogues as apophthegms, the narrative elements of these pericopes have been considered "imaginary scenes." Bultmann explains well what the issue is:

> We must keep away at first the question whether Jesus sometimes healed on the Sabbath day, or whether he used a certain saying which we find in a Controversy Dialogue in a discussion with his opponents. Of course it is quite possible that he did; indeed, very probable; but the first question

to be asked, methodologically speaking, must be about the literary form of the controversy dialogue, and its origin as a literary device. This is simply the question about the *Sitz im Leben,* which is not concerned with the origin of a particular report of a particular historical happening, but with the origin and affinity of a certain literary form in and with typical situations and attitudes of a community.[4]

Bultmann located the *Sitz im Leben* of the controversy dialogues about the Sabbath in the apologetic and polemical activities of the Palestinian church. Those who have accepted Bultmann's methodology, with the exception of Arland Hultgren, have also accepted this conclusion. Since Bultmann's time, however, there has been no lack of those who have been asking the historical rather than the formal question. Their efforts and their conclusions have been uneven.

Eduard Lohse argues that the only report that could claim historical validity is the healing of the man with the withered hand at the synagogue.[5] Willi Rordorf defends the authenticity of the report of the conduct of Jesus' disciples in the wheat field.[6] Marcus J. Borg, after pointing out the difficulties connected with the appeal to David's conduct in this particular episode, as well as with the Markan Sabbath controversies generally, insists that the story reflects "an actual historical occurrence rather than . . . the imaginary faculty of the community."[7] David Flusser considers Jesus' Sabbath activities as permissible under the law, arguing that his healings were done by the power of the word and thus no law was broken.[8] To this Geza Vermes counters that, in at least one case, Jesus did touch the sick person to effect the healing (Luke 13:10–17).[9] Anthony E. Harvey, on the other hand, thinks that the stories of healing on the Sabbath reveal no instance in which Jesus transgressed the Sabbath law, since the imposition of the hand is not work.[10] Hyman Maccoby points out that the Pharisees specifically allowed healing on the Sabbath. This must mean that the Sabbath controversies were with the Sadducees or the Essenes who, in Maccoby's view, had stricter rules for Sabbath observance.[11]

Some students of the Gospels have argued that by his conduct Jesus was not rejecting but reinterpreting the significance of the Sabbath law. Borg, for example, says that Jesus was showing his preference for deeds of mercy over the personal quest for holiness.[12] Robert J. Banks sees the issue as one of authority, rather than of legality. Commenting on the incident in the wheat field, he argues that by defending the conduct of his disciples Jesus was not in open opposition to the law, but pointing out the overriding importance of the mission of the disciples.[13] Howard C. Kee, however, considers that emphasizing the importance of the disciples' mission was the intent of the editor of Mark, rather than that of Jesus.[14] Charles K. Barrett, commenting on the healing of the man with the withered hand (Mark 3:1–6), argues that here the debate is not concerned with "the conventional dispute about what is and what is not permitted on the Sabbath," but has shifted so as to allow Jesus to single out "an egoism that is inconsistent with good Jewish piety."[15]

As already noted, Bultmann traces all these pericopes to the Palestinian church and its apologetic and polemical endeavors vis-à-vis the Jews. More recently, Hultgren has challenged Bultmann's conclusion that these pericopes share the rabbinic pattern of disputes about points of law and belong to a common social setting. He distinguishes between unitary and non-unitary stories and allows for several different life settings. Some of them, according to Hultgren, originated in the missionary and catechetical activities of the church outside of Palestine. In terms of what concerns us here, we must note that even though Hultgren gives the stories a different *Sitz im Leben,* he still assigns the controversy dialogues having to do with the Sabbath to the Christian apologetic response to Jewish criticisms. They reflect a dispute Christians were having with "outsiders."[16]

Gerd Theissen studies these narratives in connection with his structuralist work on the miracles, and classifies the miracle stories that have become controversy dialogues as "rule miracles."[17] That is, they argue for the adoption of the rule being proposed. Apparently this was not uncommon in Judaism before the rabbis agreed on the principle that "miracles are not to be mentioned."[18] This rule denied miracles and charismatic visions the power to establish halakah. Among Christians, however, what had been the case before this rule, continued to enjoy currency after it. If such is the correct setting for these stories, it is possible to see them as controversies among "insiders" who are concerned to establish what is permissible on the Sabbath. Indeed, in the context of what we know today, this seems to be the most probable social setting. These insiders appeal to the conduct or words of Jesus in order to settle disputes that Christians were having when establishing the parameters for their Sabbath observance.

The stories were valued because the circles that preserved them agreed on the authority of Jesus to establish what could be done on the Sabbath.

The Synoptic Gospels also contain stories about Sabbath observance that are not part of a controversy dialogue. Most prominent among them are the accounts of the burial and resurrection of Jesus. Mark matter-of-factly reports that on the evening of the day of preparation (προσάββατον, 15:42), Joseph of Arimathea arranged to have Jesus taken from the cross and placed in a tomb while two Marys watched. Then, when the Sabbath had passed (16:1), three women went to the tomb to anoint the body. Mark takes for granted that all readers would understand the necessity to postpone the anointing due to the Sabbath.

Matthew's account follows Mark rather closely in the burial scene, omitting Pilate's inquiry about Jesus' condition, and adding that the tomb belonged to Joseph. But he launches an argument against the slanderous rumor that the disciples stole the body. Thus, he tells of the arrangements made by the Pharisees in order to have the tomb sealed and guarded (27:62). By this means, he shows the Pharisees to be in flagrant violation of the Sabbath while, by contrast, the Christian women, who were rather anxious to anoint Jesus' body, wait until after the Sabbath to go about their business (28:1). This is a common device, used repeatedly by Josephus, by means of which the observance of those not expected to be observant is highlighted against the nonobservance of those who are presumed to be observant in order to show the piety of the former group.

Luke also follows Mark in the details of the burial, pointing out that it was the day of preparation, and the Sabbath was beginning (23:54). Then, somewhat to the reader's surprise since usually he is reluctant to mention the law and the commandments, Luke reports that the women went home and prepared the spices and ointments but "on the Sabbath they rested according to the commandment" (23:56).

Taken together, these three reports of the burial show no awareness of any Sabbath controversies. They reflect the views of Christians who are unaware that Sabbath observance is a questionable practice. It would seem, therefore, that when the story of the Sunday morning anointing became part of the Passion Narrative, and as such became part of the gospel story, the Christian communities that embedded them in the tradition saw no problem with Sabbath observance. In fact, it could be argued that these Christians wished to show the women (and themselves) as observant of the Sabbath. In the Matthean account, the redactional elaboration argues that Christians are better Sabbath keepers than the Pharisees.

Besides these references to the Sabbath, which have clear roots in the early common tradition, in the Synoptic Gospels there are four references to the Sabbath that are clearly redactional. Mark 2:21 (par. Luke 4:31) reports an exorcism in the synagogue at Capernaum that took place on a Sabbath while Jesus was there teaching. Had the event taken place on any other day, it would not have made any difference. A second instance is found in Mark 6:2. On another Sabbath, Jesus' teaching at a synagogue gives rise to opposition and the saying, "A prophet is not without honor, except in his own country, and among his own kin, and in his own house." This saying receives quite different settings in the other Gospels (cf. Matt 13:57; Luke 4:24; John 4:44). Another example appears in Luke 4:16, where Jesus' sermon in the synagogue at Nazareth is reported. Luke portrays Jesus in a pattern also found in his portrayal of Paul. To be at the synagogue on the Sabbath was their "custom." Finally, there is the Matthean expansion of the apocalyptic saying, "Pray that it may not happen in winter" (Mark 13:18). Matthew 24:20 reads, "Pray that your flight may not happen in winter or on a Sabbath."[19] Luke, for reasons of his own, omits the saying altogether. We may conjecture that, if Luke was written about 90 C.E., it was already well known that Jerusalem had not fallen in winter, thus what had concerned Mark was no longer to be feared. Matthew, on the other hand, gave the saying a new lease on life by expressing concern for the sanctity of the Sabbath, even after it was well known that Jerusalem did not fall in winter. As a redactional addition, it goes a long way towards proving that the Matthean community was observant of the Sabbath. As already noted, Matthew 27:62 points out that the Christians were more observant than the Jews.[20]

The evidence reviewed thus far would seem to indicate that the Christian communities that sustained the Synoptic tradition did observe the Sabbath, and some of them probably felt that they were doing it even better than the Pharisees. From the entombment narratives and the sayings examined above, it cannot be deduced that Christians debated whether or not the Sabbath was to be observed. On the contrary, the evidence indicates that Christians took for granted the necessity to observe the Sabbath rest.

The Synoptic Gospels, however, contain other indications that Sabbath observance was controversial. Basic evidence is provided by the two stories placed together, and in the same order, by all three Synoptics. These are the incident of the disciples plucking grain while making their way through a wheat field (Mark 2:23–28 par. Matt 12:1–8 par. Luke 6:1–5) and the story of the healing of the man with the withered hand at the synagogue (Mark 3:1–6 par. Matt 12:9–14 par. Luke 6:6–11). Bypassing for the moment the Markan account, let us review first how Matthew and Luke expand these pericopes.

Matthew enlarges the story of the disciples in the field by drawing a parallel with David's men at the tabernacle: both groups of men were hungry. He also adds, "Have you not read in the law how on the Sabbath the priests in the Temple profane the Sabbath and are guiltless?" This second biblical precedent corresponds to an ordering of priorities known from the rabbinic literature, to which Matthew gives a good christological twist by claiming, "I tell you, something greater than the temple is here!" According to Rabbi Simeon ben Menasiah, Rabbi Akiba taught: "If punishment for murder has precedence over Temple worship, which in turn has precedence over the Sabbath, how much more the safeguarding of life must have precedence over the Sabbath."[21] Both Matthew and Akiba argue on the basis that the temple has precedence over the Sabbath. However, while Akiba moves from this premise to point out that activities on behalf of those in peril have precedence over temple activities, Matthew concludes that the activities of Jesus have precedence over temple activities. In addition, Matthew appeals to Hosea 6:6, a text that also specifies activities that are given priority over temple activity[22] and one that Christians used for different purposes (cf. Matt 9:13). For the moment it is important to note the relative significance assigned to the Sabbath and the temple in the Matthean redaction, one which, as noted in chapter 1, the rabbis also made.

Luke gives the narrative a different tone by changing the charge made by the Pharisees. Rather than challenging the conduct of the disciples, the Pharisees accuse Jesus directly: "Why are you doing what is not lawful?" they ask. Like Matthew with his comparison of Jesus and the temple, by singling out Jesus' activity as unlawful, Luke is giving prominence to the story's secondary christological significance. This new emphasis is also evident in the addition of the affirmation, found in both gospels, that the Son of Man is Lord of the Sabbath. In the process of bringing to the forefront the christological motif, both gospels also omit the central affirmation of Mark: "The Sabbath was made for human beings, not human beings for the Sabbath."[23] These transformations of the account at the hands of Matthew and Luke show that with the passage of time these stories came to be used to establish the lordship of Christ, something which is tangential to questions of lawful Sabbath conduct.

Matthew alters the Markan story of the healing of the man with the withered hand by introducing Q material. In the earlier Markan version, Jesus takes the initiative and asks: "Is it lawful on the Sabbath to do good or to do harm, to save life or to kill?" Bultmann understood this to be an "organically complete apophthegm"[24] in which, following rabbinic ways of argumentation, the main saying has been turned into a rhetorical question. Matthew takes the rhetorical question, the punch line, from the lips of Jesus and puts it in the lips of the Pharisees, a frequent occurrence in the Synoptic tradition.[25] Jesus, then, answers the Pharisees with a saying from Q, of which there are three versions. Besides being Jesus' answer in this narrative, it appears as a doublet in Luke at the healing of a man with dropsy (Luke 14:1–6), and at the healing of the woman who had been suffering eighteen years a spirit of infirmity (Luke 13:10–17). The three versions of this Q saying read:

> What man of you if he has one sheep and it falls into a pit on the Sabbath, will not lay hold of it and lift it out?
> (Matt 12:11)
> Which of you having a son or an ox that has fallen into a well, will not immediately pull him out on a Sabbath day?
> (Luke 14:5)
> Does not each of you on the Sabbath untie his ox or his ass from the manger and lead it away to water it?
> (Luke 13:15)

In the Matthean setting this Q saying prompts the exclamation, "Of how much more value is a man than a sheep!" and a direct answer to the original question put forth by the Pharisee, "So it is lawful to do good on the Sabbath."

The Lukan version of the story of the healing of the man with the withered hand preserves the Markan story almost word for word, with the exception of some christological twists. It omits the comment that Jesus "looked at them in anger" and instead records that Jesus "knew their thoughts" (6:8). Luke also links other healing miracles to the Sabbath controversies using doublets of the Q saying found in Matthew. One is the healing of the man with dropsy. In this account the Pharisees are present but silent throughout. Jesus opens fire with the question, "Is it lawful to heal on the Sabbath or not?" After he has healed the man, he justifies his action by means of the Q saying (14:5).

The second Lukan miracle story with a version of this Q saying shows even more clearly Luke's hand at work. The saying is not part of the healing story itself. After Jesus' healing of the woman with the spirit of infirmity, the ruler of the synagogue, faced with the accomplished deed, rebukes the people saying, "There are six days on which work ought to be done; come on those days to be healed, and not on the Sabbath day" (Luke 13:14). To this directive Jesus responds: "You hypocrites! Does not each of you on the Sabbath untie his ox or his ass from the manger, and lead it away to water it? And ought not this woman, a daughter of Abraham whom Satan bound for eighteen years, be loosed from this bond on the Sabbath day?" The Lukan agenda is unmistakable here, and the following redactional comment makes it explicit: "As he said this, all his adversaries were put to shame; and all the people rejoiced at all the glorious things that were done by him" (13:17). Luke's use of Isaiah 61 as the paradigm for Jesus' ministry is quite evident. He came to bring release to the captives on the acceptable year of the Lord, thus causing all the people to rejoice.[26]

We may account for the reference to untying the ox or the ass from the manger by recalling the motif of the release of captives. We may note that the specification of the actions of "taking a hold" and of "lifting out" may reflect Matthew's more direct confrontation with the specifics of the oral law. The Lukan doublet that mentions a son or an ox may be softening the scene by referring to less-strenuous action for more-valuable objects, or may be credited to Luke's humanitarian concerns. Irrespective of how the specifics of each version of the Q saying are explained, it was used to settle arguments as to what could or could not be done on the Sabbath. Such arguments, of course, were important only to those who agreed on the necessity of observance.[27]

In general, it may be said that in their redactional work Matthew and Luke exhibit different concerns. Matthew seems to be concerned with establishing the relative value of the Sabbath and the temple. But this does not demonstrate a low estimation of either one. He has Jesus paying the temple tax (17:24–27) and advising people to be sure to offer their sacrifices at the temple (5:23–24). He also holds the Sabbath in very high esteem. Luke, on the other hand, uses both the temple and the Sabbath to serve his own agenda. The temple represents what is best in human piety. Jesus and his parents attend regularly and the early Christians spend the time of day in its porticoes. The Sabbath controversies bring out the significance of the Christ.

We may now turn to the Markan account of the two basic Synoptic Sabbath controversy dialogues. The story of the disciples plucking grain on the Sabbath (2:23–28), as has been noticed by many, is tainted by its artificiality.[28] It is not easy to imagine the Pharisees trailing Jesus and his disciples on the open fields on a Sabbath day. Moreover, it is somewhat of a surprise that the challenge concerns the conduct of the disciples.[29] Still, the account preserves three elements that are an integral part of the tradition: a reference to David's conduct, a Sabbath saying, and a Son of Man saying. On the last element, the christological affirmation "The Son of Man is Lord of the Sabbath," there has been some debate as to whether it came to Mark from the tradition or is a Markan creation.[30] Everyone seems to agree, however, that if it came from the tradition, Son of Man did not have titular connotations. In any case, its relation to the previous affirmation is problematic. It would seem more likely, therefore, that it is redactional.[31]

In the appeal to the conduct of David and his men, as has been noticed,[32] the analogy is not quite relevant since the two activities being compared do not belong to the same order. One has to do with cultic matters and the realm of the sacred, while the other is a question of law. Thus, as Bultmann has said, "It is a likely conjecture that the Scriptural proof was used apart from its present context in the controversies of the early Church."[33] The introduction of this analogy, however, again shows an early interest on the part of the Christian communities to discuss the relative importance of the Sabbath and the temple. Like Matthew later, Mark was already involved in a struggle with the temple.[34]

At its core the narrative contains the remarkable saying, "The Sabbath was made for human beings, not human beings for the Sabbath." This saying, as already noticed, was left out by both Matthew and Luke. There have been attempts to find a rabbinic context for it. The one suggested by most scholars, "The Sabbath was given to you, not you to the Sabbath," is the comment of a second-century teacher on Exodus 31:13, "You shall observe my Sabbaths." This baraita, however, comes from a commentary written much later.[35] Besides the problem with the dating, it is not the same to say that the Sabbath was given to humanity and to say that it was given to the Jews. In fact, it may have been this claim that prevented Matthew and Luke from reproducing it. In any case, what the saying affirms is more significant than what it denies. It stresses the gift of the Sabbath to humanity.[36] Given the general openness to the Gentiles in the Gospel of Mark, it is quite possible that the author fully intended the universalistic thrust of the saying. This would indicate that the Jewish disagreements as to whether or not a Gentile could keep the Sabbath were somewhat familiar to the Christians. Here Mark is making a strong statement in favor of the universality of the Sabbath as a gift of God. It is clearly intended against those who would restrict its benefits exclusively to the Jews.

About the Markan story of the man with the withered hand (3:1–6), it may be pointed out that the apophthegm, turned into a rhetorical question, is at its core. The matter in dispute is well defined. It is not the validity of the Sabbath per se, but what kind of activity may be lawfully performed on the Sabbath. That Mark uses the story as a milepost on the road to Calvary does not in any way change this fact. The story does not argue for the total abrogation of the Sabbath law. Rather, it serves to help Christians settle internal debates as to permissible Sabbath activities.

From the above analysis, we may conclude that there are five different kinds of references to the Sabbath in the Synoptic tradition:

Well-grounded traditional stories and redactional statements that assume the obligation of the Sabbath rest.

The aphorism "The Sabbath was made for human beings not human beings for the Sabbath."

The affirmation "It is lawful to do good on the Sabbath," or versions of it in the form of a rhetorical question.

The justification of a given activity by appeals to common sense in the care of domestic animals.

Old Testament testimonia quoted to defend activities some would judge unlawful. The analogy is to activities at the temple.

From this examination of the evidence, it is clear that within the early Christian communities Sabbath observance per se was not a matter of dispute. They took for granted the legitimacy of the Sabbath rest. What Christians debated was the kinds of activities that could be lawfully done on the Sabbath. The controversy dialogues preserved in the Synoptic tradition do not reflect attempts on the part of Jesus (or of early Christians) to declare the Sabbath obsolete or to spiritualize it because Jesus had found the Jewish way of observing it to be legalistic or unspiritual on account of the casuistry involved. These dialogues do not reflect attempts on the part of early Christians to defend themselves from charges leveled at them by Jews who insist on the validity of the Sabbath commandment. Rather, they reveal internal Christian debates trying to establish what could be lawfully done on the Sabbath. As stated at the beginning, Jesus may not have conducted himself in accordance with one or another delineation of proper Sabbath observance as set out by the rabbis. He may have exercised radical freedom in his Sabbath conduct, but his freedom was based on a recognizable respect for the Sabbath. The most radical statement attributed to him, "The Sabbath was made for human beings, not human beings for the Sabbath" (Mark 2:27), says more about human beings than about the Sabbath. Still, what it says about the Sabbath does nothing to take away its validity.

Most interpreters of the Gospels have seen these dialogues as involving disputes with "outsiders," either Jews or Jewish Christians. Lohse's comment may be quoted as characteristic of the traditional interpretation. In reference to the appeal to the example of David and his men in Mark 2, he writes, "The practice of the community, which has freed itself from the Jewish Sabbath, is being supported and vindicated from Scripture." He goes on to indicate that the saying "The Sabbath was made for human beings, not human beings for the Sabbath" means that "the absolute obligation of the commandment is . . . challenged." Later, however, Lohse concedes, "its validity is not contested in principle."[37] If the validity of the Sabbath commandment is not being contested in the most radical of all the traditional Sabbath pronouncements, how is it possible to argue that the Christian communities found themselves in conflict with their Jewish neighbors on account of their nonobservance of the Sabbath following Jesus' declaration of its obsoleteness? The evidence supports only Lohse's grudging concession. These dialogues do not contest the validity of the Sabbath. The controversies to which they bear witness were internal Christian debates as to *how* to observe it. In other words, at least some Christians, of Jewish and Gentile origin inside and outside of Palestine, continued to observe the Sabbath rest, and, like all other Jews and God-fearers of the time, were engaged in establishing what kinds of activities could be lawfully performed on the day. Those who guided their lives by the Torah, and that would involve all early Christians, presupposed the validity of the Sabbath commandment.

The evidence in the Synoptic Gospels does not support those who would like to classify the Sabbath controversy dialogues along Jew/Gentile, linguistic, and geographical delineations.[38] These gospels come from mixed Diaspora communities. To argue that generally Gentile Christians did not become Sabbath observers is, at best, misleading. Christian allegiance to Jewish institutions was not dependent on these coordinates. Greek-speaking, Diaspora Jews may have been more attached to the temple and the Sabbath, than Palestinian, Aramaic-speaking Jews. Gentile converts to Christianity may have been more attached to the Sabbath than some Jewish Christians. Attachment to the Sabbath was not determined by geographical, linguistic, or ethnic backgrounds. It would be wrong to argue on account of their Sabbath observance that Christian communities outside of Palestine, where the Synoptic Gospels took shape, must have been composed of Palestinian Jews.

6

The Sabbath in the Gospels of John and Thomas

Students of the Fourth Gospel have noted that in this gospel the treatment of the Sabbath question is different from that in the Synoptics because the issue has become intertwined with other matters that rank higher in the Johannine agenda. Most significant among these, undoubtedly, is the question of Christology. Thus, Rudolf Bultmann writes that whereas the Synoptic evangelists are concerned with the question of how far the law of the Sabbath is valid for human beings and how far it is limited by the law of love, in contrast the Fourth Evangelist is concerned only with whether or not the law of the Sabbath is binding on the Revealer.[1] Others have also contrasted the handling of the Sabbath question in the Synoptics and John. Charles K. Barrett, for example, judges that John succeeds better than the Synoptics in showing the purpose of the Sabbath healings. Whereas the Synoptics use the miracle stories to liberalize a rather harsh and impractical law, John uses them as witnesses to the accomplishment of the redemptive purpose for which the law had been given.[2] As Juergen Roloff points out, since two out of the three healing miracles found in this gospel involve a Sabbath controversy, there is no doubt that the Sabbath was an important issue for the Johannine community.[3] Rudolf Schnackenburg notes that in this gospel the Sabbath theme is obviously brought in by the evangelist and that he has Jesus introduce it "as an act of provocation."[4] Schnackenburg thus credits the evangelist for having done what, according to Willi Rordorf, had been Jesus' act.[5] That the evangelist was conscious of the Sabbath and its significance, then, is a well-recognized fact.

The first explicit mention of the Sabbath in the Fourth Gospel is in the story of the healing of the paralytic by the pool of Bethesda.[6] Form-critical studies have argued that the story of the healing does not make reference to the Sabbath and has its satisfactory ending with the paralytic walking away, carrying his pallet as proof of the healing.[7] Barnabas Lindars, detecting two sources in the story, assigns the Sabbath motif to the Galilean source, which also informs the story in Mark 2:1–12.[8] On the other hand, Jesus' threat, "Sin no more that nothing worse may happen to you" (5:14), comes from the Jerusalemite source. It reflects the later polemic between the church and the synagogue. In it, as J. Louis Martyn suggests, the paralytic has become paradigmatic of a particular kind of Jew, playing the opposite role to that of the man born blind.[9] In any case, this short dialogue in the story reflects a view of the relationship of sin to sickness that is denied in 9:2–3.[10] These observations are sufficient to demonstrate that the tradition behind the story of the paralytic at the pool is rather complex.

It would seem that the best way to look at this story is by noting the obvious connection between it and John 7:19–23, where Jesus defends his Sabbath healing by pointing out that for the rabbis the rite of circumcision takes precedence over the Sabbath.[11] On this question, H. W. Attridge's study of John 7 is quite convincing. He argues that Bultmann's reconstruction of a source as the basis of the Gospel of John "remains the most plausible, despite recent criticism."[12] According to Attridge, John 7:19–23 was connected to 5:1–16 and included the Sabbath motif already in John's source.[13] Pointing out that without the Sabbath motif there would have been no reason for the preservation of the story in the tradition, Raymond E. Brown has argued correctly for the presence of the Sabbath motif in the traditional story.[14]

If 7:19–23 belonged together with 5:1–16 in the source, the story can only be understood in terms of a Sabbath controversy dialogue. As such, it is another example of a *qal wahomer,* or *a fortiori* argument, in which the structure of the argument is if this is the case . . . how much more is that (when common sense recognizes that the argument moves from minor to major). This type of argument is also well attested to in the Synoptic Sabbath controversies (Mark 2:23–28 par. Matt 12:1–8 par. Luke 6:1–5; Matt 12:12 par. Luke 13:16). If there is an exception for circumcision, how much more there is one for the healing of the whole body. The Sabbath controversy stories in the Synoptics, as was argued in the previous chapter, show how miracle stories had been developed as "rule miracles" in order to uphold a halakic prescription. To find such a story in the tradition informing the Fourth Gospel is, therefore, almost to be expected.

Form-critically it may be argued that at its inception the story in 5:1–16 had been a miracle story with no Sabbath reference in it. What is being argued here is that, as Attridge points out in his criticism of Robert T.

Fortna, one need not insist that in the Johannine source the story still retains its original form.[15] As it came to the Johannine community, a healing of a nonemergency case was justified by an appeal to the law of circumcision, which prescribes that it must be carried out on the eighth day of birth. The rabbis had already agreed that in this case the law of circumcision had priority over the Sabbath law.[16] The argument is not too different from the one that justifies the threshing and winnowing of wheat on the Sabbath by appealing to the fact that David and his men had eaten with impunity of the bread of the presence, which was forbidden by law (Mark 2:25–26). In both cases it is pointed out that the observance of the Torah requires the ability to recognize how in some cases one element of the Torah is overruled by another.

As argued in the previous chapter, the Sabbath controversies found in the Synoptics do not show Christians, who have declared the Sabbath an obsolete Jewish feast, arguing against Jews, who insist on the validity of the Sabbath legislation. Rather, these controversies show that, for some time after the death of Jesus, the Sabbath commandment retained its validity within the Christian communities, even if the manner of its observance was a disputed matter. Whether they had a Jewish or a Gentile background, spoke Aramaic or Greek, lived in Palestine or the Diaspora, early Christians, like their counterparts in traditional Jewish synagogues, were also engaged in spirited debates as to which activities were permissible on the Sabbath and which were not.[17] The only difference was that, whereas in non-Christian synagogues the justification of a particular activity was accomplished by a halakic argument based on the words of the Torah, in Christian circles it was also possible to appeal to sayings or deeds of Jesus as supporting proof for the legitimation of a particular activity. In John 7:19–23 the *qal wahomer* claims that if "they" could do "that" on the Sabbath, "how much more" could Jesus do "this" on the Sabbath. Of course, his followers could do it too. By means of halakic arguments and "rule miracles," the early Christians argued the details of Sabbath observance.

Having established that the story of the healing of the paralytic at the pool of Bethesda came to the Johannine community as a Sabbath controversy story that ended with what is now 7:19–23, we can best read 5:17–47 as a second elaboration of the story within the Johannine community.[18] This pattern is observable in other Johannine stories. The story of the washing of the disciples' feet, for example, also received a second interpretation.[19] In John 13:12–20, by means of a collection of sayings with Synoptic parallels, foot washing is given exemplary value and teaches that the servant is not greater than the master. In John 13:6–11, however, the scene is interpreted by a well-crafted Johannine dialogue between Jesus and Peter that rides on a pun and argues that foot washing is all that is required if one is to be clean.[20]

The second explanation of the significance of the healing of the paralytic centers on the pronouncement, "My Father works until now, and I work" (5:17). As Barrett has pointed out, the Johannine coinage of the statement is evident in Father (Πατήϱ) and works (ἐϱγάζεται).[21] It is evident also that the statement presupposes some rather sophisticated acquaintance with the rabbinic discussion of whether or not God abstains from work on the Sabbath and thus keeps his own laws.[22] Philo and the rabbis had found ways to argue that, although God did not actually abstain from all work on the Sabbath, he did, nevertheless, observe the Sabbath rest. John 5:17 appropriates this argument on behalf of Jesus.

As background to a discussion of John 5:17, it should be remembered that within the Synoptic tradition a definite movement toward a christological understanding of the Sabbath is already in evidence. Luke's stories of the healing of the man with the withered hand (6:6–11) and of the woman healed at the synagogue (13:15–17) show this new interest quite clearly. The pronouncement "The Son of Man is Lord of the Sabbath" (Mark 2:28) is the strongest piece of evidence for this new interest. Even as the statement introduces a new criterion to help in the determination of who or what controls the adjudication of what is or is not permissible on the Sabbath, it says more about the Sabbath than about the Son of Man. Still, it shows that the balance is beginning to shift toward Christology.

Most commentators take John 5:17 to be a statement about the Son, ignoring what it may say about the Sabbath. Even while recognizing that the discourse that follows seems to forget it, the statement represents a justification for Sabbath activity.[23] When this is taken into account, the significance of "until now" (ἕως' ἀϱτι) becomes crucial.[24] Oscar Cullmann argues that this phrase makes clear the "termination" of the work of revelation in which God has been engaged on behalf of all creation so that "the divine Sabbath of Christ is not yet come . . . . The final rest of God has not taken place after the six days' work."[25] This interpretation, however, has been justly criticized by Brown.[26] In terms of what concerns us here, it may be pointed out that others have shown that "until now" does not indicate termination but "duration"[27] or "constancy."[28] Recognizing this, one may also question Eduard Lohse's contention that the statement declares that Jesus' work does not admit "interruptions."[29] Lohse goes on to argue that therefore the challenge is to recognize Jesus' authority to abolish the Sabbath. But Jesus' authority is not at stake. Both 5:16 and 7:21 point out that the hostility of the Jews was caused by the deed he had done and not by an unjustified claim of authority. Moreover, the question about his authority to teach, in 7:14–18, may not be interjected in the second elaboration of the miracle story now couched in 5:17–47.

To bolster his argument, Lohse appeals to the linguistic force of the Greek verb used in the redactional comment made by the evangelist in 5:18: "The reason the Jews are seeking to kill him was that he not only was breaking the Sabbath, but was also making himself equal with God." According to Lohse, in this case the verb λύω does not mean "to loose," "to untie," or "to break," but "to abolish." Thus, the anger of the Jews against Jesus, to the point that they wished to kill him, was caused not only by his "abolition" of the Sabbath, but also by his making himself equal to God. Even if it were granted that the Greek verb is capable of carrying such a connotation, it would have to be demanded by the context. It does not appear to do so in this case. Therefore, this approach to the text leads to a dead end.

Brown's comment about the redactional statement in 5:18, on the other hand, offers a more promising alternative. Brown muses on the evangelist's comment by means of a rhetorical question. Is the narrator's comment to be taken at face value or is it another example of Johannine irony?[30] The extensive use of irony in this gospel is well recognized.[31] Since the aim of the discourse that follows is to deny that the "Jewish" understanding of the equality of the Father and the Son is correct, is the reader encouraged to understand that the charges about Sabbath breaking are also incorrect? It seems likely that the evangelist is thus suggesting that "the Jews" are wrong on both counts. The Son's relationship with the Father is to be understood in terms of subordination, and his Sabbath activity is not breaking the Sabbath, but a divine way of observing it.

Brown is correct in classifying Jesus' work of giving life and giving judgment, which is described in 5:19–47 as Jesus' Sabbath activity. This discourse is truly a second elaboration of the meaning of the healing of the paralytic, which had come to the Johannine community with the halakic justification of Sabbath activity now found in 7:19–23. The discourse makes clear that the Sabbath question has been thoroughly incorporated within a christological agenda. Jesus' statement in 5:17 affirms that, in total dependence on the Father, the Son carries on the Father's Sabbath work, not that the work of the Son cannot suffer interruptions, or that the work of the Son puts an end to the Sabbath. Still, by means of this statement the evangelist has not only subsumed the Sabbath under Christology; he has also effectively given the Sabbath new eschatological significance.

The question then is, What is the eschatological significance of "until now"? The phrase, no doubt, carries a time reference. It would seem, therefore, that by means of it the evangelist is linking the Sabbath to his understanding of time.[32] The work of the Father "until now" has been synchronized with the work of the Son. This renders all time as eschatologically charged both with life and with death, as the discourse in 5:17–47 consistently argues.

Bultmann suggests that if "until now" points toward an end at all, it has to be understood in terms of 9:4,[33] the other Sabbath miracle in John where an explicit reference to time is also made. In the story of the man born blind the fact that the healing took place on the Sabbath is elaborated in a totally different context. The redactional work on this story is quite elaborate and achieves, as most modern commentators have noted, a high degree of dramatic sophistication.[34] It seems most likely that the Sabbath motif was introduced by the evangelist, who shows no interest in questions of proper Sabbath conduct. His agenda is to exhibit the blindness of the "Jewish" judgment of the Son. Still, the story makes the point that work must be done now because the time will come when no work may be done. Therefore, the Son's work must go on even on the Sabbath. This, of course, is also a motif in 5:17.

Cullmann, allowing the connection between 5:17 and 9:4, argues that the Sabbath is to be understood in terms of his own *heilsgeschichtliche* scheme, making Christ the effective midpoint in salvation history. But this would seem to make the coming of the night as the time of fulfillment, when "until now" finds its final point.[35] The text, however, makes clear that the time of fulfillment is now, during the day, during the Sabbath. The gospel wishes to emphasize that the Father and the Son work on the Sabbath, during the day. In other words, the Sabbath is not being compared with the night, when no work may be done, but with the day, when the eschatological work of giving life and giving judgment needs to be done. While the Son is on the earth, it is daytime; it is Sabbath. He is the Light of the World, and the children of the Light, who are born of God, do the works that he does.

The Fourth Gospel has a rather nuanced understanding of time, and it employs references to time to foster its theological agenda.[36] While Jesus and his disciples are people of the day, Judas (13:30) and Nicodemus (3:2; 19:39) are creatures of the night. It is not unwarranted to suggest that this gospel offers a significant counterargument to the apocalyptic expectations of the Son of Man who comes at midnight by timing Jesus' revelation of himself as the Savior of the World who reveals himself at high noon (4:6; 19:14). While the Fourth Gospel certainly views the world as a dark place where sinners die, it does not look to the future for a dramatic rescue from this evil world. Rather, it offers the opportunity to be born from above, from the Spirit, and have now, even in this world, eternal life.

By the first century, Jews had already given eschatological significance to the Sabbath.[37] Eschatological projections of the future as a perennial Sabbath are found both among Jews and Christians. Most Christians, of course, were tied to the Parousia of the Lord. Within these general futuristic speculations, the Gospel of John distinguishes itself by its emphasis on the fact that God works "until now," "while it is day." It is now that Christians who are "born of God" (1:13) must be doing the "work" the Son has been doing, and even "greater works than these" (14:12). What the Son does, Christians also do. Like the Father and the Son, they work on the Sabbath. In other words, the Johannine community has come to understand that its whole life is being lived on the Sabbath. As far as they are concerned, they have eternal life (3:15, 16, 36; 5:24; 6:40, 47, 54; 20:31). They are enjoying the Sabbath rest while doing the work of God every day of their lives. The way they see it, Jesus did not abolish the Sabbath but rather established the eschatological Sabbath among them.

The *Gospel of Thomas* is an early Christian writing with obvious connections with the Gospel of John. Even though the exact date of the final redaction of this gospel remains a matter of some debate, a consensus recognizes this collection of sayings of Jesus as beginning to take shape in the first century and in intimate contact with the traditions now found in the Synoptics and the Fourth Gospel. Thus, the discovery of *Thomas* has provoked considerable reevaluation of the development of the Jesus traditions.[38] An unquestionably early saying in this gospel warns, "If you keep not the Sabbath as Sabbath, you shall not see the father" (27b).[39] This saying has a very positive attitude toward the Sabbath. Rather than to oppose the Sabbath's authority over Christians,[40] it admonishes the day's proper observance. Most students of the saying have acknowledged its difficulties.[41] Still, scholarly efforts to enter the symbolic world of the *Gospel of Thomas* allow us to make sense of the saying.

It has been demonstrated that *Thomas* is heavily indebted to speculations based on Genesis 1–3, which were blossoming at the time in Judaism and are very much in evidence in early Christianity.[42] According to this exegesis of Genesis, the fall of Eve and Adam is to be seen in the foreground of the story. Paul also shared in this conceptual world where the fall had acquired an importance out of proportion with the passing reference to it in the Torah. He was indebted to this speculation both in the Adam/Christ typology that is essential to his Christology,[43] as well as in his claim that "what is knowable of God is clear" to all human beings (Rom 1:19). This exegesis of Genesis was widely known and shared among Jews, especially, it would seem, in Egypt.[44] According to this exegesis, Genesis 1, like Genesis 2, records a two-stage process in the creation of man. Genesis 1:27 reports first the creation of man in the image of God. Then, after the fall, this undivided being became two, male and female. Gender, particularly the female gender, is not part of the original creation and is therefore a hindrance to becoming again an undivided being in the image of God. Thus, for *Thomas,* salvation is not eschatological, but protological. Human beings must "toil" (*Gos. Thom.* 58), "seek and find" to restore the image of God in them as it was in the beginning (*Gos. Thom.* 83–84). Saying 4 describes the situation of Adam before the fall, to which all human beings must aspire. The small child seven days old "dwells in the place of life," in the Garden of Eden, as Stevan Davies has it, "on the sixth day."[45] Those who become newly born, or seven-day-old infants, also enjoy the primordial light that guides them in the world of darkness (*Gos. Thom.* 24). With its benefit they realize that the kingdom that many expect at the end is already here (*Gos. Thom.* 51, 113, 3). The newly born who enjoy possession of the image of the single-sex God are able to transit freely between the inner and the outer, the upper and the lower (*Gos. Thom.* 22). Like Adam they have dominion over the creation (*Gos. Thom.* 2). In contrast, those who fail to enter the kingdom find themselves below the birds of the air and the fish of the sea (*Gos. Thom.* 3). Saying 85 contrasts those who dwell in poverty, who in fact are poverty, with Adam "who came into being from a great power and a great wealth." The secret is to find the primordial light shining within those who are from the undivided, like Jesus (*Gos. Thom.* 61). This gospel uses a familiar Q saying to state explicitly that Jesus is not "a divider" (*Gos. Thom.* 72c). Rather, he makes possible for human beings to become undivided, in the image of God.

In view of the two distinct possibilities for human existence, either in the world of darkness and death or in the world of light and life, human beings must struggle to find the world of life. They must "seek until they find," and when they do they will find themselves at a higher level, "ruling over all things." In addition, they will also find rest. The seven days of creation began with the Spirit *moving* over the waters and ended with God *resting* on the seventh day. Appropriately, human beings who see the Father, who like Adam and Jesus have the image of the undivided God, receive the sign of the Father: "motion and rest" (*Gos. Thom.* 50). They are told: "Seek for yourselves a place of rest, or you might become a carcass and be eaten" (*Gos. Thom.* 60). In other words, the alternative, again, is to slide down the chain of being and become a lower animal that is food for those higher in the chain. The gospel's ultimate beatitude is for "the one who stands at the beginning" (*Gos. Thom.* 18) because he who stands at the beginning has the benefit of the primordial light that even preceded creation (*Gos. Thom.* 77).[46]

In light of the above, the pun at work in saying 27b may be identified.[47] To sabbatize the Sabbath is a way of life. Ignatius of Antioch uses the verb with the same sense. Of course, what Ignatius means by "no longer sabbatizing" is not at all what *Thomas* means by "sabbatizing the Sabbath."[48] For *Thomas* it means to live in the primordial time of creation week, when God was in motion and at rest. For *Thomas,* as for the Gospel of John and for Philo, the Sabbath is not a sociological marker, not even essentially a commandment, but a reality of the primordial world of the light. Those illumined by the light that shone on the first creation, before the fall, live in a different world all the days of the week.[49] Like God on creation week, they are also characterized by motion and rest at all times. *Thomas*

27b teaches that in order to see the Father[50] one must "stand at the beginning" and experience God's restful creative motion throughout the week.[51] In other words, the Christian way of life requires a return to the conditions that existed before the fall, before the division of humanity according to gender.

This understanding of the saying is also supported by its first part, which teaches the necessity to fast from the world. Thomas actually condemns fasting, praying, and the giving of alms as the piety of those who live in darkness (*Gos. Thom.* 14, 104). One can easily imagine that the gospel could have included in this category "sabbatizing one chronological day." On the other hand, those who "stand at the beginning," "fast" from the world, and "sabbatize" all time, are blessed. It is clear that both *fast* and *sabbatize* need to be understood more liberally than their strict meanings. The actions they describe are not being done on the object one normally would expect. Sabbath here is to be read as "week." The piety of the kingdom is of a different order. It demands that one not be involved in the affairs of the world. As the *Gospel of Thomas* puts it, "Buyers and merchants will not enter the kingdom" (64). It also demands the recognition that secular time cannot set the pattern for life in the kingdom. The two statements in Logion 27 are a good example of poetic parallelism. They say the same thing twice, but from two different perspectives. From the perspective of the world of light, one is "sabbatizing all days of the week" and thereby transcending them. From that of the world of darkness, one is "fasting from the world" and thereby not involved in its affairs.[52]

This way of seeing the Sabbath, as the time that participates in eternity, is not new and was not a passing fad. It was part and parcel of eschatological conceptions in Judaism, and it appears in different forms within the Christian landscape. What is peculiar to the *Gospel of Thomas* and to John is that this conception is given a protological foundation.[53] From Paul we learn that some Christians in Rome also viewed the Sabbath in this way, and the authors of the Epistle to the Hebrews and the *Epistle of Barnabas* argue for an eschatological Sabbath, even if on a futuristic, instead of a protological, basis. The communities of the Gospels of John and *Thomas* came to understand that their whole life was lived on a perennial Sabbath. Both agree that it is possible to have eternal life, to become undivided, in this life. As the Gospel of John works it out, doing his eschatological work of giving life and judgment was Jesus' Sabbath activity on behalf of those who are born of God. In this way the Sabbath has been released from the weekly chronological cycle and reattached to the primordial *beginning*.

Returning our attention to the Gospel of John, we may notice again its highly developed redactional techniques. In chapter 9 the trial of Jesus in absentia takes place because, as 9:14 distractedly explains, "it was a Sabbath day when Jesus made the clay." Unlike all other gospel stories of Jesus' Sabbath activities, this one does not include an attempt to demonstrate that the making of the clay was permissible, neither by halakic arguments nor by appeals to Jesus' special status. Here the Sabbath serves as a tool in the hands of the redactor in order to ironically turn the tables and judge the Pharisees. In the narrative, of course, the Sabbath infraction serves the Pharisees to argue that Jesus cannot be "from God" (9:16). Obviously, the story is not concerned with what is or is not permissible on the Sabbath. As the trial progresses, the accusers affirm, "We know that this man is a sinner" (9:24). But Pharisees who use proper Sabbath observance as the criterion that proves Jesus a sinner, only prove that they are "blind," and their predicament is even worse because they claim to see (9:40–41). The irony is difficult to miss and even borders on sarcasm.

The ironic undertone of the Gospel of John is patently present in the entombment and embalmment scene, where Sabbath observance is viewed as a concern of the "Jews." If one reads the Johannine narrative in parallel with the Synoptic accounts, it is easy to detect the Johannine agenda. In Mark (15:42–16:1), Joseph of Arimathea takes the initiative, asks for the body of Jesus, and after Pilate ascertains that Jesus is in fact already dead, takes the body and buries it. Then on Sunday, the women who had witnessed the burial come to the tomb in order to anoint the body. In this way Mark shows how the Christian community has fulfilled one of the most sacred obligations demanded by mercy. He also exhibits a Christian community that is concerned with observing the weekly Sabbath rest. Matthew and Luke add some details of their own to the Markan account but basically preserve the same reverence for the weekly Sabbath rest.[54]

In John, on the other hand, it is declared that "the flesh is of no avail" (6:63), even the flesh of the Son of Man. A Christian community that is concerned with the body of a dead person would be a community that is not living in the light. Consistent with this view of reality, the entomb-ment is depicted quite differently. Instead of the Sabbath being what pre-vents pious Christians from anointing the body on Friday evening, it causes the "Jews" to request that the body be removed from the cross before sundown (19:31). Out of nowhere appears a secret disciple who fears the "Jews" (Joseph of Arimathea). He asks for the body. With him is Nicodemus, a creature of the night, who supplies one hundred pounds of ointments. They embalm and bury the body of Jesus "according to the burial customs of the Jews" (19:40). As background to the whole scene the reader is reminded of the approaching hours of the Sabbath and, in an aside, is told that "it was a Great one, that Sabbath day" (19:31).[55] Accord-ing to this version of the story, Nicodemus and Joseph completed the embalming on Friday. There seems to be no need for the women to come on Sunday to do what the two men had already done. In this account, the sanctimonious overkill of the "Great Sabbath," the profuse pouring of spices,[56] the repeated references to the careful observance of Jewish cus-toms, the total absence of "true" disciples, and the fact that on Sunday Mary's journey to the tomb is not related to the anointing, make obvious that what is being described is not an act of Christian piety, but a parody of the "Jewish" misguided attachment to the material world. The ironic tongue-in-cheek tone cannot be missed.[57]

It may be concluded, then, that by the time the Fourth Gospel received its last reediting the Johannine community no longer considered impor-tant to determine the "how" of Sabbath observance within the chrono-logical cycle of days, even if this had been a preoccupation within it at an earlier time. Toward the end of the first century, like the Thomas Chris-tians, the Johannine community also understood itself to be living every day on the Sabbath. Every day they performed the works of the Son, even if in Jewish eyes they were perceived to be Sabbath breakers (5:18). For these two communities, space and time have been transcended by "eternal life now." The Johannine community explicitly came to say about the temple, "Neither on this mountain nor in Jerusalem will you worship the Father . . . The true worshipers will worship the Father in Spirit and Truth" (4:21, 23). It is possible to imagine that both the Thomas and the Johan-nine communities could have said, "Neither on this day nor on that one will you worship the Father. True worshipers worship the Father in Spirit and Truth on all days."

The conclusion arrived at by this analysis is also important because it demonstrates how a community that had experienced a traumatic break with Judaism,[58] and therefore had to reconstruct its symbolic universe, changed its understanding of the Sabbath. The shift from a concern to justify particular activities as permissible to the sarcastic parodying of such concerns as "Jewish" and as belonging to those who ignore the light reflects a dramatic turnaround. Furthermore, as a result of this "conversion" the Johannine Christians did not leave the Sabbath behind as a relic of a past they wished to repudiate. They did not throw it overboard. Rather, they gave it even more significance in their lives by making it the environment in which they lived. It is to be regretted, however, that their animus toward their former sisters and brothers turned into such sharp, and at times vitriolic, invective.

7

The Sabbath in the Letters of Paul

The three references to calendric concerns in the Pauline literature have been a puzzle for New Testament scholarship. Students have encountered serious difficulties trying to ascertain both what the texts say and how they may be related to each other. In his letter to the Galatians, Paul expresses his displeasure with the conduct of the Galatians and chides them because, having been "seduced" (3:2) by "those who perturbed" them (1:7), they were keeping "days, and months, and seasons, and years" (4:10). On account of this Paul fears that his evangelistic efforts on their behalf have been wasted and that they have ceased to be Christians. In his letter to the Romans, on the other hand, Paul very calmly encourages his readers to use their power of discernment when judging days (14:5–6), and approves their observance of "the day" according to their commitment to the Lord. Apparently, their concern for the day in no way jeopardizes their standing as Christians. In the letter to the Colossians, which was written by an admirer of Paul,[1] the author explicitly refers to the observance of "a festival or a new moon or a Sabbath" as an issue that separates Christians (2:16).

Attempts to explicate these texts have tended to see all three as referring to the same basic facts, even if some interpreters have admitted the difficulty of understanding how Paul could have heatedly opposed the Galatians for observing days and given the Romans his blessing for doing so. For example, Ernst Kaesemann writes that both Paul and the author of Colossians were dealing with a syncretistic phenomenon that threatened many early Christian communities. In all three texts this propaganda, which included both Jewish and pagan religious elements, is being condemned.[2] James D. G. Dunn, on the other hand, sees a specific reference to the Jewish Sabbath in all three texts.[3] These approaches, however, fail to explain the marked differences among the texts. The puzzle cannot be easily resolved.

The differences are very significant. For example, the calendric series in Galatians is not the one found in Colossians. These differences argue for different contexts.[4] Since only Colossians makes explicit mention of the

Sabbath, there is much room to speculate about the role the Sabbath may have in the other two texts. In both Romans and Colossians the observance of days by some results in others passing judgment upon them, but the advice the authors give to their readers is quite different. Both Romans and Galatians refer to unspecified days, but the differences are telling. While in Galatians the reference is to "days," in Romans it is to "*the* day," and while in Romans the day is viewed by itself, in Galatians the days are considered part of a calendric string. Moreover, while at Rome and at Colossae the issue of days is somehow linked to that of foods, in Galatia foods are not part of the picture. This is enough to point out that the three texts may not be understood under one rubric.

In this chapter I propose to read the two Pauline texts. The next chapter will deal with the text in Colossians. To be noted first is that there are no explicit references to the Sabbath in Paul's extant writings.[5] This silence is intriguing and becomes even more so when one recalls Paul's references to circumcision and food laws. Obviously Paul had no problem with the word *circumcision,* but his usage reveals a rather ambivalent attitude. On the one hand, he insists that it makes no difference (Gal 5:6, 15; 1 Cor 7:19). Writing to the Philippians, however, he identifies himself as having been of the circumcision (Phil 3:3), only to explain that he now considers the things that once gave him selfhood as dung (Phil 3:8). Thus, he is angered by those who make much of circumcision (Gal 2–3). They have removed the stumbling block of the cross, have fallen from grace, and have severed themselves from Christ (Gal 5:4, 11–12). In Romans, where Paul takes a rather irenic posture, he concedes that under certain circumstances uncircumcision may count as circumcision, thus granting the ritual some value (Rom 2:25–26). The context makes clear, however, that in this case Paul is arguing in Jewish terms. In summary, he spiritualized the Jewish ritual, declaring that what is of value is a circumcision which is "not visible in the flesh . . . but of the heart, spiritual, not literal" (Rom 2:28–29). In the end, he redefined it.

For Christians, Paul included, taking a position about circumcision was not only problematic, but unavoidable. Confronted with the issue, Paul made nuanced statements, taking into account who happened to be his audience. The word *circumcision* was important in his vocabulary, and in the letter to the Galatians it functions as the litmus test for a well-recognized religious point of view. It was the sine qua non of Jewish identity, and as an event in the life of a Jewish male it was an indelible mark both physically and psychologically. In addition, as Paul well knew, it preceded the giving of the law, having its roots in none other than Abraham, the father of those who believe. Still, Paul had to redefine circumcision, and he overtly did so, in order to relate it to the new situation created by the cross and the resurrection of Christ.

Paul also had to deal with the issue of foods, not only in terms of how they may get one involved with idolatry, but also in terms of purity. In Romans 14 he explicitly took a position about kashrut. He transferred the issue from the realm of being, in which things are "by themselves" (δι ἑαυτοῦ), to the realm of knowledge, in which they are humanly conceived (λογίζομαι) (14:14). He states negatively what the Markan narrator states positively, "thus he declared all foods clean" (Mark 7:19). The same point of view informs Paul's rule that a Christian could go to the home of an unbeliever and eat whatever was placed on the table before him (1 Cor 10:27). Paul did not sidestep the issue of food. He clearly denied the validity of the distinction on which purity is based.[6] He also was aware that food offered to an idol was not in any way affected by it since "an idol has no real existence" (1 Cor 8:4). In this way he again transferred the issue from the realm of being to that of knowledge, since "not all possess this knowledge" (1 Cor 8:7). For Paul the cross and the resurrection of Christ had put an end to an understanding of creation along lines that distinguished the clean from the unclean and had exposed the unreality of idols. While Paul denied the real existence of purity distinctions and of idols, he affirmed the existence of idolatry and of weaker fellow believers who possessed faulty knowledge.

In view of his deft handling of the issues of circumcision and food laws, his reticence to use the word *Sabbath* is indeed intriguing. But no argument can be built on his lack of explicit references to it. The only way to come to an understanding of the situation is to concentrate on what Paul did write.

We may best begin our search by considering the text in Galatians. In this rather intemperate letter Paul vented his frustration with the idiocy, or gullibility, of the Galatians who were, from his perspective, apostatizing (μετατίθημι, 1:6; ἐπιστρέφω, 4:9) from the gospel of the cross of Christ.

In 4:8–11 he issues a cri de coeur couched as a rhetorical question, which reveals his fear.[7] In response, he advances a rather intense argument against those who were causing a turnaround among the Galatians. Expressing his disenchantment and frustration, Paul exclaims, "You are observing days and months and seasons and years!" (4:10). The causes of Paul's annoyance with this development at Galatia are entangled in a rather complicated web. In order to untangle them, we must seek the answer to several questions: a) How was this observance connected to slavery to the "elements of the world" (στοιχεῖα τοῦ κόσμου)? b) To what, specifically, was Paul objecting? c) What is the significance, or the context, of the calendric string used by Paul?

It is quite clear that Paul was displeased with the Galatians. Modern scholarship, however, has not come to a consensus concerning what in the conduct of the Galatians was specifically objectionable. According to Heinrich Schlier, Paul's reaction was caused by the recognition that, like the Torah among Jews, law in the world at large is placed at the center of life.[8] Dunn, who thinks that the dispute had to do with the Sabbath and that Paul would not have reacted to that in itself, accounts for his reaction as an attempt to prevent Jewish sectarian infighting to enter Christianity.[9] Hans Dieter Betz, for his part, sees Paul reacting negatively to the inroads that superstition and religious scrupulosity were making among his converts.[10] Gerhardt Ebeling explains that Paul wrote against a religiosity based on nature that was not yet conscious of history.[11] Richard N. Longenecker thinks that Paul, like the Old Testament prophets, denounced legalism, but unlike them he also denounced nomism, the absolutizing of the law.[12] Robert Jewett, however, thinks that the Galatians were not attracted to the other teachers for nomistic reasons. Their fear of the cosmic powers sparked in them concerns about the mysteries of the calendar which the wisdom of the Old Testament had made manifest.[13] Frank J. Matera, who emphasizes that the celebration of feasts is in itself good, thinks that Paul objected to the use of festivals as means for the perfecting of faith.[14] Troy Martin, in a rather audacious move, argues that Paul is threatening the Galatians with a lawsuit for breach of contract since their calendric observances mark their return to paganism.[15]

In his denunciation of the conduct of the Galatian converts Paul uses the verb παρατηρέω, which in the New Testament, except here, is always used to describe close visual observation in order to entrap or to apprehend. In Mark and Luke it is used to mean to lie in wait, to watch maliciously, or to guard (Mark 3:2 par. Luke 6:7; Luke 14:1; 20:20; Acts 9:24). Josephus, however, uses this verb to refer to religious observances.[16] On the basis of the semantic force of the verb, some commentators have shifted the weight of Paul's annoyance from the calendric series to the specifics of the kind of observance the Galatians were getting into. The close observance of the physical aspects of the festivals is taken by Dunn to mean that the problem had to do with sectarian factionalism.[17] P. N. Tarazi[18] and Longenecker,[19] on the other hand, think the verb highlights the meticulous and scrupulous observance that, according to them, is characteristic of Jewish piety.

In this letter Paul draws a sharp contrast between what the human condition had been "then" and what it is "now." Referring specifically to the situation in which the Galatians had been "then," Paul points out that they had been serving those who "in nature" (φύσει) were not gods. About this assessment, without a doubt, there was no disagreement between Paul and his readers. He goes on to point out that "we," that is all human beings, "when we were children" had been "enslaved to the elements of the cosmos" (4:3). "Now," however, "through God you [and "we"] are no longer a slave but a son" (4:7). Much to Paul's frustration and anger, under the influence of other teachers the Galatians "now" wished to be enslaved to "weak and poor elements" (4:9). That is to say, the Galatians had accepted as powerful the "elements of the cosmos," which in Paul's view were ineffective and lacking in resources. In their valuation of the "elements" clearly Paul and his readers did not agree. The question before us is, How was their observance of days related to the power they ascribed to the "elements"? From the text we cannot determine what argument had been presented by the other teachers in order to induce the keeping of days. Paul's evaluation of what the Galatians were doing, however, is clear. As far as he was concerned, they were caught in a process that was bringing about their apostasy and subjecting them again to the slavery in which all humanity had been found prior to the work of God in Christ.

There would seem to be little reason to doubt that the reference to "the weak and poor elements" in 4:9 expands the reference to "the elements of the cosmos" in 4:3, to whom, Paul affirmed, "*we* were slaves" when "*we* were minors" (italics mine). By means of the illustration of the minor in the household, Paul contrasts two moments. Throughout this section the temporal contrast between "then" and "now" looms more prominently in Paul's mind than the religious contrast between Jews and Gentiles. He is interested in establishing that slavery to the elements of the cosmos "then" was the common, inescapable condition of all humanity. As a Jew he had experienced that slavery, and therefore he could not understand how anyone who had been freed from it would wish to return to it. All humanity had been "then" a minor in the house. That stage in the history of humanity, however, had come to an end "at the fullness of time" (4:4), when God accomplished two things: redemption for those who were slaves of the Law and sonship for all (4:5). It would be foolish for anyone who had grown beyond the stage of a minor to wish to return to that stage. This unthinkable reversal, as Paul understands it, is precisely what the Galatians were attempting. Doing so, however, would undo their redemption, negate their sonship, and forfeit their claim to the inheritance. In effect, it would overlook the cosmic landmark established by the cross of Christ.

The manner in which Paul equates the slavery of Jews and Gentiles while minors with the slavery to which the Galatians now wished to return helps us to identify what Paul is concerned with. Many scholars incorrectly identify the elements in this instance with rudimentary notions, or basic concepts.[20] They argue that Paul fears the Galatians are being enslaved by doctrines of rival teachers that he viewed as "elementary," or the first "rudiments" necessary for a more comprehensive understanding of the subject. Paul certainly did not think that the Torah provided only "elementary" notions of God's ways. Throughout his life he was engaged in an ongoing debate about the role of the Torah, but he never argued that the Torah deals with just the "elements" of the knowledge of God. From the Torah Paul extracted the substance of his arguments. It was from the Torah that he learned that salvation is by faith. This is quite clear in Galatians 3 and 4. Paul's estimation of the Torah indicates that identifying the elements as "elementary" Torah doctrines is incorrect. Paul thinks that the enslaving of the Galatians is being brought about not by rudimentary teachings but by the elements of the cosmos, whose reality and relative power he explicitly recognizes in 1 Corinthians 8:5. It is in reference to them that the Galatians are observing days. It is not possible, therefore, to equate the calendric concerns of the Galatians with "elementary" religious notions and think that Paul is wearied on account of the superstitious nature of their jejune preoccupations.

The lexical evidence for understanding the elements of the cosmos as astral spirits or divine beings is rather late, as has been pointed out.[21] Still, all the metaphorical ingredients for understanding the elements of the cosmos in a personified way, or as powers that subjugate humanity, were already available in Paul's time. As already noted, Paul himself alludes to them in 1 Corinthians 8:5. Even if it were granted that, in the first place, the phrase referred to the primary elements of ancient Greek physics (earth, water, air, fire, and maybe also ether), it must be recognized that these elements were understood to have cosmological power and had been personified as divinities.[22]

The identity of the elements is such a complex issue that, as J. Louis Martyn has wisely pointed out, lexicography alone cannot settle it.[23] According to him, the teachers who were perturbing the Galatians tied what they said about the law with affirmations about Abraham. In the Judaism of the time, Abraham was presented as the prototypical proselyte.[24] He was a Chaldean who had advanced along the road from the worship of the elements (polytheism) to the knowledge of the true God (monotheism). Wisdom of Solomon 13:1–5 also witnesses to the understanding that pagans are worshipers of the elements. On this basis, Martyn suggests that the rival teachers at Galatia maintained that the law-observant descendants of Abraham, who had like their ancestor also attained to the knowledge of God, possessed true knowledge of how the elements controlled the seasons. As powers that provide a basic structure to the cosmos, the elements had been arranged by the pre-Socratic philosophers in pairs of opposites (τὰ ἐναντία).[25] It was as such that the elements of the cosmos were understood by the Galatians. They controlled the balance between night and day, winter and summer, spring and autumn. Martyn's suggestion that the elements were the powers that gave to the cosmos its tensive balance is quite suggestive and helps to answer the question that has concerned us. The keeping of days, months, seasons, and years on the part of the Galatians was related to their recognition of the power of the elements to hold the cosmos together, even if under the absolute power of God. When Paul alludes to their calendric practices, he is not defining their slavery, only identifying the symptom that reveals their cosmological error. To live in such a symbolic universe, as far as Paul was concerned, was to have apostatized. The news that the Galatians were submitting to the power of the elements and, therefore, keeping days caused Paul to fear that his labors among the Galatians had come to naught (4:11).

Some interpreters think that in his dispute with the Galatians Paul made an unexpected radical move when he placed paganism and Judaism on the same level.[26] This move merits a careful review. Paul consistently argues that sin affects not only some, but all human beings. In Galatians he writes, "Scripture locked all under sin" (3:22), and in Romans he points out that "all have sinned" (3:22) and that "God has no favorites" (2:11). Still, he knows the way in which Jewish propaganda has traditionally referred to Gentiles as sinners. By definition, pagans do not know God and as a consequence they worship idols.[27] By equating the slavery in which the Galatians had been before hearing the gospel to the slavery under the elements in which they now wished to live, Paul is not contrasting or comparing Judaism and paganism. Unlike what is the case in his reference to the incident at Antioch in chapter 2, here he is not emphasizing the distinction between Jews and Gentiles, even if it may be the case that he had one or the other of them in the back of his mind. Here he is contrasting "then" and "now." "Then" everyone was a slave "locked in sin" by the Scriptures, no less (3:22). "Now" Christians are free sons with a claim to the father's inheritance. But those perturbing the Galatians were preaching a different Christian gospel which, as far as Paul is concerned, was not at all Christian because it brought with it slavery rather than freedom. As Christians, the Galatians wished to serve the weak and poor elements of the cosmos and were contemplating circumcision, as the future tense in 5:2 indicates. Paul vehemently disapproves a Christianity which, from his perspective, places individuals in the condition they had been in when they were either Jews or Gentiles. The Christianity preached by the other teachers was similar to both Judaism and paganism since it negated the freedom of the Christian "now."

If one were able with full confidence to negotiate the foggy transitions in Paul's use of pronouns from the first-person plural to the second-person singular to the second-person plural in Galatians 4:1–8,[28] one could argue that in 4:3 Paul was describing exclusively the slavery of Jews and that the minority status of a son was the peculiar condition of Jews under the Torah before "the fullness of time." The oscillating pronouns, however, make this inference impossible. Besides, in the heat of the argument Paul mixes his metaphors. He juxtaposes the contrast between the parentless and the adopted child with the contrast between the son who is a minor in his father's house (who finds himself in a situation comparable to that of the slave in the same house) and the son who is an adult. It would appear that in his efforts to win points Paul presented his argument in a manner that leaves much to be desired. It is possible, however, to determine what Paul is pointing out. The "now" established by the cross of Christ means redemption and freedom for all those who are crucified with Christ. The "then" is a past in slavery to the elements of the cosmos experienced equally by both Jews and Gentiles. His description of Jews and pagans as equally enslaved to the elements of the cosmos is, indeed, a rather surprising argumentative twist. His aim, it would seem, is to point out that the only true Christian gospel is one that brings about cosmic freedom. Paul is not arguing that the false teachers are leading his readers back to Judaism, but to a Christianity that is not Christian. In this connection it may be pointed out that throughout his life Paul never felt that he had ceased being a Jew of the tribe of Benjamin.

Having established both the connection between the observance of days and the elements of the cosmos, and also the central element in Paul's objection to the Galatians' observance of days, we now turn our attention to the significance of the calendric string "days, months, seasons and years." The first thing to be noted is that when Old Testament authors call the people's attention to the observance of the feasts, they consistently speak of "feasts, new moons and Sabbaths," which is the formula found in Colossians 2:16. The string used by Paul in Galatians is not found in the Old Testament. As a consequence, some commentators have stated that this calendric string is "not Jewish."[29] It has been correctly pointed out by Dieter Luhrmann, however, that even though this string is not the one used to call attention to the festal calendar, its origin is to be found in the Old Testament.[30] According to him, it is based on the calendric function assigned to the sun, the moon, and the stars in the creation account (Gen 1:14). In a clearly polemical thrust, the priestly authors wrote that God made the greater and the lesser lights and the stars "to separate the day from the night and to be for signs and for seasons and for days and years." This text had given rise to much cosmological speculation within contemporary Judaism.[31] Preoccupations with perfection and the advance of the soul in the path of wisdom are well documented both in Philo[32] and other sources. These themes were standard in Hellenistic spirituality. One need not characterize as not Jewish a calendric reference that is not primarily cultic but cosmological, particularly when the distinction is a modern one. According to Luhrmann, then, the observances taught by the other teachers in Galatia, which Paul's converts had began to practice, were connected to a cosmological system based on the creation story of Genesis 1.[33] By means of these observances the cosmic system was reenergized. Luhrmann's explanation fits well with Martyn's nuanced understanding of the elements of the cosmos noted above.[34] Recognizing that Paul's theology makes the cross of Christ the eschatological turning point that establishes the "now" of Christian freedom, we can see without difficulty why Paul thought that to reaffirm the Genesis creation account was a sign of apostasy from the truth of the gospel. Paul denied the cosmological effectiveness of the observances the Galatians were now practicing. He understood that by their observances the Galatians were denying the effectiveness of the cross of Christ.

In this letter Paul makes the ringing affirmation, "For neither circumcision nor uncircumcision is anything, but a new creation" (6:15). This is the eschatological equivalent to his previous ethical affirmation, "For in Christ Jesus neither circumcision nor uncircumcision accomplishes anything, but faith made effective as love" (5:6). These affirmations hold true only for those who, like Paul, live in this evil age (1:4) and are crucified with Christ (2:20–21), thus confirming the effectiveness of God's grace and denying that Christ's death was just an earthly event. When the fullness of time came, through a Jewish man God brought about redemption to the Jews and sonship to all human beings. Christ's cross is the cosmic event that brought about the new creation. Paul found himself in Christ's cross because in it "the world was crucified to me, and I to the world" (6:14). As has been already emphasized, the primary contrast in Paul's mind is not so much between Jews and Gentiles (a distinction that he clearly did not ignore), but between "then" and "now." The turning point, which he describes as "the coming of faith" (3:25), "the date set by the father" (4:2), "the fullness of time" (4:4), brought about the circumstances in which Christians live "now," the new creation (6:15). In Galatians the cross is not viewed as the historical fulfillment of the covenant. Crucifixion means death both to the world and to the self that lived in the world, so that the new creation and the new human being might live in freedom from the elements of the old cosmos fallen under sin. Within Paul's symbolic universe, calendric observances that affirm the power of the elements of the cosmos constitute a denial of redemption.

Just as it may not be said that the debate at Galatia was over circumcision, a word repeatedly found in Paul's letter to the church there, neither can it be said that it was over the Jewish Sabbath.[35] Whether or not the Sabbath was one of the days that according to the other teachers needed to be observed in order to reenergize the cosmos (and the likelihood is strong that it was), Paul's objection is not concerned with it. As Paul sees it, the question is whether or not Christians live in a new creation. Paul's clear displeasure with their calendric observances was provoked by the fact that they were symptomatic of the real issue: the eschatological effectiveness of the cross of Christ. If Sabbath observance were involved, as most likely it was, the context points out the symbolic universe within which it was operative. The calendric string Paul uses in Galatians does not call to mind the need for faithful observance of the Jewish cultic calendar, but the maintenance of the original cosmos. This distinction may seem too fine, since obviously the festal calendar is related to a cosmic structure. The reason for making the distinction is to point out the perspective from which Paul is addressing the problem. Whatever the Galatians were doing, "observing days and months and seasons and years" was understood by him to demonstrate that they were not crucified with Christ and, therefore, were still living according to the cosmological foundations of the old aeon. He had presented to them Christ crucified (3:1), but they were having difficulty in crucifying themselves with him. For Paul that was the definition of a Christian. To have "the faith of the crucified Jesus" one had to be crucified with him. Then one could live in the new creation of the Spirit.

Writing his letter to the Romans, Paul faces a different situation. He is not counteracting the influence of other teachers who have infiltrated his church with a gospel that, as far as he is concerned, is not Christian. In Romans, he wishes to bring together Christians who, while maintaining their commitment to Christ, contend with each other on practical matters, thus threatening to split the Christian community. In this letter, Paul identifies two issues, among others, that caused their meetings to turn into "disputations" (14:1). Paul reports that "some believe they may eat anything, while the weak eat only vegetables" (14:2). This disagreement does not concern us here; only the second disputed question mentioned by Paul is relevant to our theme.

According to Paul, not all Christians at Rome judge days in the same way. He writes, "One judges a day to have been set apart while another judges all days together. Let all be fully convinced in their own mind. Those who have their mind set on the day have their mind set on the Lord" (14:5–6a). The Pauline description of the situation raises three main questions. The first has to do with the identity of the days being judged; the second seeks to establish what the debate over the day was about; and the third is to determine Paul's response to the positions taken by the opposing parties.

In reference to the first question, modern scholarship has given four different answers. According to some, the dispute has primarily to do with popular pagan concerns with whether a day is *fasto* or *nefasto,* that is, propitious for important transactions or not. In all human societies organized with some kind of established priesthood, sacred days are distinguished from profane ones. Pagans had their own ways of assessing days and what should or should not be done on them. Former Gentiles who had become Christians would not have automatically left all their religious postures and attitudes behind in the baptismal waters. Thus, Wayne A. Meeks argues that, even if concerns about the Sabbath may have been included in the debate, pagan concerns with unlucky days were at the forefront of the dispute at Rome.[36]

Others have argued that the dispute cannot be characterized as centering on a pagan or a Jewish question. Superstitious concerns about the peculiar powers of different days of the year were part of the religious landscape of that age. According to Kaesemann, Paul is confronting a syncretistic religious propaganda that is making inroads in the Roman Christian community.[37]

Against these first two scenarios it must be pointed out that Paul explicitly grants that, no matter which view they held, those taking sides were doing so as servants of the Lord. "Those who have their mind set on the day have their mind set on the Lord" (14:6a). He also states that what is important is that whether they set a day apart or they do not "they should be fully persuaded in their own mind" (14:5c). It is difficult to imagine

Paul making these statements to people who are concerned with pagan unlucky days, or with a syncretistic propaganda. It is not surprising therefore that Meeks fails to quote these words and Kaesemann considers them "a typical Koine interpolation."[38] Such a conjecture, however, is not at all supported by the text, but by the desire to sustain the interpretation being proposed.

In a substantial monograph on the references to "the weak" in the letters of Paul, Max Rauer argues that the issue of days is to be understood as related to the question about food identified in Romans 14:2. From this perspective he argues that fasting on specific days was practiced by pagans, Jews, and Christians for comparable purposes.[39] Apparently at Rome, Christians were debating the merits of fasting on certain days. Several scholars have adopted Rauer's explanation.[40] As Kaesemann has pointed out,[41] however, this is an argument from silence. In all the references to food in the letters of Paul, not one involves fasting. It is, therefore, gratuitous to interject the question of fasting when the issue has to do with days.[42]

Since the three options presented above have serious drawbacks, we may profitably look at a fourth option. According to most interpreters, even if other Jewish feasts may have been within the field of vision, the debate among the Romans centered on the Sabbath.[43] The most clear defense of this view is provided by James D. G. Dunn.[44] He refers to the significance of the Sabbath in Judaism and the well-attested attractiveness it had for Gentiles, even if Jewish apologetics may have exaggerated its widespread observance among them. These factors must be taken seriously, and more importantly the text itself supports their consideration.

There is no denying that Paul's language is somewhat obscure.[45] As a consequence, determining what about the Sabbath was at issue is problematic. Most commentators, however, have not shied away from describing the situation. According to most, some of the members of the Roman community, coming from either a Jewish or a Gentile background, insisted on the sacredness of the Sabbath and set the day apart, while others considered such insistence as misdirected and viewed the Sabbath as just another day. On this account, as in the disagreement about foods, the "strong," who judged all days the same, "despised" their sisters and brothers who had outdated religious scruples, and the "weak," who respected the sacredness of the Sabbath, "condemned" their brothers and sisters for their disobedience (Rom 14:3). If such were the case, it would seem that Paul could have said about time what he said about food. Just as no food is unclean in itself (14:14), so no time is by itself sacred.

The Pauline text, however, does not support this reading of the passage. In the first place it must be noted that Paul did not write, "One judges a day as distinct, another denies the distinction." Rather, he wrote, "One judges a day as distinct, another judges all days." It does violence to the text to suggest that the debates over foods and over days at Rome were informed by a single problem: while some Christians had scruples about food and the calendar, others had none.[46] It is also a trampling of the text to suggest that while in the first clause the judging is positive, in the second it is negative. Yet, most translations of the text do this by using two English verbs, while Paul in the original Greek uses the same verb twice. The first clause is made to read, "one prefers one day over others, while another considers all days the same." Paul's language, however, emphasizes that everyone is engaged in the same activity and that their judgment is positive since they do it with the Lord in mind. According to the text, the contrast is not between some who affirm the sacredness or the special nature of a day, and some who deny such sacredness. It is found in the apposition of those who judge one day apart (παρά), and those who judge all days together (πᾶσαν). The first distinguish between days, while the second hold them together, even as they do it for the same purpose and in reference to the same Lord.

In the second place, it is to be noted that Paul wrote that "those who have their mind set on the day, have their mind set on the Lord" (14:6a). In this case he uses the verb once to include everyone. In other words, Paul affirms that all participants in the dispute are trying to do something important as Christians. They all have their mind set on the Lord. In this affirmation he also establishes that all have their mind set on "the day," not just any day. Thus, while judging days differently, everyone was concerned with "the day." This statement leaves little room for thinking that the day in question is not the Sabbath. To judge "a day" may be considered an imprecise reference. To have your mind set on "the day," in the context of a letter that is concerned with establishing that God has no favorites, is not too vague an allusion to the Sabbath.

The dispute at Rome reflects a situation similar to the one envisioned in a saying of Jesus known only from the text of the Gospel of Luke (6:5) in Codex Bezae, a sixth-century manuscript. The saying however has very early roots, even if it may not quite be the case, as Joachim Jeremias argues, that it comes from the lips of Jesus.⁴⁷ It says,

> On the same day he saw a man working on the Sabbath and said to him, "Man, if you know what you are doing, you are blessed; but if you do not know, you are accursed and a transgressor of the law."

Two things are to be noticed in this saying. In the first place it pronounces a blessing on those who do not observe the Sabbath on account of knowledge. It would appear that the knowledge in question is that the living Christ means that humans live in a new reality. Whether this should be understood, as Paul does, apocalyptically or in terms of a realized eschatology is not clear. In the second place, the saying condemns anyone who breaks the Sabbath without having this knowledge. In other words, the saying wishes to prevent the mindless neglect of the Sabbath while allowing that, with knowledge of the significance of Christ, its calendric observance is not necessary. As M.-J. Lagrange has observed, the point of view expressed in this saying fits the situation Paul faced at Rome.⁴⁸ This would be the case whether those who did not abstain from proscribed activities on the Sabbath were considering all days Sabbath, as I am arguing, or considering all days profane, as Lagrange thinks. I would argue that, since the saying condemns mindless nonobservance, it is more likely that those who have knowledge are also mindful of the Sabbath in their nonobservance.

The above considerations indicate that those who judged a day apart were concerned with the Sabbath. What remains to be determined is what those who judged all days together were doing. A few commentators have recognized that to judge all days together must be understood in a positive rather than a negative way. Martin Luther in his gloss on this text states that to those who "judge all days" every day is a feast day and a holy day.⁴⁹ Over a century ago H. C. G. Moule translated, "One man distinguishes day above day; while another distinguishes every day." He then comments that the text has

> a phrase paradoxical but intelligible: it describes the thought of the man who, less anxious than his neighbor about stated "holy days," still aims not to "level-down" but to "level-up" his use of time; to count every day "holy," equally dedicated to the will and work of God.⁵⁰

The text clearly supports this reading.⁵¹ Interpreters who think that those who "judge all days" were leveling them down do so on the basis of pre-suppositions foreign to the text. As argued above, it must be recognized that it is not the case that some were judging positively while others judged negatively. Rather, both sides were judging days in a positive way.

There is abundant evidence indicating that early Christians retained the reverence for the Sabbath that characterized contemporary Jews. One need not have been a Judaizer to take for granted the sanctity of the Sabbath.[52] Points of disagreement as to the "how" of Sabbath observance were, however, not a short list. The debates included questions as to whether Gentiles could observe it, whether the rest to be observed in it was to be total, whether God did actually observe it while continuously being involved with creation, and endless questions trying to establish which activities were lawful if it had been decided that the rest need not be total. Christians were as involved in these debates as Jews were. The only difference was that in Christian circles, questions could be settled by appeals to acts or words of Jesus, as the Sabbath controversy stories in the Gospels demonstrate. To make sense of the debate on the Sabbath at Rome, the question is, Were there Christians around 58 c.e. who considered all days Sabbath? In other words, were there Christians who leveled-up all days to the status of the Sabbath because they had their mind set on the Lord?

An affirmative answer to this question is given by the evidence presented in the previous chapter. The very early tradition found in *Gospel of Thomas* 27b insists on the need to "sabbatize the week." It is clear that these Christians understood themselves to be living the Sabbath every day. I am suggesting, therefore, that when Paul wrote to the Romans he was facing a dispute between Christians who wished to restrict the Sabbath to the seventh day of the week and others who considered all days of the week as Sabbath. In this way, the Sabbath was loosened from its ties to a twenty-four hour period within a weekly cycle. This way of understanding the Sabbath, it must be remembered, did not fade away soon afterwards as a passing fad. If, as some argue,[53] the Epistle to the Hebrews is connected to Roman Christianity it is relevant to point out that, as we shall see in chapter 9, it too understands the Sabbath as not tied to the present weekly cycle. The detachment of the Sabbath from a particular day within a realized eschatology is also found in the last edition of the Gospel of John, as has already been noted in chapter 6. In this gospel, Jesus defends his Sabbath activity by stating that he must work at all times, since he works just like the Father. Also, there is evidence that some time afterwards the Masbotheans, whose Hebraic name is a reference to the Sabbath, transmitted a tradition according to which Jesus himself had said, "in omni re *sabbatizare*."[54] This dominical command was understood to mean that all time should be devoted to the Lord. In this light, it is clear that the debate at Rome was not whether or not to observe the Sabbath, but which day was Sabbath. What I am suggesting, therefore, is congruent with what we know of early Christianity. In other words, there were debates among Christians concerning where precisely the Sabbath fit in time, given the new Christian understanding of time.

In this last section I would like to determine the position argued by Paul when he advises the participants in the debate at Rome, and whether what he said to the Romans is consistent with what he said to the Galatians. As noted above, given the shrillness with which Paul writes to the Galatians and the irenic tone he exhibits in Romans, the difference needs to be accounted for. Lagrange suggests that Paul's milder tone in Romans is due to the fact that he was confronting a less well-defined opposition. According to Lagrange, there was nothing reprehensible in either the intentions or the practices of the weak in faith. Besides, they did not constitute an organized party advocating a point of view.[55] Jewett, following Rauer's explanation that the days in question are fast days, describes Paul as the preacher of "tolerant coexistence."[56] Alan F. Segal, however, thinks that Paul's pandering to both camps is reprehensible. According to him, Paul's "diplomatic principle of conciliation" made him an apostate in Jewish eyes.[57]

Mark Reasoner argues that at Rome Paul faced a public relations problem. The position of the weak was obviously a superstition, considered such by the strong and by Paul. By writing this letter, Paul aims to prevent this superstitious point of view from becoming dominant among the Roman Christians. If such were to become the case, the non-Christians would dismiss Christianity as just another superstition. Reasoner's argument is self-contradictory. On the one hand, he points out that Christianity at Rome was viewed as another oriental superstition to start with.[58] On the other, he argues that this would be the case if the position of the weak were to become established among all Christians.[59] His interpretation fails to recognize that Paul does not advise the weak to cease doing what they were doing. Rather, he advises both the weak and the strong to be sure to do whatever they are doing "with full conviction." The ones who will have to stand before the judgment seat of God to give an account of their conduct (14:10) are not just the weak, but everyone.

Chapters 14 and 15, of course, should not be taken by themselves. Neither should they be seen as part of the "mere parenesis" found in chapters 12 to 15. According to Meeks, to do so "encourages misreading."[60] It has been recognized lately that the practical problems identified in the instructive section of Romans may have dictated the rhetoric of the more theological first chapters. Throughout the letter Paul is trying to encourage understanding and, more significantly, acceptance between those who are estranged from each other. In chapter 14 he explicitly refers to their despising and condemning each other (14:3). The chapter opens with an exhortation to welcome each other since God had welcomed them. His admonition is given weight by reminding them that they will have to stand before God's judgment (14:10c). Thus, it would seem that Paul is doing more than promoting tolerance, which can still be elitist. He wishes that God's acceptance of all be actualized in their community. Their differences in dietary and Sabbath questions was preventing this from happening.

Some interpreters have suggested that Paul wants the Romans to understand that what is troubling them are matters of no major consequence. Thus, C. H. Dodd writes that the questions of food and days are just "fads" and "taboos" that lose their significance under the light of reason.[61] Michael B. Thompson, on the other hand, thinks that the predominantly Gentile members of the Roman congregations considered dietary laws and Sabbaths "absurd."[62] For Raoul Dederen, "the mild way in which Paul deals with these weak brethren" indicates that the dispute has to do with "unessential matters."[63] F. Watson, for his part, thinks that Paul classified foods and Sabbaths as "purely optional, matters between the individual and God rather than authoritative divine commands."[64] Still, W. Sanday and A. C. Headlam identify Paul's concern to be with the Romans' "excessive scrupulousness."[65] Edward P. Sanders writes, "His negative attitude toward 'days' in Galatians does not allow us to say simply that he was against the Sabbath, since he considers it optional in Romans 14."[66]

In view of what our study of the Sabbath among the early Christians has revealed, it does not seem at all the case that Paul would agree with anyone who considered the issues he identifies in Romans 14 as unessential, a passing fad, or absurd. To say that Paul understood them as optional, requires that the rationale supporting this position be clearly understood. To the contrary, he recognized the significance of the dispute at Rome and gave it serious attention. Paul did not view the dispute at Rome as of minor importance.[67]

For its self-understanding, earliest Christianity did not debate whether to observe the Sabbath or not, the way it debated whether to practice circumcision or whether to observe the dietary laws, fasts, and prayers characteristic of Jewish piety. The *Gospel of Thomas,* Q, and the Gospel of Mark reflect Christian communities that debated the value of food laws, fasts, and prayers, but took for granted the importance of the Sabbath. Even while serving as an identity marker, like circumcision, the Sabbath had cosmic significance well beyond its social or cultic functions. Christians recognized this too. In the early stages, what was debated among them was how best to be mindful of it. The Roman Christian community was not exempt from these debates. Their dispute was not whether or not they should pay attention to the Sabbath, but whether "the day" was present in repeated twenty-four hour periods within a weekly cycle, or present in all days of the week after the resurrection of Christ.

Facing this dispute at Rome, Paul decides not to take sides openly.[68] Instead, he presents a christological and an eschatological principle as the basis for a resolution of the dispute. According to the first, the validity of any action done by a Christian depends exclusively on whether it is done "for the Lord" (14:6). The second establishes that Christians are servants who stand or fall before the judgment of the Lord (14:3, 10). It is a disappointment that Paul does not elaborate more on the question of days in the way he does on the question of food. On the question of food he makes a contrast in verse 6, and explains that no food is unclean in itself in verses 13–23.[69] He does nothing similar on the question of days.

Paul did not identify the dispute at Rome, as he did the one at Galatia, as one in which the truth of the gospel was in jeopardy. The dispute at Rome had to do with the particulars of how to live the faith. Paul's lengthy sections giving ethical instruction in all his letters, except Galatians, make clear that he understood that faith had to be transposed into life. A Christian is not a mind that understands and agrees, but a living being who acts out his convictions in everyday life. That is why Paul emphasizes that whatever is done, must be done out of "full conviction" (14:5, 14). Exactly what a person's full conviction is may be known only to God and therefore it is, like faith, a private matter (14:22). Paul, however, thinks that it cannot remain such for long. Convictions, unavoidably inform one's conduct in society. Still, it is possible for the same conviction to be reflected in diverse outward expressions. At Rome everyone agreed on the significance of the Sabbath, "having their minds set on the day" (14:6a). They were, however, giving expression to this conviction in different ways: some by observing the seventh day, others by making all days Sabbath.

Paul's explicit advice is found in a community rule and a beatitude. The first one states, "Let us . . . pursue those things which belong to peace and to the edification of each other" (14:19). Its purpose is to take care of the immediate social problem created by their disputes and personal animosities. The second reads, "Blessed are those who do not condemn themselves by what they consider approved [by the Lord they serve]" (14:22b). Neither of these sayings dictates how the Sabbath should be observed, or whether or not one should become a vegetarian. Instead, they provide the guidelines necessary for adopting a particular conduct in reference to these issues. They demonstrate Paul's trust in the intelligence and the commitment of his readers, and this trust is displayed repeatedly throughout his letters. Christians must go through the process of arriving at what they consider the conduct their master approves. Faith needs to be transposed into behavior. But Christian behavior need not be uniform. Paul insists, rather, that behavior must be "true" by coming from faith, that is, full conviction. Thus, "what is not of faith is sin" (14:23). Observing the Sabbath as present at all times or in a weekly twenty-four hour cycle, as far as Paul was concerned, were equally valid ways in which to be obedient to the Lord. It was only the Lord's prerogative to judge whether or not their behavior came out of full conviction in faith.

Even though, as some commentators claim, Paul seems to identify himself with the strong (15:1), this is not certain. As noted by Lagrange,[70] Kaesemann,[71] and others, it is not likely that the weak agreed among themselves on issues of food and days, nor that the strong did.[72] When Paul contrasts "one judges days this way, and another judges them that way," "one eats only vegetables, and another eats everything," "you condemn, and you despise," it does not follow that the first elements in these contrasts describe one well-known party and the second another. It certainly cannot be said that as one of the "strong" Paul counted himself among those who judge all days together, eat everything edible, and despise those who don't do likewise.

For Paul the cross of Christ signified the apocalyptic turning of the ages. The risen Lord was the life of the new creation brought about by the same Spirit who had created the cosmos in the beginning (2 Cor 4:6). This meant that the cosmic arrangements of the original creation were no longer what held the world together. The power of the resurrection of Christ now at work in believers was the only power worthy of human beings' attention. From this perspective, Paul affirms that the distinction between the sacred and the profane, which characterized life in the fallen creation, did not have a basis in reality (Rom 14:14). It is also true that in the new creation the Sabbath is no longer bound to its original calendric limits. This does not take the Sabbath away. It eschatologizes it. In the already/not yet of present existence in the world, it leaves the Sabbath in somewhat of a temporal limbo. Paul's position is not dictated by missionary or diplomatic expediency, but by his understanding of the new creation as already present in the risen Christ and those who are crucified with him, and not yet present in the physical and social reality in which humans live. As far as he is concerned, the Christians in Rome should be able to love each other as Christians while acting out their commitment to the risen Lord in objectively different ways of actualizing the Sabbath within the fallen creation. It should not be surprising, however, that he becomes extremely frustrated with the Galatians who, after having experienced life in the new creation by the power of the Spirit (3:2–5), are now living in the creation that has fallen under the power of the elements of the cosmos. Paul's posture and advice when addressing the Romans and the Galatians are quite different, but the symbolic universe that informs his writing is coherent. In the new creation the Sabbath is already an eschatological reality. How to locate it within the "present evil age" (Gal 1:4) is open to differences of opinion. To make it a fixture of the old creation, however, is to deny the effectiveness of the eschatological life now lived by Christians by the power of the Spirit. If Paul thought that the Galatians by their observance of days were bound to the wrong cosmology, it may be deduced that for him, in its essence, the Sabbath belonged to the eschatological world and that, as a commandment, it did not have power in the new creation.

8

The Sabbath in the Letter to the Colossians

It has not been easy to reconstruct the controversy to which the Letter to the Colossians bears witness. The only evidence at our disposal is the letter itself, and its language has been interpreted in different ways. Many proposals have been made, but as James D. G. Dunn says, "the jury is still out on the question."[1] Since the author of the letter described the teaching of those he opposes as a "philosophy" (2:8), this designation has informed most of the research. In this debate, like in the one Paul was involved in at Galatia, the relationship of Christians to "the elements of the cosmos" (τὰ στοιχεῖα τοῦ κόσμου) is also central. The writer makes an observation that could have been made by Paul. He reminds his readers, "with Christ you died to the elements of the cosmos." There is, however, a contradiction in their behavior because they are living as if they still belonged to the cosmos ruled by the elements. As will become clear, the way the Christians in Colossae are submitting to the elements is not, like in Galatia, by the observance of "days, months, seasons and years" (4:10). Rather, they are submitting to regulations that the author of the letter, rather derogatorily, describes as "Do not handle, Do not taste, Do not touch" (2:21). On account of this, the author declares, they are living "in the world." One may safely assume that the author expected them to have been living "in Christ" instead. The sarcastic description of these regulations does not allow for their identification. Still, in general, it would appear that they have to do with some form of asceticism. The author describes these regulations further in two ways: he attacks their effectiveness and their authority (2:21). In the first place, they deal with "things which perish as they are used." In this respect, their significance can be only momentary. In the second, they are formulations of human precepts and doctrines. They do not have a divine origin. Given this description of the regulations the Colossians have adopted, it is impossible to say that they come from the Torah.[2] Ascetic practices are not characteristic of the Torah, or of mainstream Judaism, even though they were part of Jewish reform movements like that of John the Baptist. Ascetic practices associated with initiation rites in the mystery cults as well as with mystical tendencies in Jewish *merkabah* speculations, apocalypticism, and religious-philosophical movements like neo-Pythagoreanism, on the other hand, are well documented.[3] The author is puzzled and asks, "Why do you submit to regulations" whose authority is human and whose effectiveness is transitory?

The specifics of these regulations are beyond us, but that their origin is not in the Torah is certain.[4] Contrary to what is the case in the controversy at Galatia, in Colossae none of the participants in the debate seeks support for their position in the Torah. In his letter to the Galatians, Paul spends much energy arguing about the purpose for which the Torah was given and its relationship to the new creation. No such references to the Torah are found in the letter to the Colossians. This makes it very difficult to think that the two disputes were similar.

The author of the letter to the Colossians, however, makes reference to "food and drink or a festival, or a new moon, or a Sabbath" (2:16). This refers, without a doubt, to matters that are regulated in the Torah. The calendric string "festival, new moon, Sabbath" is one found repeatedly in the prophetic appeals to pay heed to the obligation to observe the religious calendar.[5] Undeniably, therefore, in some way the debate was related to the Torah, even if it is not the case, like it is in Galatians, that the author condemns the other teachers, or his readers, for their use of the Torah. Commentators have consistently considered that this reference to food, drink, and festivals indicates that those teaching a "philosophy" to the Colossian Christians were imposing on them regulations about these matters prescribed in the Old Testament. According to this view, the regulations to which the author objects in 2:20–21 include the matters about food and festivals mentioned in 2:16. In other words, the other teachers were requiring the Colossians to observe the Sabbath, as part of a list of regulations related to their submission to the elements of the cosmos (a situation similar to that found at Galatia). Reacting to this imposition, the author of the letter tells them that they should not submit to these regulations in matters of food, drink, and festivals. This is taken to indicate that the other teachers are Jewish Christians who are still bound to Sabbath observances.

Other elements in the tenets of the other teachers, however, are not easily related to Judaism. Thus, there have been several attempts to interpret these tenets in terms of Pythagorean or Cynic doctrines. These attempts have a particular problem in the specific mention of the Sabbath. In his efforts to show that the "empty deceit" (2:8) taught by the other teachers is a form of Neo-Pythagoreanism, Edward Schweizer gives a very minor role to the Sabbath as a vestige of Jewish piety in a rather pagan spirituality.[6] To a large extent, the difficulty in reconstructing the debate at Colossae has been due to the problem of relating the Jewish and the non-Jewish elements in the tenets of the other teachers.

Troy Martin has taken a new approach by identifying the doctrines of the other teachers as Cynic.[7] I find his characterization of Cynicism somewhat formulaic, but his reading of the reference to the Sabbath is convincing. Martin has effectively criticized the established exegetical tradition that has given pride of place to historical polemics rather than to grammar and syntax. On the basis of a careful and convincing analysis of the text, Martin has opened up new possibilities for understanding how the author builds his argument.[8] He concentrates on finding the syntactical connection for the adversative elliptical clause "but the body of Christ" (2:17). The text of this verse has two dependent clauses. One is "but the body of Christ." The other reads "which are a shadow of things to come." Over the years the first clause has been taken to offer a contrast to the second. It is explained that a "shadow" is being contrasted with the "body." Accordingly, the author is saying that whereas regulations about food and festivals are a shadow of things to come, Christ is the real thing.

This reading, however, ignores several details of grammar and syntax. The first is that the adversative conjunction *but* can only link two clauses of the same kind. In this case the text has an independent clause "the body of Christ" and a relative clause "which are a shadow of things to come." Syntax does not allow a relative clause to be linked to an independent clause by a conjunction. Second, the traditional reading overlooks that the text says, "the body *of* Christ." To make a contrast with the "shadow," it is read as if it said, "the body is Christ." Since it is an elliptical clause, it is possible to introduce the verb *to be* in it. To make sense, however, translators and commentators take out the genitive preposition *of,* which is explicit in the original Greek. Also problematic is the way in which the verbal forms in the relative clause are understood. It does not say, "which were a shadow of what was to come." Rather, it says, "which are a shadow of things to come." In other words, the author does not say that the Old Testament festivals were shadows that have been displaced by the death and resurrection of Christ, which had already taken place when he was writing.[9] In addition to the problems in the two clauses, there is a problem with the way in which the main verb in the statement is read. The words "Let no one judge you in questions of food and drink or with regard to a festival, or a new moon, or a Sabbath" (2:16) are read to mean that the false teachers are imposing on the Colossians regulations in matters of food and festivals. *To judge* does not normally mean *to impose.*

After detailed consideration of the various ways in which the problems with the text have been (unsatisfactorily) solved in the past, Martin argues that the independent clause "but the body of Christ" cannot be linked to the relative clause "which are a shadow of things to come." Looking for a solution to the syntactical puzzle, Martin finds it by recognizing that the elliptical verb in the clause is not the verb *to be* but the main verb in the sentence, that is, the verb *to judge.* Read this way, the antithesis introduced by *but* contrasts both who should judge and what should be judged. What was taking place was that other teachers were judging the Colossian Christians on their Sabbath observance, among other things. Instead, the author insists, everyone should judge the body of Christ. What the author points out is that, when matters of eating, drinking, or festivals are involved, what needs to be judged is not "you" (that is, the one who eats or celebrates a festival), but the body of Christ. The elliptical use of the main verb indicates that what is said in the main clause is intended in the independent clause. The text, then, says: "Therefore, let no one assess [judge] you by the way in which you eat or drink, on in matters of a festival, or new moon, or Sabbath, which are a shadow of things to come, but [let everyone assess] the body of Christ [by the way in which you eat or drink, or in matters of a festival, or new moon, or Sabbath]." This reading does not make a conjunction link two unequal clauses, does not overlook the genitive preposition *of,* does not make the relative clause refer to the past, and does not understand that *to judge,* or *to assess,* is to impose observances.

The author of Colossians is not advising his readers not to allow the other teachers to impose on them the observance of the Sabbath because to do so would be to deal with shadows rather than with Christ. Rather, he insists that since they have died with Christ (2:20) and have been circumcised of the flesh (2:11–13), they have been forgiven (1:14). On matters of food, drink, a festival, a new moon, or a Sabbath, no one should judge them for doing such things, which are a shadow of things to come.

In other words, he approves their practices in matters of eating and Sabbath keeping. He defends the value of liturgical rhythms and dietary prescriptions, even as he qualifies their role. In 2:16 he tells them that they should not allow others to judge them for doing what they are doing. Then in 2:18 he tells them that they should not allow others to disqualify them for not doing what others think they should be doing.[10] The other teachers promise access to ultimate reality by means of asceticism, worship with angels, and visions. In this connection they impose regulations as to what can be handled (2:14, 20). In opposition, the author of Colossians insists that ultimate reality is in the future, when the "things to come" come. According to him, the gospel brings "hope" (1:24). Those nonsurgically circumcised in Christ have "the hope of glory" (1:27). In the meantime Sabbath observance, among other things, is quite valuable as "a shadow" of that glorious future.

The contrast in this text is not between "shadow" and "body." The contrast is between "shadow" and "what is to come." The shadow of what is to come does not refer to shadows of the Christ who has already come and made these observances obsolete. In this case, the "shadow" is the present blurred manifestation of a hoped-for future reality. In its shadow the expected future is seen as coming.

The eschatological future loomed large on the horizon of the author of Colossians. He defines the mystery in which the Colossians now have a share as "Christ in you the hope of glory" (1:27). He is concerned that they may abandon "the hope" (1:23), rather than "the faith." In the introductory thanksgiving he praises God "because of the hope laid up for you in heaven" (1:5). In view of what the future holds for them, he instructs his readers "to make the most of the time" (4:5), since the Parousia is not far away. When the expected Parousia takes place and Christ appears, the author reminds them that they "will appear in glory" as well (3:4). Rather than to find present worship with angels and visions appealing, this author has his hopes firmly tied to the glorious future coming of Christ. In reference to this future, he declares that the dietary and calendric observances his readers are involved in are a "shadow," or an intimation of the future. This is clearly a way of giving them value.

On the other hand, to designate these observances as "shadows" does, indeed, qualify them substantially. As Jean-Noël Aletti points out, "they reflect only imperfectly the eschatological realities."[11] All proleptic signs of eschatological realities can do but that. To describe such signs as a "shadow" should not necessarily be understood as derogatory, as Gunther Bornkamm has correctly pointed out.[12] As "shadows" they have a salvific function, even if they are not quite the expected reality itself. Full salvation will come with the manifestation of the saints in glory when Christ himself appears. In the meantime, those who assess the body of Christ circumcised on the cross will not abandon the traditional piety taught by Epaphras and approved by the author (2:11; 1:7).

To give further support to this reading of the text, it must be noted that "what is to come" (2:17) cannot be equated with "what spoils when used" (2:22). The ascetic regulations imposed by the other teachers, which the author ridicules as "Do not handle, Do not taste, Do not touch" (2:21), are not the practices the author tells the Colossians no one should judge them for observing in anticipation of the Parousia. The author holds what is to come in a positive light, but looks down on what spoils when used.

The way in which this author uses the metaphor of a shadow is not the same as that of the author of Hebrews, or of Paul when he writes about a type. It is not possible to equate "shadows of things to come" in Colossians 2:17 with "type of the one to come" in Romans 5:14. A type is not a shadow. The identification of something as a type depends on secure knowledge of the antitype. Adam may have been considered a prototype or an archetype before. He came to be designated a type only when Christ came to be seen as his antitype. A shadow, however, does not require discrete knowledge of the reality that projects it. As the projection of a not yet visible reality, a shadow is itself real. Besides, when the object projecting a shadow comes into full view, its shadow does not necessarily cease to be or to enhance its significance. On the other hand, it is also the case that a shadow may heighten expectations that are disappointed when it is discovered that what was projected is not what was expected.

Plato's story of the cave gave the notion of "shadow" the basic significance of being deceptive and unreal. To confuse a shadow with the real thing is to lack true knowledge. In a society where this is the case, philosophers are needed to guide the people along the path from falsehood to truth. This background is usually brought to bear in the reading of the word in New Testament texts. This is particularly the case with the Epistle to the Hebrews, which has some Platonic overtones. Careful reading of the texts, however, does not support the notion that the basic desire of the author is to contrast truth with falsehood.[13]

Hebrews 8:5 refers to "shadow and copy." The epexegetical "copy" makes clear that the intention is to contrast what is original with what is not. Thus, to say that the earthly tabernacle built by Moses in the wilderness was a shadow and copy of the heavenly one intends to take away some of its glory and show it as derivative. Still, it was only as a reproduction of the heavenly one that it had cosmic value and functioned, even if the author wishes to emphasize that it did not quite do the job it was supposed to have done. In Hebrews 9:13–14 the author constructs an a fortiori argument, known among Jews as a *qal wahomer,* the structure being: if this, how much more so is that. Arguing for the superiority of the new covenant as a means of access to God and the atoning of sins, the author states that the law had "but a shadow of the good things to come." The intention is to qualify the sacrifices prescribed in the law as inferior to the sacrifice of Christ. To state the superiority of what is better over what is good, is not to negate the value of what functioned satisfactorily once. To make his argument the author states what the law takes for granted throughout but does not quite explicitly say: "Without the shedding of blood there is no forgiveness of sins" (9:22). There is no question, of course, that the sacrifice of Christ, of which the sacrifices prescribed in the law were "but a shadow" (10:1), has already taken place. In this case as in Colossians, however, the shadow also has a future point of reference. In neither instance of the use of the metaphor "shadow" in Hebrews, is it intended to say that what is being described should not be granted reality. Instead, a shadow and copy of something should not be considered "the original" (Heb 9:23–24). In the case of temples or the priestly tabernacle, however, such is always the case. In fact, it is only as reproductions of a divine archetype that they serve as channels of communication between the human and the divine. On the other hand, to describe the sacrifices prescribed in the law as "but shadows" of the sacrifice of Christ is to see them as anticipations of it. In no single instance in the New Testament are shadows understood in the Platonic sense, in contrast to truth or reality.

To buttress my argument that the author of Colossians defends traditional Jewish views as significant within Christianity, I would like to call attention to three things in his letter.

The symbolic universe of the author of Colossians is not controlled by covenant and law,[14] but by a Christ who has brought cosmic reconciliation, forgiveness, and peace, and who will eventually manifest himself and actualize the hope of glory for the saints. In this symbolic universe circumcision is given cosmic significance. Those commentators who think that the other teachers were imposing on the Colossians Sabbath observance express surprise at their nonimposition of circumcision, yet they insist on classifying those teachers as Judaizers.[15] What they fail to realize is that the author himself is the one who throughout the letter assigns positive value to circumcision.[16] For him it was absolutely necessary, since it serves to perfect the body. Even though the author adopts the Pauline language of dying and rising with Christ at baptism, and uses it with telling effect in the advisory section, he views baptism as a circumcision of the body of flesh. This was what God did at the "circumcision of Christ" at the cross (2:11). On this basis, the reconciliation of humans with God is actualized when at their baptism they are circumcised with a circumcision made without hands, that puts off the body of flesh in the circumcision of Christ. The nonsurgical circumcision accomplished at baptism is the reenactment of the circumcision of the cosmic Christ at the cross. Thus, at baptism Christians cease to live in their body of flesh and rather live in Christ's body, which was made perfect at the cross (1:21). In this way Christians attain what the other teachers would have them attain by "rigor of devotion, self-abasement and severity to the body" (2:23). According to the author, rather than to leave the Christian "puffed up" in the fleshly mind (2:18), as the method imposed by the other teachers does, Christ's circumcision makes the baptized "perfect in Christ" (1:28). This is not at all the Pauline way of viewing circumcision. But it is very Jewish.

In the second place, the author shows a special interest in the body, that which is concrete. Thus, he states that on account of the circumcision of Christ "the whole of the Pleroma dwells in him bodily" (2:9). With this sentence he introduces a train of thought that is strung together by pointing out what God has done "in him" or "with him": in him you have been perfected (2:10), in him you have been circumcised (2:11), with him you have been buried, and in him you have been also raised (2:12), with him God made you alive (2:13), and in him God triumphed over the principalities and powers (2:15). That the pleroma, or the fullness of the divine nature, dwells in him was first said in 1:19, where the author is quoting and enlarging on, an early Christian hymn (1:15–20). In the string of things that Christians do in and with him, the author restates the case but adds the qualification bodily. In the hymn the reconciliation of all things in the cosmos (τὸ Πλήρωμα) results in all things (τὰ πάντα) now dwelling in him. As a result, "he is the head of the body" (1:18). According to 2:10b, "he is the head of all the principalities and powers" of the cosmos. The issue between the other teachers and the author of the letter is whether the perfection required for standing before God is attained through the principalities and powers, the elements of the cosmos, or through Christ who, according to the author, is their head. Not only that, but after the cross the whole of the cosmos, the pleroma, dwells in his circumcised body. That is the force of the adverb *bodily*. In this affirmation the author makes the central claim that supports his understanding of the gospel.

The author is waging a polemic against some who, according to a philosophy based on the role of "the elements of the cosmos," argued for a cosmological dualism and drove a wedge between the material and the real, the ideal and the actual. Against them, the author argues for cosmological unity. Nothing makes this point better that the stark affirmation that in Christ "the Whole of the Pleroma" dwells bodily (2:9). The author keeps the divine reality tied to the material world. This makes possible for Christians who have been baptized to participate in the pleroma that is Christ's body. The nonsurgical Christian circumcision disposed of "the body of flesh" (2:11). Thus, the circumcision performed by God on the body of the cosmos by the cross of Christ, and on the believer by baptism, means that the Christian is now "perfect" in the body of Christ and therefore reconciled, forgiven, and at peace with the cosmos.

The other teachers insisted on ascetic practices whose aim was to treat the body severely (2:23), trying to bring it under submission. The author grants that these endeavors may have "the appearance of Wisdom" (2:23) but charges that they fail to check "the indulgence of the flesh." As an alternative, the author offers a way of coming to terms with the body. It must be circumcised "by the circumcision of Christ." This is a Jewish way of dealing with the body, and a positive way of dealing with the material world. The author does not envision salvation as an escape from, or the negation of, the body. For him the problem is not the body, but the uncircumcised body. In the symbolic universe of this author, unlike the one of the author of Hebrews, the cosmic structure is understood not in terms of the tabernacle and its sacrifices, but in terms of the circumcision of the body of Christ.

Thirdly, as pointed out above, the calendric formula used by the author of Colossians is the one that was traditionally used by the prophets when emphasizing the necessity to observe the feasts.[17] The significance he assigns to the rhythms of time exhibits his view of the oneness of reality. It would seem reasonable, therefore, to identify him as one who was concerned with the Old Testament prescriptions and their function. This author does not appear to have been influenced by Paul's theology of the cross and the new creation. He is the only canonical author who explicitly calls attention to the Sabbath. He does not, however, relate the Sabbath to its origin at creation. Rather, he has effectively Christianized it by relating it to the expected Parousia. His use of circumcision as a foundational metaphor, the value he places on the body, and his appreciation for the Jewish festal calendar mark him as a Christian with strong ties to Judaism.

When the practice of religious rituals having to do with eating, drinking, feasts, new moons, and Sabbaths are to be evaluated, the author of Colossians points out, what is important is not so much to determine what they say about an individual Christian, but what they say about the body of Christ. The liturgical celebrations and dietary prescriptions do not have within themselves the power to establish the authenticity of a particular Christian. Still, they are the means for establishing the presence of the circumcised body of Christ in the community of the baptized. They also are anticipations of the eschatological realities in which Christians have their hope.

Philo also found himself defending the significance of Sabbath observance against those who "regarding laws in their literal sense in the light of symbols belonging to the intellect, are overpunctilious about the latter, while treating the former with easy going neglect."[18] Against the symbolists Philo argues that only when keeping the literal sense of the law may one gain a clearer conception of those virtues the law teaches.[19] Philo and our author, no doubt, argue for quite different things. While Philo argues for the necessity of the literal observance of laws that also have symbolic value, our author points out the anticipatory value of observances. Still, both tie the ideal intellectual world to the literal physical world against those who claim that only the ideal world has value. On this basis, as good Jews, both saw value in actual observances.

The author of Colossians was a Christian who was defending traditional ways against those who wished to make Christianity an otherworldly affair. His traditionalism is evident in his attitude toward eating, drinking, and festivals as well as in his formulation of a domestic code for the benefit of the Christian household.[20] The opposing teachers wished to do away with what they considered Jewish, and they may have claimed Paul's authority for doing it—just as Marcion did some years later.[21] Our author, on the other hand, claims Paul's authority to defend, even as he qualifies, what he considers important from the Jewish religious past. Doing this, however, he could not have been further away from Paul's understanding of the cross. Here we might point out that historical Christianity followed the advice of the author of Colossians, rather than that of Paul, when it instituted the Christian calendar and its own food and drink regulations.[22]

Our author's concerns in this regard were not different from those of the author of the Gospel of Matthew, a contemporary of his. The latter insisted that observance of the weightier matters of the law—justice, mercy, and faith—did not exonerate anyone from the obligation to tithe mint, dill, and cummin (23:23). Years after the destruction of Jerusalem, he preserved the peculiar saying, "Pray that your flight may not be ... on a Sabbath" (24:20). According to him the "righteousness that exceeds that of the Scribes and Pharisees" (5:20) includes both the performance of sacrifices at the temple and reconciliation with your sister or brother (5:23–24). The community that espoused these views as sayings of Jesus undoubtedly considered Sabbath observance, among other Jewish practices, an important ingredient of the Christian life.[22] The difference between the author of Matthew and the author of Colossians is that while the former is vitally concerned with the role of the Torah in the quest for perfection (5:17–20), the latter fails to bring the Torah as such into his argument even though he is also keenly interested in the way to perfection. He reinforces the way the Colossians were observing the Sabbath and eating and drinking, but he does not bring in the Torah as a warrant for this. The reason for this is easy to identify. Matthew is engaged in a controversy with the synagogue that is consolidating itself after the destruction of the temple. Both he and the Pharisees are claiming to be the true heirs to the riches of the Torah. The author of Colossians is engaged in a struggle with those who make no claims on the Torah.

Colossians 2:20 asks a rhetorical question somewhat similar to the one found in Galatians 4:9. The situations in Colossae and Galatia, however, were quite different. The danger at Galatia was that Christians were jeopardizing their newly acquired inheritance by failing to appreciate the significance of what God had accomplished at the cross and, therefore, they wished to live calendrically tied to the structures of the old aeon. At Colossae the problem was that Christians were being disqualified for wishing to actualize in cultic acts their eschatological hopes. Paul asked the Galatians, "But now that you have come to know God, or rather to be known by God, how can you turn back again to the weak and poor elements whose slaves you want to be once more?" (Gal 4:9). By means of this question Paul calls their attention to the God they have come to know in the work of Christ. He questions their preoccupations with the intricacies of the present cosmos and the elements that rule over it. This denies that God's new creation in Christ is a reality in their lives. In Paul' view their fear of the elements of the cosmos and their willingness to be circumcised canceled their baptism. For him baptism was not another form of circumcision, but the actualization of the crucifixion.

Our author, for his part, asked the Christians at Colossae, "If with Christ you died to the elements of the cosmos, how are you under regulations, as [are] those living in the cosmos?" (Col. 2:20). Submission to decrees that were attributed neither to the Old Testament nor to the Jesus tradition, was undoing their baptism. Thus, they were living "in the cosmos," "puffed up in their fleshly mind," rather than being perfected by "the circumcision of Christ." The decrees of 2:20 cannot be identified with "the shadows of things to come" in 2:16. It is unmistakable that while the author evaluates the latter positively, he views the former negatively. Eating, drinking, and festivals are to be considered effective means for reflecting the cosmic rule of Christ as head of the body. Writing from a Christian perspective that places its ultimate hope in the future, the author is not referring backwards to the cross of Christ but forward to the eschatological consummation. The way to the future is not by destroying, or denying, the past but by perfecting it. For this author things Jewish were valuable. Used properly, they did not focus attention on the things of earth, but rather served as pointers to the things above (3:2). By contrast, those who wished "to abduct" the Colossians and make them follow their unchristian philosophy (2:8) while claiming to open up heaven for visions and worship with angels, are charged with keeping attention on the realm below and the fleshly mind (2:18).

That Christians maintained the necessity of Sabbath observance and supported it by appeals to Jesus or Paul should not be considered Judaizing. No one has directed such charges at Matthew. Similarly, neither the other teachers at Colossae nor the author of Colossians should be charged with Judaizing. They were not the spiritual descendants of the rival teachers at Galatia.[24] The author of Colossians, even though he does use a few Pauline ideas, is not a good disciple of Paul. His understanding of baptism as a cosmic circumcision of the flesh that results in forgiveness (1:14; 2:13) is quite non-Pauline. His description of the cross as what takes away "from the middle the signed document" (2:14) has no echoes of elaborations in the undisputed letters of Paul. Moreover, the context in which he establishes the significance of Christ is solely cosmological rather than both historical and cosmological as in Paul.

Both the other teachers and the author of Colossians were concerned with the way to perfection, which, as noticed above, was also a concern of the author of Matthew (Matt 5:48; 19:21). According to those who imposed ascetic practices, the Colossians should abandon their Jewish ways and adopt the regulations they had devised in terms of a cosmos ruled by "principalities and powers." The author of Colossians ridicules their regulations as providing for only temporary satisfaction. He recognizes that on account of the "self-abasement" they inflict, many see wisdom in them (2:23). Their appeal, however, is an "empty deceit" (2:8). They fail because they do not take into account that in order to grow to perfection one must be connected to the circumcised body (2:11) of which Christ is the head (1:18, 2:19).

According to our author, the cosmos belongs to Christ both by creation and by reconciliation (1:15–20). The mystery of life is "Christ in you the hope of glory" (1:27). The only philosophy that counts is the one "according to Christ" (2:8). It teaches that perfection is not to be found in asceticism and rigorism but in the community of love. The cultic realm, on the other hand, is only a shadow of the Christian's future life in the presence of God. Its significance is found in that it makes the body of

Christ visible and thereby its assessment possible. Perfection is not a private matter to be sought in individual humility but a corporate matter that is visible when all are "knit together in love" (2:2). The Colossians, who once were involved in practices that activated the wrath of God still to come (3:5–7), must "now put away: anger, wrath, malice, slander, and foul talk," etc. They must "put on . . . compassion, kindness, . . . Forgiving one another, . . . and above all these put on love, which is the bond of perfection" (3:8–14). Like the author of Matthew (18:21–22), this author considers forgiveness to be an indispensable ingredient of life in the body of Christ, and perfection to be found only in the power of God's forgiveness and love.

Before moving on to the household code, the author concludes the first string of ethical instructions with the exhortation "And let the peace of Christ rule in your hearts, to which indeed you were called in the one body" (3:15). It is clear that the author is concerned with the dispute going on between those who observe the Sabbath and those who condemn them for doing so. His running theme is forgiveness, reconciliation, and peace. The peace found in the one body, as the editorial addition to the hymn in chapter 1 explains, is the cosmic peace brought about by Christ's death on the cross (1:20). Therefore, the body that is to be assessed as they observe the Sabbath is the body that unites the humanity and the cosmos as one. The author does not advise his readers to abandon earthly practices in order to become otherworldly. Rather, he takes seriously the necessity to live in the body "a life worthy of the Lord" (1:10). He bases his vision of perfection on things that are above but that are lived in the body, recognizing that all liturgical activity is only a shadow of the presence of God. Perfection is not found in the careful scrutiny of human activity or the ascetic escape from the world of sense, but in the perfection of forgiveness, love, and peace brought about by God's reconciliation and triumph on the cross. The body of the cosmos has been made perfect by the circumcision of Christ. Only those who appreciate this body, in which the pleroma of divinity is pleased to dwell, give to the Sabbath its proper role in their lives, recognizing its ability to anticipate the eschatological future.

The advice the author of Colossians gives his readers is quite straightforward: "Let no one assess you on questions of food or drink, or in matters of a festival, or new moon, or Sabbath" (2:16). An anti-Judaic, and anti-Jewish Christian, exegetical tradition, however, has consistently turned

146 A Day of Gladness

around this advise to read, "Let no one impose on you the observance of the Sabbath." In whatever way the Colossians were eating, drinking, celebrating feasts, new moons, and Sabbaths, according to this author, they were concretizing the body of Christ. The author, however, makes a distinction between the head and the body. As in several other matters, in this also he moved along paths that, as far as we can tell, Paul would not have taken.

In Paul's symbolic universe, created by the resurrection of Christ, the distinction between sacred and profane did not have a basis in reality (Rom 14:14). The Sabbath could not be bound to limits within a calendric system. On this basis, Alan Segal has argued that in Jewish eyes Paul had become an apostate.[25] The Christianity that saved his letters, on the other hand, softened this angular portrait and painted him as a traditional Jew. According to the Acts of the Apostles, Paul went to Jerusalem to give alms and offerings in the temple and was found at a synagogue every Sabbath. All rumors about him not being an observant Jew were patently false (Acts 24:17; 13:14, 42–44; 16:13; 17:2; 18:4; 21:20–25). Besides, he had understood Christ in terms that were primarily cultic and high priestly, as presented in the Epistle to the Hebrews. Sociologically, he had been a conservative who imposed the silencing of women in the churches, patterned the Christian communities after the patriarchal household (1 Tim 2:11–12, and its echo in 1 Cor 14:34–36), and saw the twelve apostles as the foundation of the church (Eph 2:20; Col 1:27).[26] Religiously, he had endorsed the celebration of the Jewish feasts and Sabbaths, as I have argued the author of Colossians, writing as Pseudo-Paul, affirms. In this way, Paul's admirers saved him from oblivion, confirming him as the apostle to the Gentiles, even while presenting him as a rather traditional Jew.[27] The author of Colossians belongs to a generation of Christians who claimed the authority of the apostles in order to institutionalize a more conventional Christianity.

9

God's Sabbath in the Epistle to the Hebrews

The Epistle to the Hebrews remains one of the most intriguing writings in the New Testament. Several aspects contribute to its appeal to modern scholarship. Once it became almost universally accepted that the letter had not been authored by the apostle Paul, questions of authorship and of the religious and cultural milieu of the epistle have been studied with some enthusiasm, but no significant consensus has emerged. In a review of the literature on the epistle, J. C. McCullough concludes by saying that it was precisely in these areas that the "most progress has been made and the most promising work has been done."[1] The religious and cultural milieu of this letter, however, remains as elusive as ever. This is quite evident by the options available for understanding the notion of God's Sabbath celebrations, or God's rest, in the epistle. The student of this question is confronted with the following spectrum of views. At one end is Ernst Kaesemann's argument that the rest is to be understood in terms of the Gnostic concept of the pleroma out of which the human soul originated and to which it wishes to return. While on earth, the soul finds itself suffering the continuous perils to be encountered on the journey back home.[2] James W. Thompson posits that the epistle needs to be read within the background of platonic metaphysics, in which the realm of being is contrasted with the realm of becoming, where existence is characterized by change and decay. Those who love wisdom, who are also lovers of God, strive for being. This point of view is evident in the dominical saying in Matthew 11:28, which characterizes the goal of life as rest, as well as in the writings of Philo of Alexandria.[3] Otfried Hofius, for his part, thinks that the epistle shares the symbolic universe of those who believe in apocalyptic visions of inheriting the new heaven and the new earth, or of entering God's heavenly temple.[4] Finally, George W. Buchanan identifies the dream of sharing God's rest as one that Christians who were heavily influenced by the Qumran covenanters had for an earthly political future in Jerusalem.[5]

Any summary of interpretative options, like the one above, has, of course, problems of its own. The most obvious is that justice is not done to the individual interpreters, and sometimes their arguments are made to fit the spectrum created for their presentation; thus, the nuances provided by their authors are ignored. Still, the above spectrum of views serves to demonstrate the lack of consensus as to the cultural milieu of the epistle. According to Harold W. Attridge, the two options at both ends of the spectrum are less convincing because their proponents do not provide the necessary evidence to create a probable "religio-historical construct" of the cultural situation in which the epistle made its argument.[6] This leaves as viable the Philonic and the apocalyptic options. They, however, are not free from significant problems.

Thompson's analysis of the motif "the rest of the wise" in the writings of Philo, as Gerd Theissen has demonstrated,[7] does not do justice to the various ways in which Philo uses this notion. Besides, Thompson may be claiming too much when he affirms that the epistle is a "philosophical treatise,"[8] the first Christian one. Even if the author proves himself acquainted with philosophical terms, he does not come across as a philosopher. On the other hand, Thompson himself argues convincingly that Hofius fails to take full account of the nuances to be found in the apocalyptic universe of *4 Ezra*. At the core of Hofius' argument is the claim that the eschatological rest envisioned by the author of Hebrews can be understood only in spacial terms, as taking place in a materialistic new Jerusalem. The apocalyptic literature of the time, however, also contains references to the rest of the righteous, which can only be understood in temporal terms.[9] Thus, while it may be too much to claim that the author is the first Christian philosopher, his acquaintance with philosophical concerns cannot be denied. Similarly, while it may be too much to say that he is an apocalyptic visionary, his acquaintance with apocalyptic speculations about the temple must be acknowledged.[10]

One's conclusion as to whether the Sabbath rest envisioned by the author of Hebrews is best understood in apocalyptic or in middle platonic terms is somewhat determined by whether one understands the rest as a present or a future possibility for Christian believers. On this question, again, interpreters have come to different conclusions. C. K. Barrett argues that the eschatology of Hebrews is distinguishable as early Christian because the rest is viewed as both a present and a future reality.[11] Attridge, on the other hand, emphasizes that the author sees the rest as a present possibility.[12]

In an attempt to understand what the author of the Epistle to the Hebrews envisioned as God's Sabbath celebration, I would like to find the answers to three questions. First, what is the author trying to elucidate for his readers when he introduces the notion of God's rest? Second, why does the author exhort them "to enter" God's rest? And third, in view of the argument, in which symbolic universe did this author dwell?

The text that draws our attention is Hebrews 3:1–4:11. The section begins with a comparison between Moses' and Jesus' faithfulness (3:1–6). According to the author, while Moses in ancient times had been faithful as a "servant" *in* God's house, "in these last days" Jesus, as God's "Son," had also been faithful *over* God's house (3:2,6a). This comparison and contrast pivots on the better status enjoyed by the Son who is over the house and who, therefore, should not be confused with the servant who labors in the house. The point of the comparison is then brought out: "we" are the house over which the Son is faithful. In other words, the argument is for self-definition: We are not faithful followers of Moses, but the house over which Jesus keeps faithful watch. This definition, however, is true only if a condition is met. The house over which Jesus is faithful are those "who hold fast to the boldness and the boastfulness of hope" (3:6b).[13] The section thus alerts the readers that their privileged position as God's house is conditional on their holding fast to, or not giving up, hope. Their hope, moreover, must be characterized by boldness and boastfulness, in other words, by its capacity to provide confidence.

In view of the conditionality attached to their self-definition, the author issues a warning in the words of Psalm 95:7c-11:

> Therefore, as the Holy Spirit says, "Today, when you hear his voice, do not harden your hearts as in the rebellion, on the day of testing in the wilderness, where your fathers put me to the test and saw my works for forty years, Therefore, I was provoked with that generation, and said, 'They always go astray in their hearts; they have not known my ways.' As I swore in my wrath, 'They shall never enter my rest.'" (Heb 3:7–11)

Why does the author bring in the words of the psalm in his warning to his readers?

Gerhard von Rad asserts that the psalm is quoted because it already made a distinction between God's rest and the rest that the people of Israel had enjoyed when living in the land as a result of God's grace.[14] By denying that they had entered God's rest when they entered the promised land, the psalm clearly distinguishes between these two experiences. Life in the land is not life in God's rest. But when the author of Hebrews introduces the warning pertinent to the conditionality attached to being God's house, he does not build his case on the difference von Rad points out. Thus, even if the observation about the psalm is correct, it does not seem to be the reason for the introduction of the words of Psalm 95 at this point.

The reason for the quotation from the psalm is explained quite differently by R. Reid.[15] The quotation is dependent on the fact that in 1:5 the author has quoted Psalm 2:7, "Today I have begotten thee." The text is structured according to a *gezera shawa,* an expansion of thought accomplished by bringing in another text using the same word.[16] The epistle's first section begins in 1:5 with the word *today* from Psalm 2:7. The second section begins in 3:7 with the word *today* from Psalm 95:8. Of course, if the quotation from the psalm introduces a new section in the epistle, the point about being the house over which Jesus is faithful would not be directly related to the quotation. This way of understanding the rationale for introducing the words of Psalm 95, therefore, fails to take into account the force of the author's "therefore, as the Holy Spirit says." The "therefore" links directly the conditionality of the status of Christians as God's house with the warning not to loose this privileged status.

F. F. Bruce explains that Psalm 95 has two parts. The first proclaims the benefits obtained by those who worship God (1–7b). The second warns that only those who have an obedient heart can worship acceptably.[17] He then locates Psalm 95 as one sung in Second Temple times to welcome the Sabbath. This reconstruction of the psalm is suggestive but, unfortunately, also conjectural. Besides, there is no evidence that in antiquity authors were careful to retain the contextual allusions present in the originals they were quoting. Therefore, this reconstruction of the rationale for bringing in Psalm 95 to the author's mind fails to convince.

Thompson points out that the quotation from the psalm serves to buttress and to explain both the affirmation and the warning offered by the author when he reminds his readers that "we" are the house over which Jesus is faithful but then points out that this status was not guaranteed. To make his case, Thompson appeals to Psalm 95:7a, "For he is our God and we are the people of his pasture and the sheep of his hand." It is difficult to see how the reason causing the author to quote this particular psalm is found in words that the author did not quote. This argument from silence is inadequate.

In view of the unsatisfactory answers already given, I would like to explore a different approach to the question at hand. In the first place it must be noted that the author credits the words of the psalm to the Holy Spirit, rather than to David. And by means of them he is warning his readers about the consequences attached to a "hardened heart," which causes "going astray." But the author is particularly interested, it would seem, in the force of the "today," which he wishes to apply to his generation. In the Deuteronomic tradition the opportunity to enter into a covenant with God has been transferred from the generation that left Egypt led by Moses to the generation that entered Canaan under Joshua's leadership (Josh 24:15). In the book of Deuteronomy the guise of the Mosaic speeches covers very thinly the fact that the opportunity for deciding the future is a responsibility that King Josiah's generation needs to assume. The author of Psalm 95 and the author of Hebrews obviously did not understand the Deuteronomic traditions in this way. The author of Hebrews, however, thought that since at the time of the writing of the psalm the Holy Spirit issued a challenge to David's contemporaries with his "today," the author could now, "today," issue a challenge to his own contemporaries. He sustains his right to do so by pointing out that the "today" granted to David's generation demonstrated that the "today" offered to Moses' generation had not come to an end (4:7–8). This means that "today" was still in effect for the benefit of the author's contemporaries. In other words, the "today" of the Holy Spirit is an eternal "today," which is present even now. In view of this, the author advises his readers to "keep exhorting one another each day, as long as it is called 'today'" (3:13).

The urgency of "today" is demanded by the conditions that, from the perspective of the author, were threatening the community. He seems to have in mind something specific; otherwise he would have used a hypothetical subjunctive. Instead, he uses the emphatic "lest there be in any of you" and an object clause with the imperative (3:12).[18] Apparently, some members of the community had what the author considers a "wicked, faithless heart," and, therefore, he extends to them the Holy Spirit's "today" of opportunity.

F. F. Bruce thinks that the author of Hebrews is working in terms of the traditional understanding that a generation consists of forty years, and that a forty-year probationary period before the entry into God's rest is envisioned here. Making a connection to Luke 9:51, where Jesus' journey to Jerusalem is described as an "exodus," Bruce argues that the forty-year probationary period would come to an end about 70 c.e.[19] This suggestion, however, gives to the author of Hebrews an interest in apocalyptic timetables that is not in evidence elsewhere in the epistle. On the other hand, it would seem that "today" has for him apocalyptic urgency, since he understands his generation to be living in "these last days" (1:2). He is also quite concerned because he fears that some might be forfeiting "such a great salvation" (2:1), even though Christ's "second appearance apart from sin and for salvation" (9:28) is now at hand.

As Thompson suggests, the "today" of Hebrews has the future in view, while the "now" of Paul has for its point of reference the past "when faith came."[20] The future perspective is in evidence when the author points out that while "the word of hearing" had not profited the generation in the wilderness, it was profiting those among his contemporaries who believed (4:2). The evangelization that was taking place "in these last days" was similar to that which had taken place before the entrance of the Israelites into the promised land. As is well recognized, in this epistle the continuities and discontinuities between the old and the new covenants are rather fluid. It appears that while covenantal arrangements may suffer changes, typically the dramatis personae in the history of salvation remain the same. In the author's view, the "today" of Moses' days, which according to Psalm 95 was still in effect in David's days, had reached even "these last days," which included the imminent second appearance of the Son. As O. Bauernfeind expresses it, "'today' is the road from promise to fulfilment."[21] "Today" does not refer to the past. It represents a historical present which can be the foundation for the future. "Today" marks the cruciality of the present within the continuum of God's eternity.

In the second place, the author quotes Psalm 95 because it contains a divine oath. In view of the conditionality under which a Christian community may be God's house, this oath served the author in two ways. On the one hand, an oath of the "living God" (3:2) guarded the entrance to God's rest, denying to some access to it. On the other hand, the oath affirmed the promise that some will actually enter God's rest. By stating God's oath in the third person rather than the second, the author of Hebrews indicates that it did not include everyone. At the time of the spying of the land, when the people of Israel listened to the negative report of the ten spies and identified with it, God swore that none of them would enter the land (Num 14:23).[22] Numbers 26:63–65 confirms that all those numbered at Sinai, except Joshua and Caleb, died in the wilderness. But Deuteronomy 12:9–10 reestablishes the expectation of living in the land where the Lord "gives you rest from all your enemies round about, so that you may live in safety." The author of Hebrews chooses to bypass this reaffirmation. In fact, with a contrary-to-fact conditional sentence, he denies it: "For if Joshua had given them rest, God would not speak later of another day" (4:8).

Why did the author overlook that, even if the generation who came out of Egypt failed to enter the land, Caleb, Joshua, and the next generation did enter? He seems to ignore that Chronicles repeatedly states that when the Israelites refrained from frequenting the high places and the groves they enjoyed rest in the land.[23] He feels compelled to insist that, contrary to what anyone might say, till his own day none of God's people had entered God's rest. The strong language of God's oath in Psalms 95:11, "they shall never enter," suited his purpose well. Von Rad is right: the language of the psalm was appropriated by the author because the psalmist had already distinguished God's rest from enjoying rest in the land.[24] In this connection, it must be noted that while Psalm 95 was not used much by apocalyptic visionaries of the time,[25] the hope of an eschatological rest was given a wide range of metaphorical expression in apocalyptic and rabbinical literature.[26] The exhortation of the author of Hebrews must be understood within this context. In conclusion, it may be said that the author introduced Psalm 95 into his text in order to establish that within the fragility of historical existence faithfulness is of the essence.

The argument of this section of Hebrews is built by means of a *gezera shawa*, where a second scriptural text using the same word is brought forward to explain the first one.[27] In order to interpret the notion of God's rest in the psalm, the author brings in a text from the Torah that uses the same word. That he could use Genesis 2:2 in this way demonstrates that the author based his argument on the LXX, rather than the Hebrew text.[28] Genesis 2:2 not only provided the interpretation for the notion of God's rest but also established that beyond God's oath there was a divine promise of rest. This was pivotal to the exhortation given by the author of Hebrews. What had prevented people from entering God's rest had not been God's oath, but their own disobedience (3:18; 4:11), and "lack of faith" ('απιστιά, 3:19). This contrasted radically with the "faithfulness" (πίστισ) exhibited by Moses and Jesus (3:2). This clarification of the reason for the failure of previous generations is essential to the argument.

Now, if the above is the case, it may legitimately be asked whether the opportunity to enter being made available to the author's contemporaries is dependent on the faithlessness of previous generations. Did some have to fail for others to get the chance? To answer this question Hebrews 11 must be brought into view. In this chapter, the author gives a long list of those who did not lack faith; in fact, they are considered the paragons of faith. The author makes clear, however, that even though they had been "attested through faith" (11:39), they did not receive what they had been promised. He explains that the failure of the patriarchs, judges, prophets, and martyrs of old to receive the promise was not due to a failure of theirs, but to God's desire not to reward a few when many should be sharing in the reward. As the author puts it, the "perfection" of the faithful of previous generations could not take place without "us."[29] This means that neither the failure of the generation of the exodus, nor the successes of the heroes of faith, have altered the effectiveness of the promise. Thus the invitation to enter, extended as an exhortation to the present generation, is not dependent on the failure of previous generations to take advantage of the offer. The promise to enjoy God's rest still stands, even though no one has entered it yet, because of the nature of the promise and God's plan to include "all," at least all those who are faithful.

The author of Hebrews balances God's oath that the faithless shall never enter with God's purpose that the faithful shall not be "perfected" without "us." Both God's oath and the announcement of God's purpose are followed by an exhortation. The difference between these two exhortations is most telling. Following the oath that the faithless shall never enter, the author writes: "Let us fear" God's evaluation of our lives (4:1). This motif is echoed in 10:21: "It is a fearful thing to fall into the hands of the living God." On the other hand, following the long list of those who exercised faith with boldness and boastfulness, the author exhorts: "Let us put off every extra weight . . . and let us run the race set before us with patient endurance" (12:1). Whether he is presenting a negative example that calls for becoming fearful, respectful, and attentive, or presenting positive examples and urging for more effort and patient endurance (a prominent apocalyptic virtue), he is guided by his understanding of what God is doing. In other words, his description of God's purposes and actions reveals his symbolic universe, and any comprehension of the text must take this universe into account.

Quoting Genesis 2:2 to illumine Psalm 95:11, the author argues that ever since God completed his work of creation God has been enjoying a Sabbath rest. God lives a perennially joyful Sabbath celebration, a σαββα-τισμόσ.[30] For this author the ongoing rest of God takes place on a different plane, one that is not affected by what is going on in the world. God's rest, which began at the conclusion of his creation of the world, did not take place at some time now buried in a chronological past. It is a permanent reality in the life of God. On account of the permanent nature of God's rest, the author sees the possibility of entering this rest open to successive generations living in chronological time.

In 3:13 the author first suggests that the promise of entering God's rest is still open, and advises his readers: "Exhort one another every day, as long as it is called 'today.'" In chapter 4 the author returns to the implications of "today" and elaborates on what he assumed in 3:13. Verses 4–8 point out that "they," those who proved faithless in the wilderness, became the object of the divine wrath and therefore would not enter God's rest. To the author, however, this only means that "others" are going to enter God's rest, since the Holy Spirit offered another "today" to David's generation many years later. In this way, the *gezera shawa* in 4:3–4 functions not only to define God's rest but also to prove that the invitation to enter is still in effect. It turns out, however, that with the passage of time and the coming of the Son the promise has become "better" (7:19), even though God's rest is not part of the world that suffers change and that can be improved.

As already stated, the author of Hebrews differentiates God's rest from living in any particular time or space. The *gezera shawa* in 4:3–4 appeals to the understanding of rest in Genesis 2:2 precisely to argue the point. In

4:1–2 the author states that the promise is still in effect and that even though "they" failed to enter, "we, the believers, are entering." In order to make the contrast between "they" and "we," the author defines God's rest. It must be pointed out in this context that the contrast never becomes one between Jews and Christians, but between those who lack faith and those who are faithful.

The progression of the argument on the definition of rest merits careful attention. First, the author points out the reason why previous generations, who were evangelized, did not benefit from the message of the gospel. They did not have "the hearing of faith" (4:2). This calls for a repetition of the oath barring them from entering. Then, the author adds, "although his works came to be from the foundation of the world" (4:3c). In other words, both the works of God and the rest of God have been in existence since the beginning. Therefore, people's failure in the past cannot be justified by saying that God's rest was not yet prepared and made available; it has been available since the foundation of the world. According to this author, the eschatological future is not dependent on the completion of Christ's work, either before or after the resurrection. Jesus' death and resurrection have a function in his symbolic universe, but it is not that of establishing the conditions necessary for a dramatic cosmic victory. What makes the eschatological future available is God's sabbatical celebration, which has been taking place since the foundation of the world. In this view of things, both God's evangelization of succeeding generations and God's sabbatical rest are divine activities that transcend historical particularities and distinctions between the old and the new. The strongly adversative "although" ($\varkappa\alpha\acute{\iota}\tau o\iota$)[31] with a genitive absolute in the original Greek makes clear the author's intention to highlight that, in spite of the fact that God has finished God's work and has been enjoying a sabbatical celebration ever since, God nevertheless swore that the faithless ones would never enter it. The oath was that "they" would be barred from entering not something God would eventually bring about in the future but something which had been available since the foundation of the world.

Even if in Psalm 95 the "works" of God that should have sparked faith in those who traversed the wilderness clearly refer to the miracles accompanying the exodus, the author of Hebrews makes them refer to the creation of the world. Thus, while the author of Psalm 95 contrasts God's works with God's rest, the author of Hebrews transfers both of these activities from the mundane to the cosmic sphere. For him, God's work and God's rest are related to creation. The way the author introduces the quotation from Genesis 2:2 is telling: "He has somewhere spoken of the seventh day in this way." In other words, the seventh day is the day when God rests. But this seventh day belongs to the archetypal time when creation took place. The "seventh day" is God's sabbatical celebration, God's σαββατισμοῦ.

The passage under review begins with the statement, "we are the house of God if we hold firm the boldness and boastfulness of hope" (3:6). The exhortation to take care lest disobedience, or faithlessness, render "us" subject to God's disqualifying oath includes an admonition to exhort one another because God's promise to enter stands beside God's oath barring the entrance. The passage ends affirming that "a Sabbath celebration, therefore, remains for the people of God" (4:9). The pivotal point in the whole presentation is the presupposition that the hope of the people of God is based on what God is doing, celebrating the Sabbath ever since creation. God's activity, however, is not immanent. It takes place in the order of the hypostatic.[32] Humans only have an inkling of it by faith and hope.

The author of Hebrews uses the Greek word *hypóstasis* three times (1:3; 3:14; 11:1) with the meaning it had acquired in Stoic philosophy. It had become useful to distinguish between prime matter, which is being as such, and that being that is actualized and therefore has attributes and faculties. The distinction is primarily a conceptual one that helps in the description of reality when the dualism of matter and form, essential to Platonism, has been rejected. For the Stoics all being is material, even the being of God. But not all material being is of the same sort. Thus, there is the being that has attributes, and there is the being that is primal and eternal, which is the foundation for all other being. Neither of these is the being that is phenomenologically present in the world and available to the senses. In the philosophical vocabulary *ousía* referred to being, *hypóstasis* referred to actualized being. *Hypóstasis* "designated the rise of existence out of the ground of being." It spoke of "the reality which is not immediately apparent."[33] The Stoics used the Greek term to designate what is materially differentiated in the metaphysical world. In Hebrews the term refers to reality that is not phenomenal, corruptible, or movable but that is "hoped for" and "invisible." It is what faith believes in and hope waits for (11:1). In this universe the future will not bring about the creation of a new heaven and a new earth, or the restoration of the garden of Eden, but the future will be lived in the immovable metaphysical world that is prior to, underneath, the phenomenologically changeable world in which human life is presently lived. As Helmut Koester states, the word does not as much define faith (11:1) as it establishes "the character of the transcendent future things."[34] What has risen out of the ground of being to hypostatic existence is real in the manner that counts, even if it is not now available to those who live in the world of sense perception. But it is now in some way available to those who live by faith and have the boldness to hope.[35]

The "therefore" introducing the final exhortation in 4:9 fully confirms our interpretation of the passage. According to 4:3, "we who are faithful are entering that rest." Then 4:10–11 tacitly grants that "we" have not yet ceased from our labors, meaning that "we" have not yet entered God's rest. The author interjects an exhortation, "Let us, therefore, strive to enter that rest." This places the author and his readers within the historical process where faith and hope are essential. According to the author, in faith one refrains from doing certain things and boldly does others, because what is now not apparent, but is hypostatically real, will become manifest at the soon-to-take-place second coming of the Son (9:28). That is why, for this author, hope rather than wisdom is the anchor of the soul (6:19). His argument is that when God ceased working he entered his rest, and when those who have faith and hope cease from their labors they will enter God's rest. As Attridge correctly points out, what "distinguishes Hebrews from similar reinterpretations of the divine rest as a heavenly reality in Philo or *Joseph and Asenath*" is that its author "keeps clearly in view a future eschatological consummation."[36] It is not at all the case that in 4:10 the author envisions the attainment of wisdom as the benefit of entering into God's rest at the end of one's labors, or that "the rest into which believers enter is the complete fulfilment of God's work in them and their work in God."[37] The tension left by the author between the affirmation of a present experience of rest (4:3) and the injunction to strive to enter the rest (4:11) is similar to the well-documented tension between the indicative and the imperative in Paul's writings.[38] Those who by faith and hope experience God's sabbatical celebrations now have "come to Mt. Zion, and to the city of the living God, the heavenly Jerusalem, and to innumerable angels in festal gathering, and to the assembly of the firstborn who are enrolled in heaven" (12:22–23a), but the fragility of their experience in the movable world is in no way comparable to actually celebrating Sabbath with God in the "kingdom that cannot be shaken" (12:28). Reflecting on the significance of the shaking of Mount Sinai on account of the divine epiphany, the author recalls the words, "Yet once more I will shake not only the earth but also the heaven" (Hag 2:6). Then he elaborates, "This phrase, 'Yet once more,' indicates the removal of what is shaken, as of what has been made, in order that what cannot be shaken may remain" (12:27). This is the removal of the phenomenological world so that the hypostatic world may remain. Offering to God "acceptable worship with reverence and awe," Christians do "not come to what may be touched" (12:18), the earthquake and the fire that shook Mount Sinai, but to "our God [who] is a consuming fire" (12:29). Worshiping in the company of angels, the author of Hebrews, like the covenanters of Qumran, experiences awe at the breaking of cosmological barriers, sharing in the invisible world that cannot be touched. But he knows that hope is the anchor of the soul and that faith is what makes the unseen visible, and therefore he must strive to enter God's sabbatical celebration when the world is shaken and that which is not shakable remains.

It has been noticed that there are some significant similarities but also a few differences between the Epistle to the Hebrews and the Letter of Barnabas. Referring to the question of their eschatological perspective, Barrett asserts that even though the author of Hebrews is closer to Pseudo-Barnabas[39] than to Philo, there are some basic differences between these two authors. The most notable, according to Barrett, is that while Pseudo-Barnabas ties the Sabbath to an eschatological timetable, the author of Hebrews does not.[40] Barrett also thinks that a significant contrast between the two is that while Barnabas exhibits a rather universalistic eschatology, Hebrews has a more personal understanding of salvation. Both of these contrasts are suggestive, but they need to be examined. In this final section I would like to explore the relationship between these two early Christian writings.

In Barnabas 15 there is an unusual elaboration of the Sabbath. The passage, as has been noticed, is not easily understood due to several factors. Among them are the appeal to nonexistent quotations from Scripture and the distortion of existing ones, the arbitrariness of allegorical interpretations, the shift of pronouns whose antecedents are, at best, elusive, and the introduction of an eighth day whose relation to the seventh is enigmatic since it seems to be none other than the seventh. Students of the Apostolic Fathers have also noticed that Pseudo-Barnabas is the only writer of the second century who introduces his discussion by identifying the Sabbath as one of the ten commandments. All of his contemporaries whose writings have survived exclude the Sabbath from among the commandments while asserting the Christian obligation to observe the ten commandments.

Pseudo-Barnabas also makes clear that observance of the commandments is essential to the Christian life. Giving a rather long catalogue of the things required of those who walk in "The Way of Light," as opposed to those who walk in "The Way of the Black One," he makes this belief explicit (19:2). He also repeatedly affirms the wisdom of Moses in giving the laws. However, he argues throughout that in the writings of Moses and the prophets God had already "made all things plain to us beforehand that we should not be shipwrecked by conversion to their law" (3:6). This could only introduce a situation whose resolution would remain problematic. Pseudo-Barnabas' preferred option is to point out that due to "their lust of the flesh" the Jews failed to understand the meaning of the commandments. In agreement with the author of Hebrews, he also points out that the Jews had been evangelized. In disagreement with him, however, he maintains that there is nothing wrong with the law.[41] The writers of Scripture already had in mind the allegorical meaning of their words. Thus, their words stand true as expressions of the divine will, which may be correctly understood and followed.

Quoting the Genesis text, "And God made in six days the works of his hands and on the seventh day he made an end, and rested in it and sanctified it," Pseudo-Barnabas turns the quotation into an apocalyptic chart of world history. The text means that "in six thousand years everything will be completed," and that "when his Son comes he will destroy the time of the wicked one, and will judge the godless, and will change the sun and the moon and the stars, and then he will truly rest on the seventh day" (15:4–5). This allegorization of the creation week serves the author to establish a key element to his views on the Sabbath. Not even God has truly rested on the Sabbath yet. He will do so "well" (καλῶσ) only when the seventh millennium arrives, after the destruction of evil.

This premise establishes the author's basic contention. If not even God fully enjoys the Sabbath rest now on account of the presence of evil in the world, can sinful humans actually have a "sanctified rest" (καταπαυόμενοι ἁγιάσομεν) now? Obviously, this is impossible because the commandment states, "Sanctify also the Sabbath of the Lord with pure hands and a pure heart" (15:1). Nowhere in Scripture is such a commandment found, but Pseudo-Barnabas has no problem with putting it this way if it serves to further his argument. Given the nature of the commandment, no human being is capable now of observing it, since having pure hands and a pure heart are preconditions to it. On this point he is willing to bet his whole view of Christianity. "If, then, anyone has at present the power to keep holy the day which God made holy, by being pure in heart, we are altogether deceived" (15:6). This is, of course, a contrary-to-fact conditional sentence. And Scripture itself says so: "Your new moons and Sabbaths I do not accept" (Isa 1:13). This means that "now" all Sabbath observances are unsatisfactory. "We shall sanctify it while resting well (καλῶσ καταπαυόμενοι ᶜαγιάσομεν αὐτήν) when we shall be able to do so when we ourselves have been made righteous and have received the promise, when there is no more sin, but all things have been made new by the Lord. Then we shall be able to sanctify it, having ourselves been sanctified first" (15:7). According to the argument so far, under present circumstances no human being is able to observe the commandment to sanctify the Sabbath, and God does not quite rest "well" on it. This situation will change in the seventh millennium, when the Son comes. Then we shall be sanctified, lawlessness will no longer exist, and both God and we will be able to rest well sanctifying the Sabbath. In this way Pseudo-Barnabas has eschatologized the Sabbath within a millennial schema,[42] and made the observance of weekly Sabbaths now both misguided and impossible. Sinners who pretend to sanctify the Sabbath have been shipwrecked in the law. A spiritual understanding of the law sees that its purpose is to promote sanctification, not ritual purity. The author makes this argument more explicit in reference to the food laws in chapter 10.

The authors of Hebrews and of the Epistle of Barnabas have disconnected themselves from the weekly Sabbath by eschatologizing its true nature. They also agree, therefore, that no human being has yet received the promise or is yet able to enjoy fully the Sabbath rest. The symbolic universes within which they understand things, however, are quite different. Pseudo-Barnabas looks forward to "the beginning of *another* world, . . . when I [God] will give rest to all things" (15:8).[43] The Sabbath commandment, it would seem, was intended all along for that world, not our current one. Even God is looking forward to the arrival of the seventh millennium in order to fully rest on the Sabbath. The author of Hebrews, on the other hand, like the author of the *Gospel of Thomas,* sees things in terms of the finality of protology. God has been enjoying a perfect Sabbath celebration since the foundation of the world. The world God created has hypostatic discreteness and is unshakable. The Sabbath is a reality of that world, and when the world of change and suffering is removed the faithful will enter into God's Sabbath rest. The Sabbath is not as much a commandment as a way of life. So far, no one has yet received the promise; no one is yet fully enjoying God's Sabbath celebrations. On this last point the authors of Hebrews and of the Epistle of Barnabas agree. The contrast between these authors is that between the Sabbath as a reality in an already created perfect and eternal world and the Sabbath as belonging to a world not yet made. For both of them, however, resting on the Sabbath is the ultimate experience, which is denied now to humans but to which they should certainly aspire.

10

The Sabbath among the Jews and Christians

The commandment to abstain from work on the Sabbath soon became a central feature of Jewish life in antiquity. Even if its origins are not quite clear, the presence of this commandment among the Ten Commandments enshrined at the core of the Mosaic legislation gives it a singular place in Judaism. Specifically, the commandment is not only negative, forbidding work. It positively commands "to sanctify" the Sabbath. The two versions of the commandment found in the Pentateuch, however, differ not only in the way they call attention to the Sabbath, Exodus 20 saying "remember," while Deuteronomy 5 reading "observe," but also in the rationale given for it. While Deuteronomy recalls God's liberation of the Israelites from Egyptian slavery, Exodus calls attention to God's rest at the completion of creation. Still, the two accounts agree that the intention of the remembrance, or the observance, is "to keep it holy," "to sanctify it." As Pseudo-Barnabas perceptively noticed, this is asking quite a lot from sinful humans. Those who see themselves tied to the yoke of the law, however, have not been stingy in their efforts to find the way of keeping this commandment.

Of the two rationales given for it, undoubtedly the priestly linkage of the Sabbath to creation is the one that captured the imagination of the Jews. Since God in the beginning rested on the Sabbath and sanctified it, humans must ritually repeat this divine archetypical act. By resting and sanctifying the Sabbath, humans transcend the monotony of human life in time and center their lives on the life of God. As such, the Sabbath is a cosmic gear, synchronizing the activity of humans with the activity of God. It is a cosmic center facilitating communication between the human and the divine realms. Given the Sabbath's cosmic setting, it is impossible to overemphasize its hold on the religious imagination of Jews. There could not be a symbolic universe within which a religious Jew felt comfortable without the Sabbath. This does not mean, however, that all Jews gave to the Sabbath the same symbolic significance or agreed among themselves as to the way in which it was to be sanctified.

The desire to make certain that the sanctity of the Sabbath was established and no work was done on it was paramount. It placed a premium on the determination of which activities fell under the definition of work. Another way of stating this, and the most common way of talking about it, was to establish whether a particular activity was or was not permissible on the Sabbath. This, of course, meant that it had been determined that the commandment did not require total inactivity. Philo argues that this is the case with God. God is the Creator at all times. Such is his nature; therefore, he cannot do otherwise, even on the Sabbath. The difference between the first six days of the week and the seventh, then, is not that while on the first six God is actively creating, on the seventh he is inactive. The difference, rather, is in the kinds of activity God is engaged in during the first six days and on the seventh. On this day, God instead of making mortal things creates "the happy and blessed things." The rabbis also understood that God was active on the Sabbath. There were, however, differences among them as to what exactly God did on this day.

Not surprisingly, Philo reports that there were many Jews who thought that as a day of leisure the Sabbath provided a good opportunity for sports and entertainments. For most Jews, however, the way to observe the Sabbath commandment needed to be worked out with care, allowing for the requirements of particular situations. For some, it was the most important of the commandments. Its observance could cover failures in the observance of others, and full compliance with this commandment on the part of all Israel would trigger the coming of the Messiah. This understanding of the Sabbath, as the anvil on which Israel's devotion to God is hammered into shape and finally perfected, gives to Sabbath observance supreme value in the religious landscape of Judaism.

The attitude of Jews toward the Sabbath ran the gamut of a rather wide spectrum. To the far right there were those who took the command extremely seriously and did nothing on this day. To make sure they were at rest, they spent the day immobilized. For them it was primarily a negative commandment. To the far left of the spectrum were those who understood the Sabbath to be a reality of the world of perfect forms, where seven is the perfect number. Its presence in the material world in which humans work is purely symbolic. Therefore, as a command, it is not to be taken literally. Its function is to call attention to the reality of the immaterial world.

Philo tried to chart a path that avoided the extreme of those who thought that observance is not required because the Sabbath belongs to the uncreated world, and those who are concerned only with its observance in the material world, overlooking that the Sabbath is a basic structural element in nature. The Sabbath was already a reality before the creation of the material world and, of course, before the giving of the Sabbath commandment. For Philo, to observe the Sabbath is to change one's activity from the material to the contemplative life. In this way humans follow the pattern established by God, and God facilitates this shift by making wisdom available in greater abundance on the Sabbath. Sabbath observance is for the contemplation of God's activity and the examination of one's conscience. While the first is done principally at the synagogues, which are schools of virtue, the second is done privately in the council chamber of the soul.

Since Philo finds the otherworldly aspects of the Sabbath the most worthy of consideration, he seems to have been under attack from those who considered most important the actual material observance of abstention from work. In reference to the symbolists, with whom he fully agrees on seeing the Sabbath as a symbol of uncreated things, he disagrees with their disregard for actual observance, and he gives a list of impermissible things they are doing. Moreover, he charges them with exposing those who take the Sabbath seriously as a pointer to the uncreated to the wrath of those who live tied to the material world. Those who insist on the practical rather the metaphysical aspects of the Sabbath may not see the difference between the symbolists and himself, leaving him vulnerable to charges of nonobservance. Philo wishes to make clear that for him it is a question of both/and, not one of either/or. According to him, the symbolists make things difficult for those who agree with them only in part. They also confuse non-Jews. Therefore, he finds their conduct reprehensible.

Philo draws a contrast between those who call the Sabbath "Virgin" and those who call it "Seasons." He fully identifies himself with the former and thinks the latter are somewhat misguided. In this case, however, he does not attack those who call it "Seasons" and are concerned only with the practical details that need to be established for its proper observance in the material world. Still, his drawing of the contrast illumines our understanding of the range in the spectrum of Sabbath views.

Philo also illustrates the relationship of the Sabbath and its observance by comparing it to that of the body and the soul. He insists that observance is a precondition for the proper appropriation of its meaning. It is impossible for the meaning of the Sabbath to exist apart from its observance. The metaphor, however, cannot be pushed. In reference to the body and the soul, Philo is clear in his teaching that the proper way to conduct one's life is to aim at the extrication of the soul from the body. Philo also makes a distinction between the Sabbath and the laws governing its observance. Ultimately, for him, the Sabbath is not law. He views the Sabbath not as an institution within creation but as a reality prior to creation, one that makes possible for those within creation to escape the created world. He makes a rather nuanced series of distinctions about the Sabbath. As a reality in the uncreated world the Sabbath is that seven that is equal to one. As a reality in the created world the Sabbath is that seven that follows six. Many years later the Sabbath became law. But the law given by Moses needs also to be distinguished from the laws for its observance given by other ancient worthies whose authority, according to Philo, "also merit respect."

The origins of the community of covenanters at Qumran, at least in part, are related to the desire to observe the Sabbath and the feasts at the correct time. The adoption of the lunisolar calendar by the Hasmonean High Priest Jonathan in 150 B.C.E. sparked a bitter debate as to whether the Sabbaths in this calendar were really the holy times prescribed in the Torah. The covenanters withdrew from the orbit of the temple in Jerusalem and its feasts in order to sanctify the Sabbath at the appointed time according to the traditional solar calendar of 364 days. In other words, Judaism also knew controversies over the proper time in which to observe the Sabbath. No amount of care in the performance of the prescribed sacrifices or the abstention from work was worth anything if it was done on the wrong day.

The Dead Sea Scrolls provide clear evidence that prior to the destruction of the temple the covenanters conducted spirited communal worship on the Sabbath. In it the singing of liturgically assigned psalms was a major component. On the other hand, both Philo and Josephus view the Sabbath as an opportunity for the self-improvement of the community and the individual by means of study, discussion, and introspection. On the Sabbath at the synagogues Jews debated the meaning of the law, an activity that is essential if the law is to be the effective guide of the life of the community. These different pictures of what was done on the Sabbath when the community came together have fueled a considerable debate on the nature of the synagogue and the development of a liturgy in it. When considering the evidence from the Dead Sea Scrolls, however, we must remember that the covenanters were in open revolt against the temple, its priesthood, and its services. Their Sabbath worship was their explicit alternative to what was taking place at the temple. It cannot be assumed that the covenanters provide evidence of what took place at the synagogues prior to 70 C.E. Our review of the evidence does not support the notion that when Jesus, Paul, and other Christians went to a synagogue on a Sabbath they participated in a Jewish worship service.

Those who were concerned with the material observance of the injunction against work spent some effort distinguishing what is from what is not work. This preoccupation brought about the great expansion of halakah. These prescriptions were concerned, in the first instance, with establishing which activities were permissible, but also with making the observance of the Sabbath not an "impossibility," as some Christians later charged. As a result, *Shabbat* is the largest tractate in the Mishnah.

Since God is not inactive on the Sabbath neither should God's people be. This necessitated the establishment of the limits within which one could act. To be determined were the distances people could travel from their places of residence, the burdens they could carry within their places of residence, whether or not a particular object could be taken in or out of a place of residence, etc. In reference to these questions it also became important to define what constituted a place of residence. It would seem that in spite of the many disagreements in these matters, Jews respected the legitimacy of each other's opinions. This was most in evidence among the rabbis, even if on occasion there were some serious feuds between them. Ultimately, every Jew had to follow the ruling that proved his willingness to obey.

Most Jews considered it obvious that the preservation of one's life could not take precedence over the Sabbath. Philo laughs at the idiocy of an Egyptian official who thought that on a Sabbath the Jewish community would help with preventing a dike from breaking. Common sense would dictate that such a civic emergency would undoubtedly take precedence over the commandment. Philo leaves no doubt that this is not the case. Josephus reports that toward the beginning of the Maccabean War, Judas established that it would be counterproductive not to fight on the Sabbath. This was after the Syrians had massacred a large number of men, women, and children who had hid in a cave and remained passive when attacked. Judas' argument was that a living Sabbath observer is better than a dead one. Josephus reports that it became the common policy that it was permissible to fight on the Sabbath if an enemy attacked. This policy, however, seems to have been ignored by every Jew who was attacked on a Sabbath. In every case Josephus reports that those under attack thought they should not fight. Besides, Agatharchides argues that on account of the Jews' unwillingness to fight on the Sabbath they have lost their freedom. Faced with the charge that keeping the Sabbath is a bad practice that jeopardizes the future of the nation, Josephus forcefully argues that, if the choice is between safety and obedience to the commandment, obedience represents the path of virtue and must be preferred to safety. This, of course, contradicts Judas' argument which, according to Josephus, instituted the policy that it was preferable to fight than to let oneself be unceremoniously killed on a Sabbath.

Philo's view that Jews should go to the synagogue on the Sabbath rather than help with civil emergencies agrees with the notion that it is preferable to suffer martyrdom than to fight on the Sabbath. Cases like these, of course, create the dilemmas by which human souls are tried. It would seem, then, that many Jews considered obedience to the Sabbath law more valuable than one's life. This explains, to some degree, why there is no evidence of overt efforts to rescind the death penalty for Sabbath offenses, even if there were some efforts made to limit the circumstances where it applied. In any case, it seems clear that Josephus' report that from the time of the Maccabees till his own days all Jews had a common policy concerning fighting on the Sabbath is not to be trusted. While many Jews chose martyrdom over breaking the Sabbath, it is well known that Jews were sought-after mercenaries in many foreign armies. It is difficult to think that these mercenaries adhered to any kind of policy on Sabbath fighting. Whether fighting for their homeland, or on foreign armies, it would seem that Jews followed their own rules of observance.

Both Philo and Josephus point out that the observance of the Sabbath by Gentiles proves that the Sabbath is not just a discrete Jewish institution. It is a universal marker embedded in nature and intended for all nations. With careless disregard for his own credibility, Josephus reports that in every city there are schools where on the Sabbath Jews and non-Jews spend their time developing the life of virtue. The widespread observance of the Sabbath on the part of Gentiles throughout the world, according to Josephus and Philo, is an argument for the superiority of the Mosaic constitution. The rabbis, on the contrary, held that the Sabbath belonged exclusively to the Jews. It was the signet ring that marked them as the bride of God. For them the Sabbath is to be seen within the context of God's covenant with Israel. A non-Jew who keeps the Sabbath is an interloper in the bridal chamber where Israel enjoys intimacy with God. Neither Philo nor Josephus looks at things from the perspective of a covenant theology. According to them, the benefits of the Sabbath are intended for all humanity. Its positive aspects, rather than its negative injunction concerning work, is what distinguishes the commandment. It fosters the life of virtue and the attainment of wisdom, bringing about the consolidation of the community.

In Second-Temple Judaism the Sabbath also acquired an important eschatological role. This was understood both in terms of its connection to the exodus from Egypt and to creation. As a day that marked the Israelite's liberation from slavery in Egypt, the Sabbath anticipates the age to come. As a day that sealed the completion of creation, the Sabbath institutes the age to come. The eschatological connection worked in two ways. As the rabbis declared, every Sabbath is a portion of the Messianic era. On the other hand, the Messianic era will come only when all of Israel faithfully observes a Sabbath. As a proleptic anticipation of that perfect age to come, the Sabbath made essential qualities of the divine realm available in this life. Philo emphasizes peace, freedom, and wisdom. Josephus sees the Sabbath river as a channel of the waters of salvation already available within the Roman Empire. Marqah extolls the Sabbath as the source of life. The rabbis praised the conjugal ecstasy of the Sabbath. The covenanters of Qumran found that in the Sabbath the boundaries of the material world could be broken so that humans could worship God together with the angels. As a platform on which to stand before God, the Sabbath allowed humans to transcend cosmic limitations and be with beings of higher spheres closer to the throne. In this way the Sabbath provides now what is expected to be the case in the age to come. Josephus, who had a rather this-worldly eschatology, ties his hopes for the future to Titus' triumph. Philo, who has a more philosophical mind-set, understands that the limits broken on the Sabbath are in the amount of wisdom the mind can comprehend.

This presentation amply demonstrates the wide spectrum of opinion on the Sabbath among Jews in antiquity. At one end of the spectrum we find those who thought that in order to be faithful to the commandment they should remain immobilized for the duration of the day. Moving toward the center there were those who were primarily concerned with the negative aspect of the commandment but thought that not everything one does is work. It was of the essence, for them, to determine which activities constituted "work." Some among these insisted on limiting the significance of the commandment to its prohibition to work, thus denying it any place in the immaterial world. Others thought that the Sabbath involved a change from one kind of activity to another. They sought not just to find out what could not be done because it was "work," but to determine what fosters the contemplative life. This means that, for example, negotiations for the education of one's child could be done on the Sabbath. For them the commandment was primarily positive, and they sought to observe it by spending the day in the synagogues as schools for the study of the Torah and the development of the life of the soul. On the other end of the spectrum, some thought that within the material world the Sabbath is only a sign of the uncreated world. Its purpose is to enlarge the understanding, not to stop any activity. Within this spectrum, most saw that it had eschatological significance, which gave it cosmic transcendence. Also, some gave to creation week revelatory value as the paradigm for the history of the world, thus obtaining from it an eschatological timetable. Others understood its transcendence to be a door to the heavenly realms even now. The richness of the variety of views on the Sabbath is, undoubtedly, one of the clearest signs of the vitality of Judaism in the Roman world.

The references to the Sabbath in the Synoptic Gospels reveal that in the early stages of the Christian oral tradition some healing miracles became transformed into Sabbath controversy stories whose purpose was to determine permissible Sabbath activities. These stories appeal to the authority of Jesus to establish whether a particular activity can be performed on the Sabbath. In them, a saying or an act of Jesus gives a Sabbath ruling that is accepted as binding. This could have been the case only in observant communities. That the Christians who preserved these traditions were observant of the Sabbath is also evident in the entombment stories. They take for granted that everyone agrees with the necessity of postponing the embalming until Sunday. The stories establish the piety of the women who did not violate the Sabbath by their actions. All the evidence in these gospels show that for these Christians it was not an issue whether or not they should observe the Sabbath. Instead, they were concerned with not violating it with an impermissible act. This, however, is not true of the Johannine version of the entombment, in which there is no embalming of the body by pious Christian women.

While the Synoptics share the same controversy stories and entombment account, they also exhibit some concerns characteristic to each. Mark, for example, is the only one to have the saying "The Sabbath was made for humans, not humans for the Sabbath" (2:27). The saying may be understood to point out that Sabbath observance should not make human life burdensome. The saying can also be understood to say, however, that the Sabbath is a gift for humankind, not an exclusive privilege available only to Jews. Given Mark's explicit openness to the Gentiles, it is quite probable that the saying was intended to affirm the Sabbath's universal implications.

The author of Luke/Acts repeatedly brings Jesus and Paul to the synagogue on the Sabbath and makes the point that attending the synagogue was their custom. For persons whose piety is beyond question this is only to be expected. This author clearly wishes to make the point, in particular about Paul, that he was an observant Jew. In his account of the Sabbath healings, he brings out that the Sabbath is a day for deliverance, thus linking the Sabbath to the words of Isaiah that serve as the text for Jesus' sermon at the synagogue in Nazareth (Luke 4:16–20). The observance of the Sabbath represents the arrival of "the acceptable year of the Lord," when the oppressed find freedom. This is the leitmotif of his gospel. The author of Matthew, for his part, is concerned with the "higher righteousness that exceeds that of the Scribes and the Pharisees" (5:20). According to him, Sabbath observance should not be disrupted by anything, including the troubles that accompany the apocalyptic end of the present age. To that end he hopes that the Parousia will not take place on a Sabbath (24:20). He repeatedly looks at the Sabbath in relation to the temple and is explicitly anxious about perfect obedience to the Sabbath commandment.

The author of the Letter to the Colossians, like the author of Matthew, is also concerned that nothing should prevent Christians from observing the Sabbath. His letter is an attempt to convince his readers that what other teachers are trying to get them to do is an "empty deceit" that is not "according to Christ" (2:8). At issue is the way to perfection. In order to attain it, the other teachers at Colossae had given a series of regulations whose origin and content is impossible to determine. The author of Colossians caricatures them as "Do not handle, Do not taste, Do not touch" (2:21). By means of "rigor of devotion and self-abasement" they are to avoid "the indulgence of the flesh" (2:23) in order to attain worship with the angels and visions (2:18). The author judges this way to perfection as misguided. Instead, he prescribes "the circumcision of Christ" (2:11), which takes care of the problem of life in a body of flesh. In terms of signs of devotion, he prescribes that they continue to observe "festivals, new moons and Sabbaths," which are "a shadow of what is to come" (2:16–17). They should not allow anyone to judge them on account of this manifestation of their piety. What needs to be taken into account is "the body of Christ" to which they belong. Their piety is to bear fruit when Christ appears in glory (3:4). What the other teachers propose is in reference not to Christ, but to the "elements of the cosmos." For this author Sabbath observance, as a shadow of the coming of Christ in glory, is the most legitimate form of worship. He endorses a piety guided by calendric rhythms derived from the Old Testament but redirects its significance away from the temple to the future age. He proves to have similar interests to those of the author of Matthew not only in his concern with perfection, but also in his concern for the temple and its festivals.

The Epistle to the Hebrews, the Letter of Barnabas, and the Gospel of John, each in its own peculiar way, envision the Sabbath in eschatological terms. While Hebrews and Barnabas share a futuristic eschatology, John understands that eternal life is already a present reality.

For the author of Hebrews, God's Sabbath celebrations belong to the immovable world, while humans live in the movable world, where change and suffering is everywhere. Ever since God created the world and completed his activity by resting on the Sabbath, God has been enjoying a perpetual Sabbath rest. Humans are invited to enter that rest, but none of them has yet really entered it. Thus, while God has given an oath that some will never enter, repeatedly God has been issuing the invitation to enter. This means that in this shakeable world Christians must live by faith and hope. In this view, the Sabbath belongs to the original, unshakeable world. As such, it is fully in existence but not yet available to humans.

While both Philo and the author of Hebrews single out the fact that ultimately the Sabbath celebration belongs to God, they differ in rather significant ways in their views of what it means for the lives of human beings. Philo finds in this the basis for arguing that humans, just like God, must spend the Sabbath doing divine things, contemplating the uncreated, gaining in wisdom. In other words, Philo finds an argument for becoming a philosopher, a lover of wisdom. The author of Hebrews, on the other hand, finds in this the basis for arguing that humans must be faithful believers in "Jesus, the apostle and high priest of our confession" (3:1). It is an argument for living in suffering, patiently enduring until the "second appearance" of the Son, when he will save "those who are eagerly waiting for him" (9:28). Only then will they at last "enter God's rest."

The author of Barnabas shares with the author of Hebrews the notion that it is impossible for humans now to enjoy a Sabbath. But the reason for this is quite different. He points out that the commandment asks for the sanctification of the Sabbath. This is impossible for humans to do on account of their sinfulness. At the Parousia, however, when God sanctifies those redeemed from the world of sin, it will be possible for humans to observe the Sabbath. Like the author of Colossians, the author of Barnabas links the Sabbath to the Parousia. But, while the author of Colossians argues that the observance of a Sabbath now is a shadow of that glorious future, the author of Barnabas argues that the Sabbath now cannot be kept by anyone; as a matter of fact no Jew has actually ever kept it. When the commandment was given, its purpose was to provide an eschatological promise for Christians. The fulfillment of this promise, according to Pseudo-Barnabas, will take place according to a chiliastic scheme in the seventh millennium.

A quite different eschatologizing of the Sabbath took place in the latter stages of the composition of the Gospel of John. The oral traditions received by the Johannine community included Sabbath controversy stories that, like those in the Synoptic Gospels, were intended to establish that certain activities could be performed on the Sabbath. According to John 7:19–23 those things that contribute to a healing can be done because the rabbis allow circumcisions to be performed. In chapters 5 and 9, however,

John is concerned with something altogether different. Like Philo, some rabbis, and the author of Hebrews, the Johannine community speculates about how God may rest while working on the Sabbath. John takes for granted that on the Sabbath God works, and that when God works it is day. For this gospel what needs to be believed is that the Son and the Father are one, that Jesus is God. To make this claim, according to John, Jesus states that he works on the Sabbath, just like God does (5:17). Since those born from above (3:5) do the works of Jesus, and even greater works than he ever did on earth, those who have eternal life live in the day and work at all times. Cessation from labor comes with the night (9:4), not with the Sabbath. Fitting the Sabbath within his realized eschatology, the author of John no longer sees the Sabbath as a marker in time. It has lost its anchorage in the seventh day of the week. Rather, the Sabbath is the day in which eternal life is lived now.

For the author of Hebrews, on the other hand, God's Sabbath is a reality into which believers have not yet entered, even if by faith and hope they can claim it. Hebrews and John share a proclivity to speculate about God's work and rest. For John, work is done while it is day; cessation from work comes with the night. The children of light, therefore, work also on the Sabbath, just as God does. For Hebrews, God's eternal rest has been available within creation since the time when he completed his work, and believers will not enjoy God's rest until they cease from their own labors. For Hebrews, the works of believers, like the works of Jesus, are the works of faith, which with boldness, boastfulness, and patient endurance dramatize the fact that human life is still lived within the contingencies of history. In John, God's Sabbath is an eternal day in which those born of God live and work out their eternal life now. In Hebrews, God's Sabbath is an eternal day in the realm of immovable reality. Believers have in it only an "immovable hope" (Heb 10:23). Living in the movable world, believers who have their consciences perfected may taste the power of the world to come (6:5), but God's rest is to be found in what will remain when the movable world is finally removed and the hypostatic, metaphysical world is revealed. In John, the existence of believers is what has eschatological significance. Since faith can be had only by those who are born of God, the presence of believers here and now demonstrates God's consummation of the work of giving life. Thus, while believers live *in* this world, they are not *of* this world.

Saying 27 of the *Gospel of Thomas* also considers the Sabbath a way of life rather than a time period. It juxtaposes fasting from the world with "sabbatizing the Sabbath." In Hebrew, in Greek, and in Coptic, the three languages in which the saying was transmitted, the word *Sabbath* may also mean "week" as, for example, in the expression "first of the Sabbath" meaning "first [day] of the week." Taking this usage into account, saying 27 is not an incoherent redundancy, but a pun. Read correctly, to sabbatize the week is a perfectly clear directive. The two statements in saying 27 are parallel expressions of the same thought. They enjoin nonparticipation in the life of the world at all times. In fact, the *Gospel of Thomas* disapproves of the traditional piety of fasting, praying, and the giving of alms. Instead, it recommends fasting from the world, not just from foods, and sabbatizing the week, not just a twenty-four hour day. In the language of the *Gospel of Thomas*, to fast from the world and to sabbatize the week means not being "a buyer and a merchant" (64).

Paul's angry reaction to the news that some in Galatia were "observing days, months, seasons and years" (4:10) is out of joint with his equanimous advice to the Romans allowing for different ways of expressing their obedience to the Lord in reference to their concern for the Sabbath (14:5, 6). It is noteworthy that while the author of Colossians uses the calendric string well known from the Old Testament prophetic calls to responsible observance of the feasts, Paul uses a calendric string that is unique. Also, while the author of Colossians thinks that his readers are subjecting themselves to the "elements of the cosmos" by ascetic regulations that have "the appearance of wisdom" (2:23), Paul thinks that the Galatians are enslaving themselves to the "elements of the cosmos" by means of calendric observances. While the author of Colossians thinks that the observance of feasts, new moons, and Sabbaths makes an eschatological statement, Paul thinks that the observance of "days, months, seasons and years" on the part of the Galatians makes a cosmological one. The calendric string in Galatians does not have the festal cycles in view. Rather, it refers to the cosmic arrangement described in Genesis 1:14. According to those perturbing the Galatians, the observance of days was tied to the maintenance of the cosmic structure established at creation and sustained now by the "elements of the cosmos." It would appear, then, that Paul's intemperate reaction was provoked by his view that to sustain the cosmic arrangements of the fallen creation is to deny the effectiveness of Christ's cross and resurrection to put an end to that creation and to inaugurate the new creation. To insist that human life is to be lived in reference to the powers that rule over the fallen creation is to affirm the permanence of that creation. That is why, as far as Paul is concerned, both in Judaism under the law and in paganism, one lives in slavery. The observance of days in reference to the "elements of the cosmos" negates the reality of the new creation brought about by the resurrection. While the author of the Letter to the Hebrews tied the eschatological significance of the Sabbath to the original creation, and Pseudo-Barnabas tied it to the seventh millennium, Paul deftly tied it to the cross of Christ.

Writing in a different vein, in his Letter to the Romans Paul reports that some "judge a day apart" while others "judge all days" together, or as equal to each other (14:5). In other words, Christians at Rome did not agree as to when one was to observe the Sabbath. While some observed it during one day, the seventh of the week, others observed all days as Sabbath. This, together with differences of opinion about foods, had divided the community to the extent that they were not welcoming each other as sisters and brothers, and when they came together the meetings turned into confrontations. That some at Rome considered all days Sabbath should not cause surprise. So did the Johannine community and those who transmitted saying 27 of the *Gospel of Thomas*. What may be unexpected is Paul's reaction to this situation. As expected, his basic concern is for unity in the fellowship of Christians. Paul considers that both groups are eager to do something positive with "the day," and that both are acting "in the Lord" (14:6a). His direct command is that they should "welcome" the one with whom they disagree (14:1). The foundation for unity, however, is not uniform practice in matters of food or Sabbath observance. Rather, it is the unity of faith as trust and commitment to obedience. As far as Paul is concerned, those who observe the Sabbath on the seventh day may continue to do so, and those observing it all days of the week may also continue with their practice. What all must do is be convinced that what they are doing is what the Lord requires of them (14:5c), conscious that they will have to stand before the judgment seat of God (14:10). As noted above, this is a very Jewish position on the matter. Paul did not idealize uniformity in Christian practice. To sin is not to observe the Sabbath at the wrong time, but to observe it without faith (14:23). According to Paul, the

Christian lifestyle is "walking in love," mindful of the sister or brother "for whom Christ died" (14:15). This is Paul the Jew at his radical best.

Contrary to what some have said, the New Testament does not have a polemic against the "Jewish" Sabbath. Not even in Galatians, where Paul angrily objects to their calendric observances, does he object to its Jewishness. As to the reason why the other teachers at Colossae objected to the Sabbath observance of the recipients of the letter, the evidence is not sufficient for a determination. Still, it is noteworthy that the Torah plays no role in the debate. The New Testament shows that the Sabbath occupied a prominent position in the early Christian communities. Among Christians there were significant debates concerning the Sabbath, similar to those taking place among the Jews at the synagogues. Four issues may be identified in broad outlines.

The Gospels witness to debates among Christians concerning the determination of permissible Sabbath activities. Christians did not have an agreed upon list of what could and could not be done. What distinguished these debates was that those who participated in them appealed to the deeds or the words of Jesus to establish the paradigms for lawful Sabbath activity. They had acquired another source of authority with which to settle Sabbath questions. In the second place, the Letter to the Colossians reflects a debate between the author and some other teachers with the Colossians in the middle. The issue of the debate is which piety leads to perfection. While the other teachers insist on imposing ascetic regulations that will facilitate worship with the angels and visions in a state of paroxysm (2:18, 23), the author argues for a traditional Jewish piety that includes Sabbath observance. This means that in this community some questioned the validity of observance. Thirdly, the Letter to the Romans reports a debate in which the issue is not whether or not the Sabbath is to be observed. Rather, while everyone is concerned with observing the Sabbath, there is disagreement as to when it should be observed. While some insist that it must be limited to the seventh day of the week, others consider that as Christians they live continuously on the Sabbath. Finally, in the Letter to the Galatians Paul is engaged in a heated argument against the position being adopted by the Galatians, who are being persuaded by other teachers to recognize the significance of the "elements of the cosmos" (4:3, 9) as those who rule over the world. In their efforts to be cosmologically correct the Galatians were "observing days, months, seasons, and years" (4:10). Even though this calendric string is not the one associated with the keeping of the Jewish festal calendar, some kind of Sabbath observance may have been involved. Paul is openly opposed to this behavior on the part of his readers because by affirming the cosmic structure of the fallen creation, they were negating the effectiveness of the cross of Christ, which put an end to that creation. For Paul the new creation accomplished by the Spirit at the resurrection was what the gospel announced (6:15). While Paul would allow the Romans to observe the Sabbath as servants of Christ, he would not allow the Galatians to observe it as servants of the "elements of the cosmos." The problem for Paul is that the Galatians viewed the Sabbath within the wrong cosmology. These debates were concerned with whether, how, when, and in reference to whom the Sabbath was to be observed.

The identification of these debates facilitates the construction of a spectrum of early Christian views on the Sabbath. To the far right of this spectrum one finds those teaching a different Christian gospel to the Galatians. They saw the cosmic arrangement of the original creation as the key to salvation and thought that observing the Sabbath as a way of keeping the "elements of the cosmos" in balance was essential. To the far left we find the author of Hebrews, who thought that the Sabbath was not part of the phenomenal world but a reality in the hypostatic world where only God now enjoys its rest. While this is a way of affirming the significance of the Sabbath, it effectively removes it from the immediate human horizon, something which the author of Barnabas also did.

Moving from the left toward the center, one finds the late redaction of the Gospel of John and the early tradition embedded in the *Gospel of Thomas* where, like in Hebrews, the Sabbath has lost its chronological anchorage in time, but humans do benefit from it now. According to this view, by being born from the Spirit humans live now in a sabbatical cosmos. Living on the Sabbath, those who believe do not participate in the life of the world. They are at odds with the world. This view gives to its realized eschatology a sabbatical quality. Pseudo-Barnabas, as noted, considers it impossible for humans to observe the Sabbath now since they cannot sanctify the day until they themselves are sanctified at the eschaton.

Thus, he also gives to the Sabbath purely eschatological significance in a chiliastic scheme where the world of human history lasts six millennia and the seventh is the Sabbath. In effect, this author does two things: he sanctifies the Sabbath out of the reach of humans and then allegorizes it into a chiliastic view of history.

Among those who were concerned with the weekly Sabbath, the teachers who disqualified the Colossians for observing it clearly thought that by doing this the Colossians were failing to take advantage of the more mystical ways of attaining to God. They may have thought that new times required a new piety and condemned them for following a traditional approach.

Paul had a rather broad view on this matter. For him it was clear that the cross of Christ had put an end to the slavery in which all humanity had been living in a fallen world. The power of the Spirit who raised Christ from the dead now empowered everyone who through baptism participated in the cross and the resurrection. For him, though, the situation was complex because even though the new life in the Spirit was the common experience of Christians, human life continues to be lived in a world in which demonic forces are also quite evident, and this will be the case until the Parousia. In view of this basic understanding of the situation, in his Letter to the Romans Paul allows that Christians, who as servants of Christ their Lord live by the power of the Spirit, may in fact demonstrate their obedience with integrity while conducting themselves differently. The Roman Christians are breaking their communities apart on account of their different views on the Sabbath. While some agree with the view that those who live with the Risen Lord live in a perpetual Sabbath, others insist that the Sabbath is a period of twenty-four hours that recurs every seventh day. Paul tells these Christians that if that is what they are fully convinced of, then they should follow their convictions and serve Christ faithfully while welcoming each other as sisters and brothers. Their different Sabbath views should not cause the rupture of their communities.

While adopting this laissez-faire attitude with the Romans, Paul takes a rather belligerent stance against the Galatians who, by observing days, months, seasons, and years show that they are still bound to a cosmos not affected by the cross of Christ. It would appear, then, that Paul's stance in Galatians is not against the Sabbath per se. He violently objects to a Sabbath observance that is not Christian. When it has been integrated to what one understands to be the "obedience of faith" (Rom 1:5; 15:23), Sabbath observance is a perfectly legitimate way of demonstrating one's discipleship. Since he allows Christians to demonstrate their obedience while giving the Sabbath different temporal content, however, it would appear that Paul in effect understands that, in its essence, the Sabbath belongs neither to the fallen nor to the new creation, but to that world where God dwells.

Sabbath Views of Early Christians

Hebrews	The Sabbath is a reality of the hypostatic world. As such, it is available now only to God. The faithful will have full access to it at the second appearance of the Son.
Barnabas	No one has ever been able to sanctify the Sabbath on earth. The Sabbath must be understood allegorically in a chiliastic scheme.
John	Like the Father and the Son, believers live now an eternal Sabbath and do in it the work of God.
Thomas; The Strong in Rome	After the Christ event, all time is Sabbath in the Lord.
The Judges at Colossae	Sabbath observance does not belong to Christian piety. (There is no evidence of what they thought of it.)
Paul	Believers may observe the Sabbath, but its calendric identity is relative because the creation in which the Sabbath was fixed calendrically has been crucified.
Luke/Acts	Sabbath observance is an exemplary sign of liberating piety fully exhibited by Jesus and Paul.
Mark	Believers piously observe the Sabbath and are concerned with establishing permissible activities. It is God's gift to all, not just the Jews.
Matthew; The Weak in Rome	Christ demands a higher righteousness that specifically includes Sabbath keeping.
Colossians	The Sabbath must be kept even in the face of opposition. It anticipates the eschatological realities believers hope for.
The Galatian Perturbers	The Sabbath belongs to the cosmic structure of Genesis and must be kept.

On the Sabbath question, like on many others, Luke/Acts represents the branch that eventually became mainstream Christianity. In these books Jesus and Paul are depicted as faithful Sabbath keepers who on the Sabbath, as was their custom, were found at the local synagogue. Acts also indicates that Paul was eager to observe the Jewish feasts. The fateful trip to Jerusalem, which led to his imprisonment, came about on account of his desire to be in Jerusalem for the Passover. From Paul's Letter to the Romans we learn that his motive for going to Jerusalem was quite a different one. He felt obliged to take there personally the monies he had been collecting for the poor. On the other hand, the author of Colossians would fully agree with any Christian who went to Jerusalem to celebrate the Passover.

To the right of center, the oral traditions found in the Gospels reveal Christians who were concerned with establishing which activities were permissible on the Sabbath. As the entombment accounts in these same gospels make clear, the Christians who told them were Sabbath observers who took for granted the necessity to postpone the embalming until the Sabbath had passed. While these gospels show particular emphases of their own, they all reflect observant Christian communities.

In a similar vein, the "weak in faith" at Rome and the author of Colossians insisted on giving the seventh day its due as the Sabbath, even in the face of opposition. Exactly how those who insisted on the sanctity of the seventh day at Rome understood its Christian significance we are unable to determine. The author of Colossians explains that it is "a shadow of things to come" (2:17). As an anticipation of the conditions to obtain at Christ's Parousia, the Sabbath acquired an identifiable Christian connotation. At the extreme right, the other teachers at Galatia insisted on the cosmic stability of the original creation, of which the Sabbath was a calendric marker.

As pointed out in the introduction, R. E. Brown suggests that the linguistic, geographic and religious grid most commonly used to map early Christianity should be used with caution. For him, a more fruitful way of mapping early Christianity would delineate how different Christians related to the central institutions of Judaism. Thus, Brown places Christians on a grid that shows whether they followed all Mosaic regulations, or some, or none, and whether they participated in the temple sacrifices, some of the feasts, or none. In this study I have endeavored to show that this approach to our understanding of early Christianity is helpful and merits wider attention. The spectrum of Christian views on the Sabbath that I have attempted to draw may also serve as a grid on which to chart early Christianity.

In conclusion, it may be said that Christian attitudes toward the Sabbath were as varied as those found among Jews. Christians disagreed as to its temporal content, its calendric limits, its cosmic identity, and its eschatological referent. They argued whether Gentiles could or should observe it. They speculated as to the quality of life it promotes. They wondered how humans could sanctify it while living in a sinful world. In any case, it is evident that very few Christians dared to dismiss it outright. On account of this, the Sabbath offers a valuable window through which to view Jewish-Christian relations in the first century. More than any other element in the religious life of early Christians, the Sabbath demonstrates the firmness of the ties that bound Christians with Jews. It is most revealing that Christians did not feel they could establish Sunday as a day of worship with its own roots in the resurrection of Christ, with no connection to the Sabbath. Even Paul, who insisted on the radical freedom of the new creation, granted the Roman Christians the freedom to observe the day so long as they were mindful that they would be judged by the Lord. Christians considered it essential to their liturgical life and their theological vision to show how, in their own way, as Christians, they observed the Sabbath. Even if the tragedy of 70 C.E. made it easy for Christians to separate themselves from the temple in Jerusalem, it has not been that easy for them to break away from the Jewish temple in time. Its sanctity is based on a vision of reality that transcends the material world ruled by the sun, the moon, and the stars. It is based in the unshakeable world in which God now rests and humans hope to live.

Notes

Introduction

1. Mircea Eliade, *Cosmos and History: The Myth of Eternal Return* (New York: Harper Torchbooks/Bollingen Library, 1954), 23.

2. See A. Green, "Sabbath as Temple: Some Thoughts on Space and Time in Judaism," in *Go and Study: Essays and Studies in Honor of A. Jospe,* ed. S. Fishman and R. Jospe (Chicago: University of Chicago Press, 1983), 67–91.

3. Horace, *Sat.* 1.9.65–70; Juvenal, *Sat.* 6.159, 542–547; 14.96–106; Ovid, *Ars* 1.75–76; Persius, *Sat.* 5.182–183; Suetonius, *Tib.* 32; etc. H. J. Leon says that "the observance of the Sabbath was one of the best known Jewish customs in the Roman world" (*The Jews of Ancient Rome* [Philadelphia: Jewish Publication Society of America, 1960], 3).

4. Samuel Belkin, *Philo and the Oral Law: The Philonic Interpretation of Biblical Law in Relation to the Palestinian Halakah* (Cambridge: Harvard University Press, 1940); Sidney Hoenig, *The Great Sanhedrin: A Study of the Origin, Development, Composition, and Function of the Bet ha-Gadol during the Second Jewish Commonwealth* (Philadelphia: Dropsie College for Hebrew and Cognate Learning, 1953); Samson Helfgott, "The Sabbath in the Classical Writers," (D.H.L. diss., Yeshiva University, 1974); David Flusser, *Jesus* (New York: Herder and Herder, 1969); Geza Vermes, *Jesus the Jew* (New York: Macmillan, 1973); Hyman Maccoby, *Early Rabbinic Writings* (Cambridge: Cambridge University Press, 1988).

5. Robert Goldenberg, "The Jewish Sabbath in the Roman World up to the Time of Constantine the Great," *ANRW* 19.1:420.

6. Willi Rordorf, *Sunday: The History of the Day of Rest and Worship in the Earliest Centuries of the Christian Church* (Philadelphia: Westminster, 1968; German original, 1962).

7. Samuele Bacchiocchi, *From Sabbath to Sunday: A Historical Investigation of the Rise of Sunday Observance in Early Christianity* (Rome: Pontifical Gregorian University Press, 1977).

8. Donald A. Carson, ed., *From Sabbath to Lord's Day: A Biblical and Theological Investigation* (Grand Rapids, Mich.: Zondervan, 1982).

9. Ibid., 359–68.

10. Paula Fredriksen, *From Jesus to Christ: The Origins of the New Testament Images of Jesus* (New Haven: Yale University Press, 1988), 107–8.

11. Gerd Theissen, *The Religion of the Earliest Churches,* trans. John Bowden (Minneapolis, Minn.: Fortress Press, 1999), 32.

12. Raymond E. Brown and John Meier, *Antioch and Rome* (New York: Paulist, 1983), section 1.

Chapter 1: The Sabbath in Early Judaism

1. W. G. Lambert and A. R. Millard, *Atra-Hasis: The Babylonian Story of the Flood* (Oxford: Clarendon Press, 1969), lines 206–7, 221–22.

2. The reference to the Sabbath in the Covenant Code, considered to be the earliest Israelite law, makes the point that the Sabbath's purpose is "that your ox and your ass may have rest, and the son of your bondmaid, and the alien, may be refreshed" (Exod 23:12).

3. For the history of the Sabbath in the Old Testament, see Niels-Eric Andreasen, *The Old Testament Sabbath: A Tradition-Historical Investigation* (Cambridge, Mass.: Scholars Press, 1972).

4. See André Dupont-Sommer, "L'ostracon araméen du Sabbat," *Semitica* 2 (1949): 31, and Bezalel Porten, "The Religion of the Jews of Elephantine in Light of the Hermopolis Papyri," *JNES* 28 (1969): 116–21. For the Aramaic text see, Franz Rosenthal, ed., *An Aramaic Handbook: Porta Linguarum Orientalium* (Wiesbaden: Harossowitz, 1967), 12–13.

5. Victor A. Tcherikover, ed., *Corpus Papyrorum Judaicarum* (Cambridge: Cambridge University Press, 1957–64), 1:29, 3:43–87.

6. Porten, "Religion," 117, 121.

7. Ovid, *Ars* 1.75–76; Persius, *Sat.* 5.182–183; Petronius, *Fragmenta,* 37; Juvenal, *Sat.* 6.159, 542–547; 14.96–106; Horace, *Sat.* 1.9.65–70; Suetonius, *Aug.* 76.2; Tacitus, *Hist.* 5.4.3; Plutarch, *Superst.* 3, *Quaest. conv.* 4.6.2; Martial, *Epig.* 4.4; Frontinus, *Strat.* 2.1.17; Seneca, *Ep.* 95.47, De superst. (in Augustine, *Civ.* 6.11); Pompeius Trogus, *Epitoma,* 36.2.14–16 (in Justinus, *Historia Philippica*); Meleager, *Anth.* 5.160. See J. H. Michael, "The Jewish Sabbath in the Latin Classical Writers," *AJSL* 40 (1924): 117–24.

8. Philo, *Somn.* 2.123–124.

9. *m: Ned.* 3:9.

10. *b. Shabb.* 118b.

11. *Exod. Rab.* 25:12; *m. Ta ʿan.* 1:1.

12. *Pesiq. Rab.* 27:4.

13. *Mek. Shabb.* 1.105–6. Jacob Z. Lauterbach, *Mekilta de-Rabbi Ishmael,* Schiff Library of Jewish Classics (Philadelphia: Jewish Publication Society of America, 1933–35), 3:204.

14. Abraham Heschel, *The Sabbath: Its Meaning for Modern Man* (New York: Farrar, Strauss and Young, 1951).

15. *Deut. Rab.* 1:21.

16. *"Between Me and the Children of Israel.* But not between Me and the nations of the world." *Mek. Shabb.* 1.110–11. Lauterbach, *Mekilta,* 3:204.

17. CD 11:14b–15a.

18. See Peder Borgen, "Aristobulus and Philo," in *Philo, John and Paul: New Perspectives on Judaism and Early Christianity,* BJS 131 (Atlanta: Scholars Press, 1987), 7–19, and N. Walter, *Der Toraausleger Aristobulus,* TU 86 (Berlin: de Gruyter, 1964), 166–71.

19. Philo, *Mos.* 2.17–23; *Spec.* 2.50; Josephus, *C. Ap.* 2.38–39.

20. *b. Shevu'ot* 20b.

21. *Jubilees* represents a rewriting of Gen 1 – Ex. 14. It claims to have been dictated to Moses on Mt. Sinai by an angel of the presence. It is to be remembered in this connection that copies of *Jubilees* were found among the Dead Sea Scrolls.

22. See Shemaryashu Talmon, "The Community of the Renewed Covenant: Between Judaism and Christianity," in *The Community of the Renewed Covenant: The Notre Dame Symposium on the Dead Sea Scrolls,* ed. Eugene Ulrich and James VanderKam (Notre Dame: Notre Dame University Press, 1994), 10–13.

23. See S. T. Kimbrough Jr., who argues that the stricter rulings found at Qumran are not due to sectarian origins but represent the normative Jewish tradition at an early stage ("The Concept of Sabbath at Qumran," *RB* 5 [1966]: 483–502). He follows George Foote Moore, *Judaism in the First Centuries of the Christian Era: The Age of the Tannaim* (Cambridge: Harvard University Press, 1927), 2:27–32. For a different approach to the issue, see Barbara Thiering, "The Biblical Source of Qumran Asceticism," *JBL* 93 (1974): 432–33.

24. The same question has been posed in reference to the Samaritans who, as it happened, did not have a truncated history but rather have survived uninterruptedly until our own time. On account of this they will be given separate consideration in a following chapter.

25. S. Talmon, "The Calendar of the Covenanters of the Judean Desert," in *The World of Qumran from Within* (Jerusalem: Magnes Press, 1989), 148; and James VanderKam, "2 Maccabees 6, 7a and Calendrical Change in Jerusalem," *JSJ* 12 (1981): 54, and VanderKam *Calendars in the Dead Sea Scrolls: Measuring Time* (New York: Routledge, 1998).

26. Philip R. Davies, "Calendrical Change and Qumran Origins: An Assessment of VanderKam's Theory," *CBQ* 45 (1983): 80–89.

27. According to H. Bietenhardt, the rulings at Qumran are stricter than those in the rabbinic tradition in terms of the time at which the Sabbath begins, the participation in idle talk, the distance allowed for travel, the opening of a sealed vessel, the carrying of medicines, the removal of dust in one's dwelling,

the carrying of an infant in and out of one's house, and the help to be given someone who has fallen in deep water ("Sabbatvorschriften von Qumran im Lichte des rabbinischen Rechts und der Evangelien," in *Qumran Probleme: Vorträge des Leipziger Symposium uber Qumran Probleme von 9 bis 14 Oktober 1961,* ed. H. Bardtke [Berlin: Akademie Verlage, 1963], 56–60).

28. Mark 3:6 states that after the healing of the man with a withered hand the Pharisees held counsel with the Herodians as to how to kill Jesus. John 5:18 reports that after the healing of the man by the pool of Bethesda and his declaration "My Father is working still, and I am working," "the Jews" wished to kill him not only because he broke the Sabbath but also because he made himself equal to God. Obviously the first reason was enough. In the apocryphal *Gospel of Nicodemus* 1–2, the accusation before Pilate is breach of the Sabbath by healing the sick. Such is the currency of later polemics. These polemics are also in evidence in Tertulian's description of Jesus as a Sabbath-Destroyer, *Spect.* 30.

29. Rabbi Akiba in *Mek. Shabb.* 1.64–79. Lauterbach, *Mekilta*, 3:201–02.

30. Also to be taken into account is that *The Manual of Discipline* (1QS, 7) does not specify any penalty for Sabbath infractions.

31. See Erwin R. Goodenough, *An Introduction to Philo Judaeus* (New Haven: Yale University Press, 1940), 194. For a discussion of the issue, see Edward P. Sanders, *Jewish Law from Jesus to the Mishnah* (Philadelphia: Fortress Press, 1990), 16–19.

32. *m. Sanh.* 7:8.

33. *m. Ker.* 1:1.

34. *m. Shabb.* 11:6.

35. *m. Ker.* 1:1.

36. Another institution for which there is no biblical warrant is the lighting of the Sabbath lamps. The rabbis, however, gave Moses credit for it, *Midrash Lekach Tov, Vayakhel 8.* The attempt to establish the authority of particular institutions by assigning to it great antiquity is well known in most cultures. This is most evident also in the case of the Sabbath. In second-temple Judaism it was widely held that the patriarchs kept the Sabbath, even if the case of Abraham, the archetypal proselyte, was sometimes debated. The Torah, of course, knows of no Sabbath observance until the giving of manna to the Israelites in the desert. See Robert M. Johnston, "Patriarchs, Rabbis, and Sabbath," *AUSS* 12 (1974): 94–102.

37. See Solomon Zeitlin, "The Takkanot of Erubim. A Study in the Development of the Halakah," *JQR* 41 (1951–52): 351–61.

38. *De Princ.* 1.3.4.

39. *b. ᶜErub.* 51a; *Mek. Vayassa,* 6.18–22. Lauterbach, *Mekilta*, 2:122.

40. *Num. Rab.* 2:9; *b. ᶜErub.* 41b.

41. *m. ᶜErub.* 4:1, 3; 5:7.

42. CD 11:16–17a.

43. *m. ᶜErub.* 4:7.

44. Kimbrough, "Sabbath at Qumran," 501–2.

45. See Michael Fishbane, *Biblical Interpretation in Ancient Israel* (Oxford: Clarendon Press, 1985), 128–33.

46. CD 11:11.

47. Robert M. Johnston, "The Rabbinic Sabbath," in *The Sabbath in Scripture and History,* ed., Kenneth A. Strand (Washington: Review and Herald Pub. Assoc., 1982), 75.

48. *m. Shabb.* 7:2, cf. *b. Shabb.* 97b, and *Mek. Shabb.* 2.12–14. Lauterbach, *Mekilta,* 3:206.

49. *m. Betzah* 1:1; *b. Betzah* 2a-4b; *b. Shabb.* 43a.

50. *b. Shabb.* 150a.

51. *Mek. Amalek,* 3.108–10. Lauterbach, *Mekilta,* 2:169.

52. *b. Shabb.* 130a; *b. Yevam.* 14a.

53. *b. Shabb.* 130b.

54. *m. Tem.* 2:1.

55. Josephus, *B.J.* 5.564–566.

56. *m. Ned.* 8:6; 3:10; *b. Ketub.* 62b; 65b; *b. Nid.* 38a, b; *b. B. Qam.* 82a.

57. *Pesik. Rab.* 23:8.

58. *b. Rosh Hash.* 19a.

59. Roman sources refer to Jews fasting on the Sabbath. See, Josephus, *C. Ap.* 2.40.

60. *b. Rosh Hash.* 14b.

61. See Shemuel Safrai, "The Temple," in *The Jewish People in the First Century,* ed. Safrai and M. Stern in cooperation with D. Flusser and W. C. van Unnik (Assen: van Gorcum, 1974–76), 2: 885–91.

62. Heather A. McKay casts a broadside against this assumption (*Sabbath and Synagogue: The Question of Sabbath Worship in Ancient Judaism,* EPRO 122 [Leiden: Brill, 1994]). Unfortunately her study deals with the Sabbath in a very superficial manner and overreaches by imposing her point of view on the second century.

63. E. P. Sanders, *Judaism: Practice and Belief, 63 BCE–66 CE* (Philadelphia: Trinity Press International, 1992), 198.

64. Ibid., 202.

65. See J. Gutmann, ed., *Ancient Synagogues: The State of Research* (Missoula, Mont.: Scholars Press, 1981); L. I. Levine, ed., *Ancient Synagogues Revealed* (Jerusalem: Israel Exploration Society, 1981); L. L. Grabbe, "Synagogues in Pre-70 Palestine," *JTS* 39 (1988): 101–10.

66. *Legat.* 132–165.

67. *Vita,* 272–303; *B.J.,* 2.284–292.

68. Acts 16:13, 16.

69. Juvenal, *Sat.,* 3.296; Cleomedes, *De motu.,* 2.1.91; Artemidorus Daldianus, *Oneir.* 53.

70. Josephus, *A.J.* 4.212; see also *Vita,* 271, 294.

71. C. K. Barrett, ed., *The New Testament Background: Selected Documents* (San Francisco: Harper and Row, 1989), 51.

72. *m. Rosh Hash.* 4:7; *m. Taʿan.* 3:9. See J. A. Smith, "The Ancient Synagogue, the Early Church and Singing," *Music and Letters* 65 (1984): 1–16, and "First Century Christian Singing and Its Relationship to Contemporary Jewish Religious Songs," *Music and Letters* 75 (1994): 1–15. Also James McKinnon, "The Exclusion of Musical Instruments from the Ancient Synagogue," *Proceedings of the Royal Musical Association* 106 (1979–80): 77–87, and "On the Question of Psalmody in the Ancient Synagogue," *Early Music History* 6 (1986): 159–91. I owe these references to Prof. Charles Cosgrove.

Archaeological evidence from the excavations of ancient synagogues also indicates the lack of a liturgical function prior to the middle of the second century. The architecurally fixed Torah shrine does not appear before 175 c.e., and it does not become common until 250 c.e. See L. Michael White, *Building God's House in the Roman World: Architectural Adaptation among Pagans, Jews, and Christians* (Baltimore, Md.: Johns Hopkins Press, 1990), 95.

73. *m. Meg.* 3.4.1–5.

74. Carol Newsom, *Songs of the Sabbath Sacrifices: A Critical Edition* (Atlanta: Scholars Press, 1985). See Lawrence Schiffman, "Merkavah Speculation at Qumran: The 4qSerekh Shirot ʿOlat ha-Shabbat,'" in *Mystics, Philosophers and Politicians: Essays in Jewish Intellectual History in Honor of Alexander Altmann,* ed. J. Reinharz and D. Swetchinski, DMMRS 5 (Durham, N.C.: Duke University Press, 1982), 15–47, and J. Baumgarten, "The Qumran Shabbat Shirot and Rabbinic Merkhabah Traditions," *RQ* 13 (1988): 199–213.

75. *m. Tamid* 7:4.

76. Irenaeus, *Haer.* 5.28.3.

77. Among Christians, Justin Martyr (*Dial.* 80:5, 121:3), Irenaeus (*Haer.* 4.16.1; 5.30.4; 5.33.2), and Hippolytus (*Comm. Dan.* 4.23.4–6) identify the Sabbath with the seventh millennium. Cerinthus (in Eusebius, *Hist. eccl.* 3.28.2), Papias (in Ibid., 3.39.12), and Tertullian (*Marc.* 3.24.5–7) do not explicitly do so.

78. *b. Sanh.* 97a.

79. *Gen. Rab.* 11.

80. Philo, *Cher.* 87.

81. The quotation from Ps 95 "They shall never enter my rest" is elaborated with the insistence that it is God's rest (3:16–4:10). See chapter 9.

82. Barnabas 15 is treated in chapter 9.

83. *1 En.* 18:16; 20:6 describes the period for the punishment of the "stars of heaven who transgressed the commandment of the Lord at the beginning of their rising." The completion of this period is said to require ten thousand years. Again, here seven plays no role.

84. One may also note that the section ends with what Rabbi Samuel b. Nahmani said in the name of R. Jonathan. When he was asked, "What is meant by, 'but at the end it shall speak and not lie'? He answered 'Blasted be the bones of those who calculate the end.'" The answer is a pun on the Hebrew words "it shall speak" and "blasted be" which are phonetically very similar, *b. Sanh.* 97b.

85. *Othiot de Rabbi Akiba,* cited by Theodore Friedman, "The Sabbath: Anticipation of Redemption," *Judaism* 16 (1967): 443.

86. Ibid., 443–52.

87. *t. Shabb.* 16:21; cf. *b. Shabb.* 12a; 170b.

88. *b. Shabb.* 12a.

89. *t. Shabb.* 16:22.

90. See Jacob Z. Lauterbach, "The Sabbath in Jewish Ritual and Folklore," in *Rabbinic Essays* (Cincinnati: Hebrew Union College Press, 1951), and K. Hruby, "Le sabbat et sa célébration d'après les sources juives anciennes," *L'Orient Syrien* 8 (1963): 72–79.

91. *m. Shabb.* 5:1.

92. *Gen. Rab.* 12:6–11; *Yalkut Be-Ha'alotcha,* beginning, cited by Friedman, *Sabbath,* 450.

93. *b. Ber.* 67b.

94. See Elliot K. Ginsburg, *The Sabbath in the Classical Kabbalah* (Albany: State University of New York Press, 1989), 59.

95. Pagan authors saw in the Sabbath an excuse for idleness. Jewish authors, particularly Philo and Josephus, felt the need to explain that the Sabbath had nothing to do with idleness, or with self-control.

96. See Gerhard von Rad, "There Remains a Rest for the People of God: An Investigation of a Biblical Conception," in *The Problem of the Hexateuch and Other Essays,* trans. E. W. Trueman Dicken (New York: McGraw-Hill, 1966), 94–102.

97. Augustine, *Confessions,* 1.1.

Chapter 2: Philo on the Sabbath

1. Eduard Lohse, "Sabbaton," *TDNT* 7.10.

2. Ronald Williamson, *Jews in the Hellenistic World: Philo* (Cambridge: Cambridge University Press, 1989), 4.

3. Erwin R. Goodenough, *By Light Light: The Mystic Gospel of Hellenistic Judaism* (New Haven: Yale University Press, 1935), 84.

4. Alan Mendelson, *Philo's Jewish Identity,* BJS 61 (Atlanta: Scholars Press, 1988), 61.

5. Goodenough, *Introduction,* 208.

6. Goldenberg, "Jewish Sabbath," 429.

7. Goodenough, *Introduction,* 83.

8. M. Friedlaender identifies these Jews as members of a rather large religious party with members in Palestine and maybe elsewhere. Rabbi Eliezer of Modin referred to them when he condemned those who study the Torah and do good works but reject circumcision and the feasts (*Die religioesen Bewegungen innerhalb des Judentums im Zeitalter Jesu* [1905; reprint, Stuttgart: Magnus, 1980], 81). One may agree that this phenomenon may not have been restricted to Alexandria, but it is impossible to determine its size and nature. It is incorrect, therefore, to say that "all Jewish varieties of opinion with the single known exception of certain groups in the early Christian church shared a concern for the proper observance of the Sabbath," as Goldenberg affirms, ("Jewish Sabbath," 429).

9. Borgen, *Philo, John and Paul,* 67.

10. The discussion is not limited to the Sabbath. It takes into account also circumcision and temple worship. In *Prov.* 1.34 he deals with circumcision, Sabbath, and purity laws.

11. See Belkin, *Oral Law,* 200–201.

12. See chapter 1 concerning impermissible activities in Judaism.

13. In *Spec.* 2.250, Philo says that the other Israelites "were staying very quietly in their tents" and discovered the transgressor when he returned with the firewood in his arms.

14. According to Philo, this is the beginning of the tradition, still being carried out in his own day, for teaching the duties to God and to fellow humans in the synagogues (*Mos.* 2. 215).

15. Belkin, *Oral Law,* 195–201.

16. Ibid., 198.

17. Colson, *Philo* (LCL) *ad loc.,* suggests that "perhaps" this is his meaning.

18. Belkin, *Oral Law,* 203.

19. The main references to the Sabbatical Year are: *Decal.* 158–164; *Spec.* 2.71, 86–107; 4.215–217; *Virt.* 97–98; *Praem.* 154–157; *Hypoth.* 7.15.

20. On more than one occasion while commenting on the Sabbath, Philo notes that life is full of ups and downs. He seems to see the Sabbath not only as a symbol of freedom (from work), and of equality (within creation) but also of the futility of human attempts to control the future.

21. Philo is eager to correct the misconception of the Sabbath as a day of idleness. Sabbath observance is not the indulgence of laziness (*Mos.* 2.216; *Spec.* 2.60–61).

22. Harry Wolfson, *Philo: Foundations of Religious Philosophy in Judaism, Christianity and Islam* (Cambridge: Harvard University Press, 1947), 1: 80.

23. Both Wolfson, *Philo,* 1:95–96, and Williamson, *Jews,* 4, argue that Philo's exposition of the laws may have seen the light of day, in the first instance, as oral instruction in these schools. For a discussion of the nature and the curriculum of these schools, see Alan Mendelson, *Secular Education in Philo of Alexandria,* HUCM 7 (Cincinnati: Hebrew Union College, 1982), 32–33.

24. On the other hand, Philo can also argue that the Sabbath provides an opportunity for togetherness (*Conf.* 30).

25. The expression is used in the LXX of Lev. 16:31, and 23:32.

26. D. R. Schwartz, "Philonic Anonyms of the Roman and the Nazi Periods: Two Suggestions," *SPhilo* 1 (1989): 63–69, attempts to identify this official as Philo's nephew Tiberius Julius Alexander, an apostate Jew, but this is highly hypothetical.

27. Philo's explanation of the significance of numbers is that Moses "always adhered to the principles of numerical science, which he knew by close observation to be a paramount factor in all that exists. He never enacted any law great or small without calling to his aid and as it were accommodating to his enactment its appropriate number" (*Spec.* 4.105).

28. See F. E. Robbins, "Arithmetic in Philo Judaeus," *CP* 26 (1931): 345–61; K. Staehle, *Die Zahlenmystik bei Philon von Alexandreia* (Leipzig: Tuebner, 1931), and Horst Moehring, "Arithmology as an Exegetical Tool in the Writings of Philo of Alexandria," *SBLSP* 13 (1978): 191–227.

29. A similar, though shorter, exhibition of the possibilities of the number seven is found in *Leg.* 1.8–15, which opens with the words, "Nature takes delight in the number seven." Elsewhere, contemplating the temptation of expounding one more time all the possibilities of the number ten, Philo says he will limit himself to pointing out the facts because "brevity of speech is liked by us" (*QE.* 2.84). At times one wishes he had been true to his likes.

30. For Philo's dependence on his predecessor, Aristobulus, see Borgen, "Aristobulus and Philo," 7–19. N. Walter posits the existence of a collection of poetic passages useful for arithmological elaborations from a Pythagorean perspective (*Toraausleger,* 166–71). According to this theory, an Alexandrian Jew extracted from this collection the entries concerned with the number seven, "perhaps" because he was seeking to argue that Sabbath observance was expected from all human beings. This collection, then, was available to Aristobulus. In its particulars this reconstruction remains highly hypothetical, but that Philo

worked within a larger Hellenistic Jewish tradition in which Aristobulus was a main figure seems certain. See Abraham Terian, "A Philonic Fragment on the Decad," in *Nourished with Peace: Studies in Hellenistic Judaism in Memory of Samuel Sandmel,* ed. F. E. Greenspahn, E. Hilgert, and B. L. Mack (Chico, Calif.: Scholars Press, 1984), 173–82.

31. The phrase is used by Philo, appropriately enough, seven times, *Opif.* 89; *Mos.* 1.207; 2.210, 263–266; *Spec.* 1.170; 2.59, 70. The importance attached to the celebration of imperial birthdays makes the apologetic intent of the phrase obvious.

32. *Pace* C. K. Barrett, "The Eschatology of the Epistle to the Hebrews," in *The Background of the New Testament and Its Eschatology,* ed. W. D. Davies and D. Daube (Cambridge: Cambridge University Press, 1956), 369.

33. Moehring, "Arithmology," 210, considers this "the most sweeping *interpretatio graeca* of the Sabbath" in Philo. He explains, "Philo here interprets what he sees as an historical event as a revelation of a cosmic fact." One must take into account, however, that Philo is arguing for the prophetic revelatory powers of Moses.

34. The exchangeability of the number and the day is most evident in that Philo rarely writes about the Sabbath. Most often he writes about seven. Whether he has in mind the number, the day, or the Sabbatical Year is left for the reader to determine from the context.

35. Philo's use of six and seven as numbers of creation have been the object of much study. See Valentin Nikiprovetzky, "Problèmes du 'Récit de la création' chez Philon d'Alexandrie," *REJ* 124 (1965): 271–306, and David T. Runia, *Philo of Alexandria and the Timaeus of Plato* (Leiden: Brill, 1986), 553–55.

36. Philo suggests that "perhaps because by reason of the constant and repeated destructions by water and fire the later generations did not receive from the former the memory of the order and sequence of events in the series of years" (*Mos.* 2.263).

37. In another connection, Philo states that he "does not blame" (αιτια-σαμενοσ) the literalists since "perhaps the truth is with them also" (*Conf.* 190). By contrast, he does blame (μεμφαιμην) the symbolists (*Migr.* 89).

38. Colson, *Philo* (LCL) *ad loc.,* conjectures that αει may have been present in the text before αορατωσ, in which case it would read: "Him who ever works invisibly." This would agree with Philo's notion that God never ceases creating since on the Sabbath God "does not cease making, but begins the creating of other things" (*Leg.* 1.18).

39. This was a common charge leveled by outsiders. Augustine reports, "Seneca also censures the sacred institutions of the Jews, especially the Sabbath. He declares that their practice is inexpedient because by introducing one day of

rest in every seven they lose in idleness almost a seventh of their life, and by failing to act in times of urgency they often suffer loss" (*City of God* 6.11). The same charge is made by Juvenal who explains that the Jews "gave up every seventh day to idleness, keeping it apart from all concerns of life" (*Sat.* 14.105).

40. It would seem that Philo has forgotten that no manna fell on the Sabbath. More likely, he is pointing out that the double supply of manna received on Friday, which did not spoil, required more trust. Peder Borgen suggests, "the explanation must be that here the manna is understood to be the wisdom of the Jewish philosophy which has its primary place just on this day in the assemblies of the synagogue" (*Bread from Heaven: An Exegetical Study of the Concept of Manna in the Gospel of John and the Writings of Philo,* NovTSup 10 [Leiden: Brill, 1965], 113). This allegorical interpretation of Philo, however, is not convincing.

41. Mary Douglas, *How Institutions Think* (Syracuse, N.Y.: Syracuse University Press, 1986), 57.

Chapter 3: The Sabbath among the Samaritans

1. Rita Egger, *Josephus Flavius und die Samaritaner,* NTOA 4 (Goettingen: Vandenhoeck und Ruprecht, 1986).

2. See, for example, S. Lowy, "Some Aspects of Normative and Sectarian Interpretations of the Scriptures: The Contribution of the Judean Scrolls toward Systematization," *The Annals of Leeds University Oriental Society* 6 (1966–68): 98–163. On the Samaritans and the Sabbath, see pp. 111–13.

3. This is recognized by Frank M. Cross, "Aspects of Samaritan and Hellenistic History in Late Persian and Hellenistic Times," *HTR* 59 (1966): 201–11; F. Dexinger, "Limits of Tolerance in Judaism: The Samaritan Example," in *Jewish and Christian Self-Definition,* ed. Edward P. Sanders (London: SMC Press, 1981), 2:88–114; J. D. Purvis, "The Samaritan Problem: A Case Study in Jewish Sectarianism in the Roman Era," in *Traditions in Transformation: Turning Points in Biblical Faith,* ed. B. Halpern and J. D. Levenson (Winona Lake: Eisenbaums, 1981), 323–50.

4. Cross, "Aspects," 207–8.

5. This is the opinion of those listed in note 3 above.

6. J. A. Montgomery, *The Samaritans, the Earliest Jewish Sect: Their History, Theology and Literature* (Philadelphia: J. C. Winston Press, 1907; reprint, KTAV, 1968), 156.

7. For the archaeological evidence of the hellenization of Samaritans in Palestine, see F. M. Cross, "Papyri of the Fourth Century B.C. from Daliyeh," *New Directions in Biblical Archaeology,* ed. D. N. Freedman and J. Greenfield (Garden City, N.Y.: Doubleday, 1969), 45–69. For evidence of the Samaritan Diaspora, see A. T. Kraabel, "New Evidence of the Samaritan Diaspora has been

found at Delos," *BA* 47 (1984): 44–46, and A. T. Anderson, "Mount Gerizim: Navel of the World," *BA* 43 (1980): 217–21. For openness to Hellenistic influences by first-century Samaritans, see Harold W. Attridge, "Historiography," in *Jewish Writings of the Second Temple Period,* ed. M. E. Stone, CRINT 2, (Philadelphia: Fortress Press, 1984), 165–66, where he analyses Pseudo-Eupolemus, the "anonymous" Samaritan. Further discussions may be found in A. D. Crown, "The Samaritan Diaspora to the End of the Byzantine Era," *Australian Journal of Biblical Archaeology* 2 (1974–75): 107–23, and "The Samaritan Diaspora," *The Samaritans,* ed. A. D. Crown (Tuebingen: Mohr, 1989), 195–217.

8. H. G. Kippenberg, *Garizim und Synagogue: Traditionsgeschictliche Untersuchungen zur samaritanischen Religion der arameische Periode,* RVV 30 (Berlin: de Gruyter, 1971): 175–87; Jarl Fossum, "Sects and Movements," *The Samaritans,* 334; S. J. Isser, *The Dositheans: A Samaritan Sect in Late Antiquity* (Leiden: Brill, 1976), 84–95, 109–10.

9. *Princ.* 1.3.4.

10. As Isser, *Dositheans,* 26, points out, Dositheus was one among several who opposed allowing two thousand cubits of traveling on the Sabbath.

11. Jeffrey M. Cohen, *A Samaritan Chronicle: A Source-Critical Analysis of the Life and Times of the Great Samaritan Reformer Baba Rabbah,* SPB 30 (Leiden: Brill, 1981). J. Macdonald, *The Samaritan Chronicle II: From Joshua to Nebuchadnezzar,* BZAW 107 (Berlin: Toepelmann, 1969), contains only the biblical sections.

12. Another important element in the story is the friendship between a Samaritan and a Judean woman. The woman told her friend about the plot against Baba Rabbah. At the end the story reports that when the inhabitants of the hill opposite the tower were slain this woman was spared and that she joined the Samaritan community.

13. This was in direct opposition to the explicit ruling of *Jubilees* and to the Tannaim.

14. The chronicle depicts the Judeans as breaking the Sabbath by fighting. Using Sabbath observance as a way to demonstrate one's piety and reveal the lack of piety of those one despises is a practice well documented in the writings of Josephus. See the discussion in chapter 4.

15. See Philo, *Spec.* 2.250–251; *Mos.* 2.214; *Sifre Num.* 113 (15:32); *b. Sanh.* 35a.

16. M. Gaster overstates the case, affirming that all Samaritans rejected "the principle of the Erub" (*The Samaritans: Their History, Doctrines and Literature* [Oxford: Oxford University Press, 1925], 77). Isser correctly writes, "Origen noted that Dositheus rejected the concept of *erub,* or Sabbath limits" (*Dositheans,* 102).

17. G. Wedel, *Kitâb aṭ-Ṭabbâḥ des Samaritaners Abu ᶜl-Hasan aṣ-Sûri. Kritische Edition und kommentierte Uebersetzung des ersten Teils* (Ph.D. thesis, Berlin, 1987), folios 28b-29b, 32b, 34b. He classifies works that are not permissible on the Sabbath under five categories: looking at, hearing, speaking, running, and counting (26 a-b).

18. In part this is related to the relationship of Sabbaths with festivals, as reported by Abu ᶜl-Fath, a fourteenth-century chronicler, *Abu ᶜl-Fath b. Abi ᶜl-Hasan ʾaṣ-Samiri, Annales samaritani quos ad fidem codicum manuscriptorum Berolinensium, Bodlejani, Parisini, edidit et prolegomenis instruxit Eduardus Vilmar* (Gotha, 1865). Selected fragments from Vilmar's edition appear in translation in Isser, *Dositheans,* and in J. Bowman, *Samaritan Documents Relating to Their History, Religion and Life* (Pittsburgh: Pickwick, 1977). Translators have read Abu ᶜl-Fath's words differently. Whereas Isser reads: "would celebrate a feast only on the Sabbath day, even if this would involve moving it from its proper time to another. They did not take their hands out of their sleeves" (*Dositheans,* 79), Bowman translates: "They kept no Festival but the Sabbath day, and if it were shifted from its proper time to another time, they would not even put out their hands from their sleeves" (*Documents,* 167). Isser gives the translation of Lee Scanlon, which is to be preferred.

19. Abu ᶜl-Hasan argued that, besides being released from the Sabbath prohibitions in order to perform his cultic duties, the high priest was also released from the observance of the requirement of fasting on the Day of Atonement. In this way both Sabbath requirements and Day of Atonement requirements were overruled. On this day the high priest had to eat of the offering, as Aaron had done (*Kitâb aṭ-Ṭabbâḥ,* 194b-195b).

20. Z. Ben-Hayyim, *The Literary and Oral Traditions in Hebrew and Aramaic among the Samaritans* (Jerusalem: Magnus, 1957–77), 1:258, 260n. 2.

21. British Museum, Oriental MS. 1159, 107. Folio 31 a–b. A similar inference is drawn in *Lev. Rab.* 12.1.

22. See Yitzhak D. Gilat, "On Fasting on the Sabbath," *Tarbiz* 52 (1982): 1–15.

23. See Leon Nemoy, "Al Quirqisani's Account of the Jewish Sects and Christianity" (translation of "Book of Lights and Watch-Towers"), *HUCA* 7 (1930): 344n. 62.

24. Folio 27 a-b.

25. British Museum, Or. Ms. 1156, 167–69.

26. Fossum, "Sects and Movements," 351.

27. Ibid., 334.

28. Isser, *Dositheans,* 104.

29. Vilmar, 157; Isser, *Dositheans,* 79; Bowman, *Documents,* 167.

30. For a more extended discussion, see Herold Weiss, "The Sabbath among the Samaritans," *JSJ* 25 (1994): 252–73.

31. Iain R. M. Boid, *Principles of Samaritan Halachah*, SJLA 38 (Leiden: Brill, 1989), 328, italics his.

32. J. Macdonald, ed., *Memar Marqah: The Teaching of Marqah*, BZAW 84, 2 vols. (Berlin: Toepelmann, 1963).

33. A. Broadie, *A Samaritan Philosophy: A Study of the Hellenistic Cultural Ethos of the Memar Marqah*, SPB 31 (Leiden: Brill, 1981), 235. Broadie may have overvalued the work when he wrote: "Had Marqah written in Greek, and not in Samaritan Aramaic, he would surely have found a niche long ago in standard histories of philosophy" (237).

34. Macdonald notes that the Samaritan translators of the fourteenth century failed to understand this passage, and that the Arabic versions are confused. He writes: "Marqah connects Sabbath with creation in this sort of way without specifying what he means. Apparently his students and readers understood without further explanations" (*The Theology of the Samaritans* [London: SCM, 1964], 301).

35. This is noticeably different from Philo's concept of the Sabbath as a reality preceding creation, already present in the eternal world as the number seven. See chapter 2.

36. The garden as the place of renewal is prominent in Augustine's *Confessions*, 2.1; 8.8. Marqah, after all, was almost a contemporary of Augustine. See M. R. Miles, "Infancy, Parenting and Nourishment in Augustine's Confessions," *JAAR* 50 (1982): 349–64; M. Suchocki, "The Symbolic Structure of Augustine's Confessions," *JAAR* 50 (1982): 365–78; D. Capps, "Parabolic Events in Augustine's Autobiography," *ThT* 40 (1983): 260–72; and J. Houle, "The Mystical Journey and the Garden Archetype in the Confessions of St. Augustine," *Studies in Formative Spirituality* 9 (1988): 63–77.

37. Broadie concludes: "The Memar, as has been shown, is permeated with philosophical ideas found in the works of Plato, Aristotle, the Stoics and Philo, and it is a probability approaching certainty that Marqah knew, even if only at second hand, the works of these thinkers" (*Philosophy*, 237).

38. See chapter 2.

39. One may wonder whether this is in any way connected with the Dosithean practice of praying only while standing in water, as reported by Abu ⁽l-Fath, Vilmar, 157; Isser, *Dositheans*, 79; Bowman, *Documents*, 167.

40. This is comparable to Philo's treatment of the Sabbath at times. On one hand, he distinguishes the Sabbath both from the law and the commandments given by Moses and from the rules for their observance given by other ancient

worthies whose authority merits respect. On the other, he insists that the Sabbath is a law and as such needs to be literally obeyed. See chapter 2.

41. He, for example, lists the seven warnings against the oppression of the sojourner, the seven against the oppression of orphans, and the six against the oppression of widows in order to have a total of twenty warnings, a multiple of ten.

42. It may be recalled that a Thanksgiving Psalm from Qumran (1QH VIII) considers Truth (rather than the Sabbath) to be the trees and the fountain in the Eden of glory, approachable only by those who seeing discern, and considering believe.

43. The Hebrew text reads "the name" rather than "in the name."

44. Rabbinic literature also elaborated this aspect of the Sabbath, *Gen. Rab.* 17:5, "The Sabbath is an unripe form of the world to come." Cf. *Gen. Rab.* 44:17 and *b. Ber.* 57b.

45. Macdonald notes that MS A reads: "light and wellbeing," 2: 183.

46. The contrasts between garden and city, nature and culture, are overdrawn in both O. Keel, *Das Hohelied* (Zurich: Theologischer Verlag, 1986), and H.-J. Heinevetter, *Das Hohelied als programmatische Komposition*, BBB 69 (Frankfurt: Athenaeum, 1988).

47. See Francis Landy, *Paradoxes of Paradise: Identity and Difference in the Song of Songs* (Sheffield: Almond Press, 1982), 202.

48. P. Briant, *Rois, tributs, et paysans*, Annales de l'Université de Besançon (Paris: Les Belles Lettres, 1982), 454–55.

49. On account of this feature, Landy describes the garden of the Song of Songs as "Noah's ark of the vegetable kingdom" (*Paradoxes*, 192). The profusion and variety of botanical species to be found in them is commented upon by Arrian, *Anab.* 6.29.4, and Xenophon, *Oec.* 4.13–14.

Chapter 4: The Sabbath in the Writings of Josephus

1. For a convenient listing of all of the edicts protecting the civil and religious rights of Jews, see Jean Juster, *Les juifs dans l'empire romain: leur condition juridique, économique et sociale* (Paris: P. Geuthner, 1914), 1:132–52, and C. Saulnier, "Lois romaines sur les juifs selon Flavius Josephe" *RB* 87 (1981): 161–98. Goldenberg gives a list of those that explicitly mention the Sabbath: the decree of Dolabella to the Ephesians and surrounding cities issued in 43 B.C.E., *A.J.* 14.226–227; the letter of the magistrates of Laodicea agreeing to the decree of Gaius Rabirius, *A.J.* 14.242; the letter of Publius Servilius Galba to the magistrates of Miletus reaffirming a previous decree being ignored by the magistrates, *A.J.* 14.244–246; the decree of Halicarnasus professing adherence to

what obtains at Rome, *A.J.* 14.256–258; the decree of Ephesus which states that the matter is of importance to Rome, *A.J.* 14.262–264; the decree of Augustus Caesar, *A.J.* 16.162–163; the letter of Agrippa to the Ephesians, *A.J.* 16.167–168 ("Jewish Sabbath," 416–18). To these should be added a letter of King Demetrius to Jonathan, *A.J.* 13.52.

2. When questions of actual wording are not at issue, one must agree with the judgment of Emil Schuerer, G. Vermes, and F. Millar that "no one today doubts the essential authenticity" of Josephus' evidence on this matter (*The History of the Jewish People in the Age of Jesus Christ* [Edinburgh: T and T Clark, 1973], 1:53n. 19).

3. As Michael Grant points out, local populations no doubt resisted the granting of special privileges to the Jews among them (*The Jews in the Roman World* [New York: Scribner, 1973], 33, 60, 76). See T. Rajak, "Jewish Rights in the Greek Cities under Roman Rule," in *Judaism and Its Graeco-Roman Context*, vol. 5 of *Approaches to Ancient Judaism*, ed. W. S. Green (Atlanta: Scholars Press, 1985), 19–36.

4. Max Radin, *The Jews among the Greeks and Romans* (Philadelphia: Jewish Publication Society of America, 1915), 179–81.

5. Alger F. Johns, "The Military Strategy of Sabbath Attacks on the Jews," *VT* 13 (1963): 482–86.

6. Hoenig, *Great Sanhedrin*, 93–98.

7. Goldenberg, "Jewish Sabbath," 420.

8. Scholars have also studied Josephus for evidence that facilitates the dating of events in Jewish history. In this connection different conclusions have been reached about the usefulness of the calendar of Sabbatical Years drawn from the works of Josephus. This study is not concerned with the Sabbatical Year in Josephus. See R. J. North, "Maccabean Sabbath Years," *Bib* 34 (1953): 501–15; B. Z. Wacholder, "The Calendar of Sabbatical Cycles During the Second Temple and the Early Rabbinic Period," *HUCA* 44 (1973): 153–96; D. Blosser, "The Sabbath Year Cycle in Josephus," *HUCA* 52 (1981): 129–39; and B. Z. Wacholder, "The Calendar of Sabbath Years during the Second Temple Era: A Response," *HUCA* 54 (1983): 123–33.

9. Leon notes that "the observance of the Sabbath was one of the best known Jewish customs in the Roman world" (*Jews of Ancient Rome*, 3).

10. *A.J.* 1.33; 3.91; 3.281; 12.4; 12.274; 13.252; 14.63; 18.318; 18.359; *B.J.* 2.456; *C. Ap.* 1.212; 2.174.

11. *A.J.* 13.252.

12. Helfgott relates Josephus' descriptions to Tannaitic and talmudic prescriptions, but exactly what can be inferred from the association of statements is not obvious ("Sabbath," diss.).

13. The same passage from Agatharchides is quoted in *A.J.* 12.6. The wording in the two quotations of the passage, however, is not consistent. Moreover, in this instance he omits altogether the explicit reference to the Sabbath and what may not be done on it. It alludes in a general way to "an untimely superstition (ἀκαιρὸν δεισιδαιμονίαν)" which made the Jews decide not to take up arms.

14. The claim that by citing Gentile authors he is enhancing the credibility of his description of the Jews is, therefore, vitiated by the freedom with which he "quotes" his sources.

15. Josephus certainly knew that the Jews had only one temple. The presence of the plural in this case could be explained as due to Agatharchides' ignorance of this fact. Another explanation might be Josephus' wish to enhance the standing of the synagogue, which he also designates a "house of prayer."

16. Philo is much more concerned with this issue. See chapter 2.

17. In the proem to the *Antiquities* Josephus claims that the high priest Eleazar was eager to supply Ptolemy II with a copy of the law, and that he is writing this work because Jews "make nothing of what is good into a secret" (1.11).

18. For the importance of memory in Josephus' views on piety, see G. Boccaccini, *Middle Judaism: Jewish Thought 300 B.C.E. to 200 C.E.* (Minneapolis, Minn.: Fortress Press, 1991), 175–76; 241–50.

19. H. St. J. Thackeray, *Josephus,* Loeb Classical Library (1961), 4:461.

20. See F. W. Danker, *Lexicon,* σάββατον.

21. This appears in *A.J.* 3.151–178 and, in an abbreviated form in *B.J.* 5.228–233. See A. Demsky, "When the Priests Trumpeted the Onset of the Sabbath," *BAR* 12, no. 6 (1986): 50–52.

22. Apparently, when he wrote the *Jewish War* he intended to give a more detailed account of the customs and laws relating to the temple in the projected treatise "On Customs and Causes," which he alludes to with some frequency in the *Antiquities.* He finished the small section on the matter with the words, "on these topics much yet remains to be told" (*B.J.* 5.237).

23. Here we find an explicit reference to the weekly, monthly, and yearly feasts which we suggested earlier may be the way in which Josephus construes "day of gladness, new moon and feasts" in *A.J.* 3.294. It is the usual formula in the OT for enjoining the observance of the feast. It is also the calendric string found in Col 2:16.

24. Belkin draws a contrast between Philo and the Tannaitic halakah. Philo and Josephus find in the Sabbath observance of pagans an argument for the superiority of the Mosaic legislation. The halakah considers that it is impossible

for pagans to keep the Sabbath. Those who try are adulterers. The Sabbath belongs exclusively to the Jews (*Oral Law,* 193).

25. The words omitted describe the three things not done and the one done on the Sabbath quoted earlier.

26. Josephus admired the noble death of those who would not agree to break the laws. The speeches of Eleazar to the defenders of Massada make the point (*B.J.* 7.323–336, 341–388). See A. Droge and J. Tabor, *A Noble Death: Suicide and Martyrdom among Christians and Jews in Antiquity* (New York: Harper Collins, 1992).

27. In the *Antiquities* Josephus writes, "On the seventh (day) God rested and had respite from His labors, for which reason we also pass this day in repose from toil and call it the Sabbath, a word which in the Hebrew language means 'rest'" (1.33).

28. From a rather uncritical reading of Josephus, Johns flatly affirms, "It is a well known fact that the leaders of the Seleucid armies at the beginning of the Maccabean period employed the military strategy of attacking the unresisting Jews on their Sabbath day" ("Military Strategy," 482–83).

29. Radin certainly does not accept this premise. He writes, "In the Bible there is no hint in the lurid chronicles of wars and battles that the Sabbath observance involved cessation from hostilities during time of war, and the supposition that no resistance to attack was offered on that day is almost wholly excluded. . . . That any rule of Sabbath observance which demanded this had actually developed during the post-Exilic period is likewise untenable" (*Jews,* 179).

30. 1 Macc credits the policy to the group as a whole, while Josephus credits Mattathias for having issued the policy, which the group adopted.

31. Shaye J. D. Cohen emphasizes Josephus's "inveterate sloppiness. Texts suitable for tendentious revision as well as passages which contradict his motives are sometimes left untouched. The narrator is frequently confused, obscure and contradictory. Legal and technical terms are used very loosely" (*Josephus in Galilee and Rome: His Vita and Development as a Historian,* CSCT 8 [Leiden: Brill, 1979], 233).

32. The qualification is somewhat implicit in the wording of 1 Macc 2:41, "Let us fight against every man who comes to attack us on the Sabbath day; let us not all die as our brethren died in their hiding places."

33. Radin argues that the recurring story of Jerusalem being stormed on the Sabbath "may be reasonably doubted" (*Jews,* 179).

34. This is certainly not what Josephus describes as the Jewish response to the choice between safety and obedience in *Against Apion.*

35. Goldenberg agrees that by fighting Asinaeus was overtly in violation of

the law, but then argues that Asinaeus is only applying the reasoning of Mattathias to the effect that under certain circumstances violation is better than compliance ("Jewish Sabbath," 433). As we noted above, Josephus argues strenuously that among Jews such is never the case.

36. "When their success was at its peak, their situation began to deteriorate for the following reason. Their manly qualities had raised them to the height of power; but now they diverted these to the service of lawlessness, into which they plunged in violation of the Jewish code at the bidding of lust and self-indulgence" (*A.J.* 18.340).

37. This incident also testifies that pagans observe the Sabbath.

38. This apparently conscientious act of Anilaeus in reality testifies to Josephus' sense of irony. The story of the two brothers found its way into the *Antiquities* in the first place because Josephus needed to explain how 50,000 Jews had been slaughtered in Mesopotamia. After the death of the brothers, the Jews of Nehardea found themselves exposed to those who still wished to settle accounts and had to immigrate to Seleucia, but there they were terribly persecuted and most were killed. Josephus does not tire of showing how the Deity keeps close watch on human affairs and distributes rewards and punishments.

39. This is not to say that Josephus thought that Anilaeus' lack of proper Sabbath observance was *the* cause of his downfall. It is only to say that his improper Sabbath conduct exemplified his lawlessness in a rather significant way, just like his marriage to a non-Jewish woman also did.

40. M. Herr, "The Problem of War on the Sabbath in the Second Temple and the Talmudic Periods," *Tarbiz* 30 (1960–61): 242–56, and Helfgott, "Sabbath," 63–69, follow Hoenig, who solves the problem by appealing to the historical development of halakah (*Sanhedrin,* 93). Helfgott writes, "The only approach which explains all of the references is that in general, fighting on the Sabbath was considered a violation of the law. But, in emergencies involving actual warfare the people did violate the Sabbath and fought both defensively and offensively. However, recognizing that the general rule was to prohibit fighting, the people were not anxious to violate the law even during the emergencies and their leaders had to encourage them to fight on the Sabbath." He then offers a Tosefta in corroboration (*t. cErub.* 3:5). The problem with this explanation is that it offers generalizations based on conflicting evidence.

41. Goldenberg, "Jewish Sabbath," 433.

42. It is possible to argue that later in life, when he wrote the *Vita,* his commitment to the life of piety, or his desire to present himself as pious increased.

43. As R. Marcus points out, it is difficult to reconcile the fact that the fall of Jerusalem took place at the time of the consulship of Gaius Antonius and Marcus Tullius Cicero and on the Fast Day (if the Fast Day is understood to be

the Day of Atonement, which in Jewish terms is the obvious meaning) because the consulship of Antonius and Cicero ended in June of 63 B.C.E. and the Day of Atonement is on the 10th of Tishri (in October?) (*Josephus,* Loeb Classical Library [1961], 7:480–81). One way of solving the problem is to suggest that Josephus was dependent on Strabo for the fact that the city fell on the Fast Day. Pagans erroneously thought that Jews fasted on the Sabbath. (On this point, see Goldenberg, "Jewish Sabbath," 435–42). This would mean that what Strabo described and Josephus admired actually took place on a Sabbath.

If this is the case, what Josephus describes is reminiscent of Philo's description of how Jews behaved when being forced to participate in public service during times of civil emergency. Philo makes the point by having an Egyptian official ask what he thinks are rhetorical questions but Jews understand in the opposite way. He asks: "Will you stay at home perfectly quiet? Or will you appear in public in your usual guise, with your right hand tucked inside and the left held close to the flank under the cloak lest you should even unconsciously do anything that might help to save you? And will you sit in your conventicles and assemble your regular company and read in security your holy books, expounding any obscure point and in leisurely comfort discussing at length your ancestral philosophy?" (*Somn.* 2.123–124). In the meantime the town is being sacked and razed either by armies or natural phenomena. The answer, of course, is that Jews even under these circumstances will continue doing what they always do on the Sabbath.

44. Following the development of halakah outlined by Hoenig, this would be well after Hillel's ruling that fighting was permitted (*b. Sanh.* 96).

45. He concludes the *Jewish War* with the words, τῆσ προνοίασ τοῦ θεοῦ τεκμήριον γενόμενοσ ὅτι τοῖσ πονηροῖσ δίκην ἐπιτίθησιν "becoming decisive proof that the providence of God inflicts punishment on the wicked" (*B.J.* 7.453). The proem to the *Antiquites* says that "God, as the universal Father and Lord, who beholds all things, grants to such as follow Him a life of bliss, but involves in dire calamities those who step outside the path of virtue."

46. It is significant that in this he agrees with Philo who tells of an Egyptian official who, wishing to bring about "a general backsliding" among the Jews, tried to force them to work on the Sabbath (*Somn.* 2.123–124).

47. It is well known that the Samaritans were, and still are, quite strict in their Sabbath observance, lagging in no way behind other Jews in their zeal to establish what is permissible Sabbath activity. See chapter 3.

48. See T. S. Beall, *Josephus' Description of the Essenes Illustrated by the Dead Sea Scrolls,* SNTSMS 58 (Cambridge: Cambridge University Press, 1988).

49. Ibid., 97–98.

50. Most noteworthy is that Josephus fails to mention that the Essenes

observed the Sabbath according to a different calendar, or that it may have been precisely their concern for proper Sabbath observance that caused their resistence to the calendar adopted by the larger Jewish society that wished to be engaged with Hellenistic civilization. See Talmon, "The Calendar of the Covenanters of the Judean Desert," in *The World of Qumran from Within,* 148.

51. For the description of the Samaritans in Josephus, see Egger, *Josephus Flavius,* and R. J. Coggins, "The Samaritans in Josephus," in *Josephus, Judaism and Christianity,* ed. L. H. Feldman and G. Hata (Detroit, Mich.: Wayne State University Press, 1987), 271.

52. Three times he says that it is their nature to lack integrity and become whatever seems convenient at the moment (*A.J.* 9.291; 11.341; 12.257).

53. In *A.J.* 11.342–343, they approach Alexander in order to ask for a privilege he had granted the Jews, but when Alexander asks them, they said, according to Josephus, that they were not Jews. As told, the story makes no sense.

54. It is not without justification that Coggins writes, "It is easy to see how Josephus has altered its [the Samaritan explanation of their Sabbath observance] thrust so as to discredit the Samaritans" ("Samaritans," 266). "He several times makes the point that the Samaritans varied in their attitude toward Judaism, sometimes distancing themselves from it, sometimes claiming to be an integral part of it. The point can easily be stood on its head, as an illustration of Josephus's own attitude toward the Samaritans" (257).

55. Would it not have been quite permissible for John to defend himself if attacked on the Sabbath? Of course, in this case Josephus is showing John's duplicity, since John did not really care about the Sabbath.

56. *Josephus,* 3:535.

57. *Hist. Nat.* 31.18.24 (31.11).

58. Helfgott writes, "Pliny's version appears to be more in agreement with the Jewish spirit in that the river runs for six days and stops on the seventh" ("Sabbath," 138).

59. When Tineius Rufus asked why the Sabbath was superior to any other day, Akiba answered, "The river Sambation proves it" (*b. Sanh.* 65b). This reply is elaborated in *Gen. Rab.* 11, where it is explained that for six days the river has a current strong enough to carry along stones but on Saturdays it ceases to flow.

60. "So he said, 'Behold I am making a covenant *that I will not exchange this people for another. But from you shall multitudes of righteous people go forth.* Before all your people I shall work wonders *for them when they go into exile by the rivers of Babylon. And I will have them dwell on the banks of the river Sambatyon. Such wonders* have not been performed among any *of the inhabitants of* the earth or in any nation. And all the people among whom *you dwell* will see the deed of the Lord *on that day* for what I am going to do with you is awesome'" ("Targum

Pseudo-Jonathan: Exodus," in *The Aramaic Bible: The Targums,* trans. M. Maher, MSC [Collegeville, Minn.: Liturgical Press, 1994], 2:259).

61. See Adolf Neubauer, *La geographie du Talmud* (Paris, 1868; reprint, Hildesheim: G. Olms, 1967), 33, and Louis Ginzberg, *Legends of the Jews* (Philadelphia: Jewish Publication Society, 1956), 4:317, 6:407.

62. Philo is concerned to show that the study of the law results in the attainment of wisdom. See chapter 2.

63. H. St. J. Thackeray, *Josephus: The Man and the Historian* (1929; reprint, New York: KTAV, 1967), 76.

64. Moore, *Judaism,* 1:20.

Chapter 5: The Sabbath in the Synoptic Gospels

1. Raymond E. Brown, *The Gospel according to John,* AB 29 (Garden City: Doubleday, 1966), 1:210.

2. Rordorf, *Sunday,* 62–63; H. Braun, *Jesus of Nazareth: The Man and His Times,* trans. E. R. Kalin (Philadelphia: Fortress Press, 1979), 58–61; E. Stauffer, "Neue Wege der Jesusforschung," in *Gottes ist der Orient* (Berlin: Evangelische Verlagsanstalt, 1959), 167; S. Schulz, *Die Stunde der Botschaft: Einfuehrung in die Theologie der vier Evangelisten* (Hamburg: Furche, 1967), 85; E. Schweizer, *Good News according to Mark* (Richmond, Va.: John Knox Press, 1970), 40.

3. Fredriksen, *From Jesus to Christ,* 107–8.

4. Rudolf Bultmann, *History of the Synoptic Tradition* (Oxford: Blackwell, 1963), 40.

5. Eduard Lohse, "Jesu Worte ueber den Sabbat," in *Judentum, Urchristentum, Kirche,* ed. W. Eltester (Berlin: Toepelmann, 1964), 85.

6. Rordorf, *Sunday,* 60–67.

7. M. J. Borg, *Conflict, Holiness, and Politics in the Teaching of Jesus,* SBEC 5 (New York: Edwin Mellen Press, 1984), 152.

8. Flusser, *Jesus,* 49–50.

9. Vermes, *Jesus,* 25, 231.

10. A. E. Harvey, *Jesus and the Constraints of History* (Philadelphia: Fortress Press, 1985), 264.

11. Maccoby, *Rabbinic,* 170–72.

12. Borg, *Conflict,* 148–50.

13. Robert Banks, *Jesus and the Law in the Synoptic Tradition,* SNTSMS 28 (Cambridge: Cambridge University Press, 1975), 116–17.

14. Howard C. Kee, *The Community of the New Age* (Philadelphia: Westminster, 1977), 38–40.

15. C. K. Barrett, *Jesus and the Gospel Tradition* (Philadelphia: Fortress Press, 1968), 63.

16. Arland Hultgren, *Jesus and His Adversaries* (Minneapolis, Minn.: Augsburg Press, 1979), 50–51.

17. Gerd Theissen, *The Miracle Stories of the Early Christian Tradition,* trans. Francis McDonagh (Philadelphia: Fortress Press, 1983), 106–11.

18. Ibid., 107.

19. Braun considers this text the only one in the Synoptics with a positive view of the Sabbath (*Jesus,* 58). This, however, is not quite the case. Daniel Harrington correctly sees it as characterizing the Matthean community as observant of the Sabbath (*The Gospel of Matthew,* SP 1 [Collegeville, Minn.: Liturgical Press, 1991], 140).

20. Yong-Eui Yang arrives at a conclusion on the basis of inadequate exegetical considerations (*Jesus and the Sabbath in Matthew's Gospel,* JSNTSup 139 [Sheffield: Sheffield Academic Press, 1997], 230–41). He chooses among proposed solutions on the basis of a methodologically inadequate consideration of the controversy stories in Matthew. Having decided that in the Sabbath controversies Jesus had abolished the Sabbath, he thinks that the concern of this prayer is with the availability of lodgings and provisions on the Sabbath due to the faithful observance of the Sabbath by the Jews who would have been expected to provide them. In order to sustain this explanation, it would seem, he favors a pre-70 c.e. dating of the gospel. Given the circumstances envisioned for the crisis, and Matthew's obvious concerns with the delay of the Parousia, this explanation is not convincing.

21. See Vermes, *Jesus,* 181.

22. Braun says that the quotation from Hosea was introduced to prove that casuistry as such did not apply (*Jesus,* 60), but here he is claiming too much.

23. Mark's is undoubtedly a radical statement, but the fact that it is found neither in Matthew nor in Luke may not necessarily be due to its radicalness. Their christological concerns may have been a major factor. Faced with two statements in Mark which did not fit smoothly together they chose the more christological one.

24. Bultmann, *History,* 12.

25. One of the best examples, among many, is Luke's placing of the Great Commandment in the lips of the lawyer (10:27).

26. See James A. Sanders, "From Isaiah 61 to Luke 4," in *Christianity, Judaism and Other Greco-Roman Cults,* ed. Jacob Neusner, SJLA 12 (Leiden: Brill, 1975), 1:75–106.

27. Braun maintains that these rhetorical questions are an argument against casuistry as such, but that is not the case (*Jesus,* 60). The questions presuppose casuistry.

28. See Hultgren, *Adversaries,* 112.

29. F. W. Beare, *Earliest Records of Jesus* (Oxford: Blackwell, 1962), 91–92; Schweizer, *Mark*, 70; Hultgren, *Adversaries*, 114.

30. Bultmann already raised the issue, but left it open (*History*, 16–17).

31. On the secondary character of Mark 2:28, see Vincent Taylor, *The Gospel according to Mark* (London: Macmillan, 1959), 220; C. E. B. Cranfield, *The Gospel according to Mark* (Cambridge: Cambridge University Press, 1959), 118; D. E. Nineham, *The Gospel of St. Mark* (Baltimore, Md.: Penguin, 1963), 106; F. W. Beare, "The Sabbath Was Made for Man," *JBL* 79 (1960): 135; F. Klostermann, *Das Markusevangelium*, 4th ed. (Tuebingen: Mohr, 1950), 31; Ernst Lohmeyer, *Das Evangelium des Markus*, 2nd ed. (Goettingen: Vandenhoeck and Ruprecht, 1963), 66; E. Haenchen, *Der Weg Jesu: Eine Erklaerung des Markusevangelium und der kanonischen Parallelen* (Berlin: Toepelmann, 1966), 121; Hultgren, *Adversaries*, 113–14. For a critical review of the case for inauthenticity, see M. D. Hooker, *The Son of Man in Mark* (London: SPCK, 1967), 94, 175–77.

32. See Hultgren, *Adversaries*, 111–12.

33. Bultmann, *History*, 16.

34. See Werner Kelber, *Mark's Story of Jesus* (Philadelphia: Fortress Press, 1979), 62–70.

35. *Mek. Ex.* 31.14 and *b. Yoma* 85b. See Vermes, *Jesus*, 180.

36. Maccoby thinks the saying comes from a common stock of Pharisaic maxims (*Rabbinic*, 170). This could be so if, as he says, the saying emphasizes the character of the Sabbath as a gift, which it does. But there is no Pharisaic stock of maxims pointing out that the Sabbath is not just for the covenanted people of Israel.

37. E. Lohse, "Σάββατον," *TDNT*, 7:22. Borg, while proposing a peculiar interpretation, already recognizes that the text does not support what the traditional interpretation claimed. He writes, "These violations of Sabbath law as then understood seem to be programmatic flowing out of the alternative paradigm that Jesus taught: the Sabbath was a day for works of compassion. This change did not mean that the Sabbath was abrogated; rather it was subordinated to deeds of mercy rather than to the quest for holiness" (*Conflict*, 151). While arguing from a different perspective, Maccoby makes the same point. He says, "his insistence on the Pharisaic view that healing was permitted on the Sabbath does not imply that he wished to abolish the Sabbath" (*Rabbinic*, 170).

38. As done, for example, by Bultmann, *History*, passim, and Hultgren, *Adversaries*, passim.

Chapter 6: The Sabbath in the Gospels of John and Thomas

1. Rudolf Bultmann, *The Gospel of John: A Commentary* (Philadelphia: Westminster, 1971), 246–47.

2. C. K. Barrett, *The Gospel according to St. John* (London: SPCK, 1960), 265.

3. Juergen Roloff, *Das Kerygma und der irdische Jesus: Historische Motive in den Jesus-Erzaehlungen der Evangelien* (Goettingen: Vandenhoeck and Ruprecht, 1970), 81.

4. Rudolf Schnackenburg, *The Gospel according to St. John* (New York: Herder and Herder, 1980), 2:97.

5. Rordorf, *Sunday,* 66.

6. Brown suggests that there is a reference to the Sabbath in 1:39, in connection with the reconstruction of a week leading to "the third day" in 2:1 (*John,* 1:75). The construction of a week, however, is not quite in the text.

7. All studies of this matter begin with the analysis of E. Haenchen, "Johanneische Probleme," *ZTK* 56 (1959): 1–54 (John 5:1–16, 46–50).

8. Barnabas Lindars, *The Gospel of John* (London: Oliphants, 1972), 216–18. His suggestion has been adopted by L. T. Witkamp, "The Use of Tradition in John 5:1–18," *JSNT* 25 (1985): 19–47.

9. J. Louis Martyn, *History and Theology in the Fourth Gospel* (New York: Harper, 1968), 49.

10. As pointed out by Bultmann, *John,* 243, and Brown, *John,* 1:208.

11. C. E. Hoskyns already noted that the discourses in 7:14–24 and 5:19–47 were "solemn interpretations of the same miracle" (*The Fourth Gospel,* 2nd ed. [London: Faber and Faber, 1947], 314).

12. Harold W. Attridge, "Thematic Development and Source Elaboration in John 7:1–36," *CBQ* 42 (1980): 160–70 (165).

13. Not to 5:47, as argued by J. B. Bernard, *A Critical and Exegetical Commentary on the Gospel according to St. John,* ICC (Edinburgh: Clark, 1929), 1:xix, 258; R. H. Lightfoot, *St. John's Gospel* (Oxford: Oxford University Press, 1956), 178; R. H. Strachan, *The Fourth Gospel: Its Significance and Environment,* 3d ed. (London: SCM, 1941), 81, 176, 198–204; G. H. C. MacGregor and A. Q. Morton, *The Structure of the Fourth Gospel* (London: Oliver and Boyd, 1961), 67–68; Lindars, *John,* 52. F. Spitta suggests that the connection to 5:47 was already in the source (*Das Johannes-Evangelium als Quelle der Geschichte Jesus* [Goettingen: Vandenhoeck and Ruprecht, 1910], 112–33).

14. Brown, *John,* 1:209–11.

15. Attridge, "Development," 167–68.

16. See chapter 1 above.

17. Hoskyns offers this gratuitous comment about the healing of the paralytic: "This work involves, not the violation of the law of the sabbath, but its complete overthrow and fulfilment; for its vacuum is filled with the creative, life-giving love of God" (*Fourth Gospel,* 267).

18. Attridge, "Development," 168, already suggests that 5:17–47 is an addition to 5:1–16, 7:19–23.

19. M. Wojciechowski is correct in recognizing the two interpretations but fails to convince in the determination of their origin ("La source de Jean 13.1–20," *NTS* 34 [1988]: 135–41).

20. See Herold Weiss, "Footwashing in the Johannine Community," *NovT* 21 (1979): 298–325.

21. Barrett, *John,* 5.

22. See Barrett, *John,* 213; Lindars, *John,* 218; Schnackenburg, *John,* 2:101; Brown, *John,* 1:216; Bultmann, *John,* 246.

23. Brown, *John,* 1:212, properly designates the section "Jesus on the Sabbath: Discourse on His Sabbath Work."

24. On the possible meanings of ἕως ἄρτι, see Bultmann, *John,* 245.

25. Oscar Cullmann, *Early Christian Worship* (London: SCM, 1953), 89, also as "Sabbat und Sonntag nach dem Johannesevangelium. HEOS ARTI (Joh 5,17)," in *Vortraege und Aufsaetze,* ed. K. Froelich (Tuebingen: Mohr, 1966), 187–91.

26. Brown, *John,* 2:1020, finds support in H. Riesenfeld, "Sabbat et jour du Seigneur," *New Testament Essays in Memory of T. W. Manson,* ed. A. J. B. Higgins (Manchester: Manchester University Press, 1959), 210–17.

27. C. Maurer, "Steckt hinter Joh 5.17, ein Uebersetzungsfehler?" *WD* nS 5 (1957): 130–40.

28. Bultmann, *John,* 245.

29. Lohse, "Σάββατον," 27–28.

30. Brown, *John,* 1:214.

31. R. Alan Culpepper, *Anatomy of the Fourth Gospel: A Study in Literary Design* (Philadelphia: Fortress Press, 1983); P. D. Duke, *Irony in the Fourth Gospel* (Atlanta: John Knox Press, 1985); Gail R. O'Day, *Revelation in the Fourth Gospel: Narrative Mode and Theological Claim* (Philadelphia: Fortress Press, 1986).

32. See G. Ferraro, "Il senso di *heos arti* nel texto di Giovanni 5,17," *RivB* 20 (Suppl., 1972): 529–45.

33. Bultmann, *John,* 245.

34. Most clearly shown by Martyn, *History,* 49–50.

35. Cullmann, *Worship,* 89–92.

36. J. F. Burns, "The Use of Time in the Fourth Gospel," *NTS* 13 (1966–67): 285–90.

37. See the discussion in chapter 1.

38. S. Patterson, "The Gospel of Thomas within the Development of Early Christianity" (Ph.D. diss., Claremont, 1988), and E. Richard, *The Gnostic Gospel*

of Thomas: A Lost, Secret Vision of Jesus, Yamauchi Lectures in Religion (New Orleans: Loyola University, 1993), 2–5.

39. This saying is one of the few in the *Gospel of Thomas* preserved both in a Greek and a Coptic source. The Greek text is found in P. Oxy., 1.4–11 (B. P. Grenfell and A. S. Hunt, *The Oxyrhynchus Papyri* [London: Clarendon Press, 1898], 1:3). The earlier Greek text reads, ἐαν μὴ σαββατίσητε τὸν σάββατον, literally "if you do not sabbatize the Sabbath," which seems redundant. The verb "to sabbatize" (σαββατίζω) appears only twice in early Christian literature: here and in Ignatius, *Mag.* 9.1. Ignatius' advice, however, is to do the opposite, "no longer sabbatizing, but rather living according to the Lord" (μηκέτι σαββατίσοντεσ ἀλλὰ κατὰ Κυριακόν ζῶντεσ). In the LXX this verb translates the Hebrew verb שבת when it has the specific sense of resting on the Sabbath (Exod 16:30; Lev 23:32, 26:34–35; 2 Chr 36:2). The exhortations of Thomas and Ignatius may actually not be that much at odds as first impressions would suggest. Ignatius enjoins "living according to the Lord" as better than keeping the Sabbath. Thomas argues that the whole week must be the Christian Sabbath. M. R. James properly translates the Greek in P. Oxy., 1.4–11, "If ye keep not Sabbath for the whole week, ye shall not see the father" (*The Apocryphal New Testament* [Oxford: Clarendon Press, 1924], 17). That "Sabbath" may also mean "week" is well attested. Brown, Driver, and Briggs think that attestation for the definition of שבת as "week" is problematic, indicating that the rabbis thought that the expression "first, second . . . in the Sabbath" views each day of the week as comprehended in the climactic seventh day (*A Hebrew and English Lexicon of the Old Testament* [Oxford: Clarendon Press, 1907], 992). It would seem, however, that the rabbinic understanding of the expression (also found in Philo and in the NT, Matt 28:1; 1 Cor 16:2) is a late theological elaboration of common usage which spoke of the first, second . . . day of the week.

40. T. Baarda recognizes that the saying "belonged to a very archaic Jewish-Christian tradition" with a positive attitude toward the Sabbath. The burden of his article, however, is to argue that "starting from a presumption that the present collection of sayings known as the *Gospel of Thomas* is a Gnostic florilegium" the saying cannot be read as a positive statement on the Sabbath. Baarda lists eight positive proposed renderings but rejects them all on the basis of his "presumption" ("'If you do not Sabbatize the Sabbath . . .' The Sabbath as God, or World in Gnostic Understanding [Ev. Thom. Log. 27]," in *Knowledge of God in the Graeco-Roman World,* ed. R. van den Broek, T. Baarda, and J. Mansfeld, EPRO 12 [Leiden: Brill, 1988], 180). Present discussions are questioning the classification of the *Gospel of Thomas* as Gnostic. See Michael Williams, *Rethinking Gnosticism: An Argument for Dismantling a Dubious Category* (Princeton:

Princeton University Press, 1996), and A. Marjanen, "Is Thomas a Gnostic Gospel?" in *Thomas at the Crossroads: Studies of the New Testament and Its World,* ed. R. Uro (Edinburgh: T and T Clark, 1998), 107–39.

41. R. W. Funk, R. W. Hoover, and the Jesus Seminar laconically state, "The meaning of Thom 27,2 is obscure" (*The Five Gospels: The Search for the Authentic Words of Jesus* [New York: Macmillan, 1993], 488).

42. For the argument, see Stevan Davies, "The Christology and Protology of the 'Gospel of Thomas,'" *JBL* 111 (1992): 663–82. While in agreement with Davies on the importance of Protology and the role of exegetical elaborations of Genesis in *Thomas,* I do not share his views on Thomas' Christology.

43. Rudolf Bultmann, "Adam and Christ in Romans 5," in *The Old and New Man in the Letters of Paul* (Richmond: John Knox Press, 1967), 145–65.

44. Birger A. Pearson, *Gnosticism, Judaism and Egyptian Christianity* (Minneapolis, Minn.: Fortress Press, 1990), and "Pre-Valentinian Gnosticism in Alexandria," in *The Future of Early Christianity: Essays in Honor of Helmut Koester,* ed. Birger A. Pearson (Minneapolis, Minn.: Fortress Press, 1991), 455–66.

45. Davies, "Protology," 668.

46. Elaine Pagels offers a most convincing argument for the identification of this primordial light with the primordial man who precedes the one created in Gen 1:26, which the *Gospel of Thomas* identifies with Jesus ("Exegesis of Genesis 1 in the Gospels of Thomas and John," *JBL* 118 [1999]: 477–96). In this gospel Jesus is the personified primordial light. See note 92 of chapter 1, for the explanation of the primordial light, lost with the fall of Adam and Eve, which God graciously left shining on the first Sabbath and is now ritually reenacted by the lighting of the Sabbath lamps.

47. According to Giles Quispel, the changing of an accent in the word "light" also allowed for a pun that was heavily exploited in the exegesis of Gen 1:3 ("Der gnostische *Anthropos* und die juedische Tradition," *ErJb* 22 [1953]: 195–234, and "Ezekiel 1:26 in Jewish Mysticism and Gnosis," *VC* 34 [1980]: 1–13).

48. The verb *to sabbatize* appears in early Christian Greek literature only in Ignatius' *Letter to the Magnetians,* besides the *Gospel of Thomas.* It is clear that Ignatius is contrasting the Jewish with the Christian way of life, and he is very much concerned to inform his readers that it is incongruous for a Christian to follow the Jewish way of life. As he states it, "It is monstrous to talk of Jesus Christ and to Judaize." He then makes a most astonishing claim: "For Christianity did not base its faith on Judaism, but Judaism on Christianity" (10:3). The claim comes as the final statement of an argument that the prophets of old did not live "according to Judaism" but "according to Jesus Christ" (8:1–2). The prophets, therefore, had come to a new hope (9:1) and consequently "he whom they waited for in righteousness, when he came raised them from the dead"

(9:2). Since the prophets, then, did not live as Jews, Ignatius says that they "no longer were sabbatizing but living according to the Lord's [way]" (9:1). It is clear that while Ignatius, unlike Thomas, makes an explicit distinction between Christianity and Judaism, he also uses the verb "to sabbatize" to describe a way of life. For him "To live according to Judaism" (8:1), "to sabbatize" (9:1), and "to judaize" (10:3) are synonymous. He uses these terms interchangeably to advance his argument. For Ignatius, the danger that can shipwreck a Christian's voyage is Judaism. The same is true for Pseudo-Barnabas. In the *Gospel of Thomas* this is not the case, even if it also rejects traditional Jewish piety. The danger to be avoided is to be eaten up by "the world." But in *Thomas,* unlike in the Gospel of John, Judaism is not equated with "the world."

49. It may be remembered that the rabbis also knew that the primordial light was preserved in the Sabbath, and therefore the Jews had a peculiar Sabbath countenance. The *Gospel of Thomas* makes the primordial light available to those "who stand at the beginning," not just the Jews, and in the process unlocks the Sabbath from its limitation in the seventh day.

50. It may be not totally coincidental that ancient Egyptian theology had already linked the idea of seeing the father with rest. In the pyramid of Pepi I an inscription reads, "Isis said: 'Happy are they who see the father,' and Nephthys said: 'They who see the father have rest'" (E. A. Budge, *The Book of the Dead* [Seacacus, N.J.: University Books, 1960], 83).

51. According to Baarda, C. Taylor, Evelyn White, M. R. James, J. Leipold and J. Jeremias, on the basis of the Greek text from Oxyrhynchus, translate Sabbath as week ("Sabbatize," 200). P. Brown also argues that the Coptic text allows this translation ("The Sabbath and the Week in Thomas 27," *NT* 34 [1992]: 193).

52. Baarda gives to both the observance of the Sabbath and the fasting from the world a negative sense ("Sabbatize," 192–98). In order to do this, however, he resorts to very contrived and unsatisfactory explanations. It may be recalled in this connection how Paul, on the basis of his tensive eschatology, urged Christians to buy and live as though they had no goods and to deal with the world and live as though they had no such dealings (1 Cor 7:30–31).

53. This is still the case even if one accepts Elaine Pagels' argument, "Exegesis," that the actual protological conceptions in these two gospels are not the same.

54. See the discussion in chapter 5 above.

55. Brown points out that there is no reference to "a great Sabbath" in ancient Judaism. The mention of one in the *Martyrdom of Polycarp,* 8:1, which apparently happened in February, may be dependent on this passage in John (*John,* 2:934).

56. It would seem that a great deal less than one hundred pounds of spices would have been more that enough. D. Sylva fails in his attempt to deny the presence of irony in this description of the entombment ("Nicodemus and his Spices (John 19:39)," *NTS* 34 [1988]: 148–51).

57. Wayne A. Meeks credits Paul Meyer as the first to point it out (Meeks, "The Man from Heaven in Johannine Sectarianism," *JBL* 91 [1972]: 55, n. 39).

58. Whether or not one accepts Martyn's description of the particulars of the event in his *History and Theology,* that the Gospel of John reflects a traumatic break with a Jewish synagogue is widely recognized. See Raymond E. Brown, *The Community of the Beloved Disciple* (New York: Paulist, 1979).

Chapter 7: The Sabbath in the Letters of Paul

1. Whether Colossians was written by Paul is an issue still debated by some. It seems clear to me that the evidence is overwhelmingly in favor of a pseudonymous author. Most telling is the argument from vocabulary, particularly the use of words well attested in Paul's other letters with a totally different meaning. See Eduard Lohse, *Colossians and Philemon,* trans. W. R. Poehlmann and R. J. Karris, Hermeneia (Philadelphia: Fortress Press, 1971). The evidence about the Sabbath to be presented in chapter 8 will only provide further confirmation of the soundness of this position.

2. Ernst Kaesemann, *Commentary on Romans,* trans. and ed. G. W. Bromiley (Grand Rapids, Mich.: Eerdmans, 1980), 368.

3. James D. G. Dunn, *Romans 9–16,* WBC 3 (Waco, Tex.: Word, 1988), 808–9, *The Epistle to the Galatians* (Peabody, Mass.: Hendrickson, 1993), 227–28; Dunn, "The Colossian Philosophy: A Confident Jewish Apology," *Biblica* 76 (1995): 163, 169; Dunn, *The Epistles to the Colossians and to Philemon,* NIBCNT (Grand Rapids, Mich.: Eerdmans, 1996), 33–34, 173–75.

4. See Troy Martin, "Pagan and Judeo-Christian Time-Keeping Schemes in Gal. 4,10 and Col. 2,16," *NTS* 42 (1996): 105–19, for the differences in the two series.

5. I do not think that Paul's instructions to the Corinthians to put aside money for his collection "on the first day of the week," using the Hebraism "first day of the Sabbath" (1 Cor 16:2), represents a reference to the Sabbath in his letters. Rather, it is evidence for the fact that Sabbath could mean "week." See *BAGD,* σάββατον, for such meaning of the word.

6. On this basis, A. F. Segal thinks that in the eyes of his Jewish contemporaries he must have been considered an apostate (*Paul the Convert: The Apostolate and Apostacy of Paul the Pharisee* [New Haven: Yale University Press, 1990], 236).

7. There is not a bit of irony or sarcasm here, only fear. The passage is considered ironic by H. Schlier, *Der Brief an die Galater,* KEK 7 (Goettingen:

Vandenhoeck und Ruprecht, 1949), 146; Hans Dieter Betz, *Galatians,* Hermeneia (Minneapolis, Minn.: Fortress Press, 1979), 219; and Dunn, *Galatians,* 225. Charles Cosgrove sees in it "sarcastic incredulity" ("The Law and the Spirit: An Investigation into the Theology of Galatians," [Ph.D. diss., Princeton University, 1985], 210). Juan J. Bartolomé correctly observes that there is not a trace of irony in the text. His words reveal real fear (*El evangelio y su verdad: La justificación por la fe y su vivencia en común* [Roma: Pontifical Biblical Institute, 1988], 57).

8. Schlier, *Galater,* 136–37.

9. Dunn, *Galatians,* 228.

10. Betz, *Galatians,* 217, 219.

11. Gerhardt Ebeling, *Die Wahrheit des Evangeliums: eine Lesenhilfe zum Galaterbrief* (Tuebingen: Mohr, 1981), 296.

12. R. N. Longenecker, *Galatians,* WBC 41 (Waco, Tex.: Word, 1990), 117.

13. Robert Jewett, "The Agitators and the Galatian Congregation," *NTS* 17 (1971): 212.

14. F. J. Matera, *Galatians,* SP 9 (Wilmington, Del.: Glazier, 1992), 157.

15. Troy Martin, "Apostasy to Paganism: The Rhetorical Stasis of the Galatian Controversy," *JBL* 114 (1995): 437–61.

16. Josephus, *A.J.* 3.91; 8.96; 11.296; 14.264; *C. Ap.* 2.282 (cf. Diognetus 4.5).

17. Dunn, *Galatians,* 228.

18. P. N. Tarazi, *Galatians: A Commentary* (Crestwood, N.Y.: St. Vladimir's Seminary Press, 1994), 223.

19. Longenecker, *Galatians,* 182.

20. The identification of the elements with rudimentary notions, or basic concepts, continues to find support among conservative scholars. Lightfoot, Burton, and Ramsay were the prominent defenders of this view. M.-J. Lagrange describes them as what are taught to children, but also as the religious notions that are found in nationalistic religions (*Saint Paul épître aux galates* [Paris: Gabalda, 1950], 100). Longenecker points out that, while all four uses of the term in Galatians and Colossians refer to "first principles or rudimentary teachings," in each use the meaning of the term varies (*Galatians,* 166). He fails, however, to spell out what the variations consist of. Matera argues that Paul saw the Galatians trading one rudimentary form of religion for another (*Galatians,* 152, 157). After a rather excellent presentation of the evidence, Richard E. DeMaris in the end, unaccountably, comes out in favor of this view (*The Colossian Controversy: Wisdom in Dispute at Colossae,* JSNTSup 96 [Sheffield: Sheffield Academic Press, 1994], 73, 79–83).

21. Josef Blinzler, "Lexicalisches zu dem Terminus *stoicheia tou kosmou* bei

Paulus," in *Studiorum Paulinorum Congressus Biblicus Catholicus 1961*, AnBib 17–18 (Rome: Pontifical Biblical Institute, 1963), 2:429–43; G. Delling, στοιχεια, *TDNT,* 7:666–87; Philipp Vielhauer, "Gesetzesdienst und Stoicheiadienst im Galaterbrief," *Oikodome: Aufsatze zum Neuen Testament,* ed. G. Klein, Tbu 65 (1979), 2:183–95.

22. See Eduard Schweizer, "Slaves of the Elements and Worshipers of Angels: Gal 4:3 and Col 2:8, 18, 20," *JBL* 107 (1988): 455–68, and Walter Wink, *Naming the Powers* (Philadelphia: Fortress Press, 1984). Wink states that "the divinization of the elements was a commonplace in the whole Graeco-Roman period" (74).

23. J. Louis Martyn, "Christ, the Elements of the Cosmos, and the Law in Galatians," in *The Social World of the First Christians,* ed. L. M. While and O. L. Yarbrough (Minneapolis, Minn.: Fortress Press, 1995), 20n. 13.

24. Both Philo, *Abr.* 69–70, and Josephus, *A.J.* 1.155–156, testify to this tradition.

25. This may be related to the mythological presentation of the balancing forces in nature as theogonic pairs.

26. Longenecker writes, "Paul's lumping of Judaism and paganism together in this manner is radical in the extreme" (*Galatians,* 181). George Howard criticizes attempts "to rescue Paul from equating paganism with Judaism" and insists that one must "understand Paul's equation of Judaism with paganism" (*Paul: Crisis in Galatia* [Cambridge: Cambridge University Press, 1979], 72, 76). He also writes about "Paul's apparent equation of Judaism with paganism" (71). Bartolomé correctly observes that what Paul is equating is paganism with a particular kind of Christianity (*El evangelio,* 57).

27. That this is the language of Jewish propaganda is recognized by Betz, *Galatians,* 214, 219; Bruno Corsani, *Lettera ai Galati* (Rome: Pontifical Biblical Institute, 1990), 272; Dieter Luhrmann, *Der Brief an die Galater* (Zurich: Theologischer Verlag, 1978), 71, and Bartolomé, *El evangelio,* 55.

28. J. Ziesler accurately writes of "the erratic oscillation of pronouns" (*The Epistle to the Galatians* [London: Epworth, 1992], 56).

29. Jewett, "Agitators," 207–8; Ziesler, *Galatians,* 59–60; Betz, *Galatians,* 217; and Martin, "Pagan," 112–14.

30. Dieter Luhrmann, "Tage, Monate, Jahreszeiten, Jahre (Gal 4,10)," in *Werden und Wirken des Alten Testaments,* ed. R. Albertz (Goettingen: Vandenhoeck und Ruprecht, 1980), 430–31.

31. Philo, *Opif.* 53–61; *4 Ezra* 6:45 f.; *Jub.* 2:8–10; *1 En.* 72–82; 1QS 1.13–15, 9.26–10.8; 1QHª 12:4–9; CD 3.12–16, 16.2–4.

32. *Leg.* 3.41; *Det.* 90; *Fug.* 169, 174; *Somn.* 2.226–229; *Gig.* 49; *Post.* 27–28; *Deus* 12; *Conf.* 31–32.

33. We had occasion to refer to the widespread midrashic work on Genesis 1 in reference to the protological foundations to be observed in the Gospels of John and *Thomas*. See chapter 6 above.

34. In *Galatians, A New Translation with Introduction and Commentary,* AB 33A (New York: Doubleday, 1997), 415–17, Martyn builds his argument on Luhrmann's research.

35. As Martyn correctly points out, "to attend carefully to the creational language of 4:9–10 is to see . . . that the negative side of the picture is occupied by the universally fallen creation, not by Judaism" (*Galatians,* 418).

36. Wayne A. Meeks, "Judgment and the Brother: Romans 14,1–15,13," in *Tradition and Interpretation in the New Testament,* ed. G. E. Hawthorne with O. Betz (Grand Rapids, Mich.: Eerdmans, 1987), 292–93.

37. Kaesemann, *Romans,* 368.

38. Kaesemann, *Romans,* 370.

39. Max Rauer, *Die 'Schwachen' im Korinth und Rom nach den Paulusbriefen,* BibS 21, nos. 2–3 (1923): 180–82.

40. Franz J. Leenhardt, *The Epistle to the Romans: A Commentary* (London: Lutterworth, 1961), 348–49; Raoul Dederen, "On Esteeming One Day Better Than Another," *AUSS* 9 (1971): 21–31; R. J. Karris, "Romans 14,1–15,13 and the Occasion of Romans," in *The Romans Debate,* ed. K. F. Donfried (Minneapolis, Minn.: Fortress Press, 1977), 89; and Jerome Neyrey, *Paul in Other Words: A Cultural Reading of His Letters* (Louisville, Ky.: John Knox Press, 1990), 352.

41. Kaesemann, *Romans,* 367.

42. See Mark Reasoner, *The Strong and the Weak: Romans 14.1–15.13 in Context,* SNTSMS 103 (Cambridge: Cambridge University Press, 1999), 156–58.

43. C. K. Barrett, *The Epistle to the Romans,* HNTC (New York: Harper, 1957), 259; C. E. B. Cranfield, *A Critical and Exegetical Commentary on the Epistle to the Romans,* 6th ed. (Edingurgh: T and T Clark, 1977), 2:695; Heinrich Schlier, *Der Roemerbrief,* HTKNT 6 (Freiburg: Herder, 1977), 407; U. Wilckens, *Der Brief an die Roemer,* EKKNT 6 (Zurich: Benziger, 1982), 3:83; F. Watson, *Paul, Judaism and the Gentiles: A Sociological Approach,* SNTSMS 56 (Cambridge: Cambridge University Press, 1986), 181; J. Ziesler, *Paul's Letter to the Romans* (Philadelphia: Fortress Press, 1989), 330–31; P. J. Tomson, *Paul and the Jewish Law: Halakha in the Letters of the Apostle to the Gentiles,* CRINT 3 (Minneapolis, Minn.: Fortress Press, 1990), 237, 239. B. Byrne, *Romans,* SP 6 (Collegeville, Minn.: Liturgical Press, 1996), 409; D. J. Moo, *The Epistle to the Romans,* NIBCNT (Grand Rapids, Mich.: Eerdmans, 1996), 842.

44. Dunn, *Romans 9–16,* 805.

45. Paul's vagueness has been frequently noted. Meeks ascribes it to Paul's

attempt to create a hypothetical case for heuristic purposes ("Judgment," 291). R. Jewett complains that the passage is marked by "exasperatingly vague references" (*Christian Tolerance: Paul's Message to the Modern Church* [Philadelphia: Westminster, 1982], 30). Both Kaesemann and Dunn point out that what may have been clear to the original readers is vague to those who lack knowledge of the circumstances (Kaesemann, *Romans,* 366; Dunn, *Romans 9–16,* 804). It is surprising, therefore, to learn that J. A. T. Robinson finds that Romans 14 "reveals Paul at his clearest and surest. . . . His argument has an intellectual and moral directness which makes commentary unnecessary" (*Wrestling with Romans* [London: SCM, 1979], 143).

46. As described by Meeks, "Judgment," 290, and Byrne, *Romans,* 409.

47. Joachim Jeremias, *Unknown Sayings of Jesus* (London: SPCK, 1958), 49–53.

48. M.-J. Lagrange, *L'évangile selon Saint Luc* (Paris: Gabalda, 1948), 176–77.

49. Martin Luther, *Der Brief an die Roemer,* D. Martin Luther Werke 56 (Weimar, 1938), 494.

50. H. C. G. Moule, *The Epistle of St. Paul to the Romans,* 9th ed. (London: Hodder and Stoughton, 1893), 375.

51. Frederick W. Danker translates correctly the sense of the clause as "the other holds every day in esteem" (*A Greek-English Lexicon of the New Testament and Other Christian Literature,* 3d ed. [Chicago: University of Chicago Press, 2000], 567).

52. Leenhardt follows a strange logic when he writes, "since nothing suggests that we have here to do with Judaizers we shall not regard this as an allusion to the Sabbath" (*Romans,* 348–49). Debates as to how to observe the Sabbath, as our study amply demonstrates, were endemic to Judaism and to early Christianity, and not at all a Judaizing characteristic.

53. See Harold W. Attridge, *The Epistle to the Hebrews: A Commentary,* Hermeneia (Philadelphia: Fortress Press, 1989), 10.

54. Hegesippus in Eusebius, *HE,* 4.22.5. The Masbotheans are also mentioned in *Const. App.* 6.6.4, and in Ps.-Jerome, *Indiculus de haeresibus Judaeorum (PL* 81.636c).

55. M.-J. Lagrange, *Saint Paul épître aux romains* (Paris: Gabalda, 1950), 323.

56. Robert Jewett, "The Law and the Coexistence of Jews and Gentiles in Romans," *Int* 39 (1985): 341–56 (354).

57. Segal, *Paul,* 236, 241.

58. Reasoner, *Weak and Strong,* 161.

59. Ibid., 172–74.

60. Meeks, "Judgement," 290.

61. C. H. Dodd, *The Epistle to the Romans* (London: Hodder and Stoughton, 1932), 214–17.

62. Michael Thompson, *Clothed with Christ: The Example and Teaching of Jesus in Rom 12,1–15,13*, JSNTSup 59 (Sheffield: Sheffield Academic Press, 1991), 162.

63. Dederen, "Esteeming," 32–34.

64. Watson, *Paul,* 97.

65. W. Sanday and A. C. Headlam, *A Critical and Exegetical Commentary on the Epistle to the Romans* (Edinburgh: T and T Clark, 1895), 385.

66. Edward P. Sanders, *Paul* (Oxford: Oxford University Press, 1991), 88.

67. Both Wilckens, *Roemer,* 3:115, and Dunn, *Romans 9–16,* 801, are correct in recognizing its significance.

68. Byrne describes this passage incorrectly as "an exhortation to tolerance directed to those in Rome who particularly share his own point of view" (*Romans,* 406). It is not at all the case that Paul fully identifies himself with one of the parties in the dispute. In any case, it is not at all clear that the weak and the strong were identifiable groups.

69. Meeks says that "a minority consensus" agrees that the weak and the strong are imaginary individuals created by Paul in order to give the Romans some ethical advice he thought opportune. He drew his protagonists from his experience with the Corinthians ("Judgement," 290).

This means that there was no actual dispute at Rome known to Paul. Among those who have accepted this view are Jacques Dupont, "*Appel aux faibles et aux forts dans la communauté romaine (Rom 14,1–15,13),*" in *Studiorum Paulinorum Congressus Internationalis Catholicus,* AnBib 17–18 (1963), 1:357–66; Leenhardt, *Romans,* 346; Victor P. Furnish, *The Love Commandment in the New Testament* (Nashville, Tenn.: Abingdon, 1972), 115–16; Karris, "Occasion," 83; Jouette Bassler, *Divine Impartiality: Paul and a Theological Axiom,* SBLDS 59 (1982), 163–64; Helmut Koester, *Introduction to the New Testament* (New York: De Gruyter, 1982), 2:140–41; and Wendell L. Willis, *Idol Meat at Corinth: The Pauline Argument in 1 Cor 8 and 10,* SBLDS 68 (1985), 252. As John C. Brunt points out, however, the nuanced way in which Paul contrasts those who judge from those who despise argues strongly against this view (*Paul's Attitude Toward and Treatment of Problems Involving Dietary Practice: A Case Study in Pauline Ethics,* [Ph.D. diss., Emory University, 1978], 153). Meeks summarily says that both verbs are "equivalent" ("Judgement," 295), but such is hardly the case. Besides, there are significant differences between the situation in Corinth and the one in Rome. The "weak" at Corinth are not to be equated with the "weak in faith" at Rome. At Corinth the issue is idolatry, while at Rome it is purity. No one at Corinth seems to have been concerned with days; why, then, did Paul gratuitously bring it up at Rome? In an effort to link Rom 14 with 1 Cor 8–10, Meeks identifies "full conviction" (Rom 14:5, 14) with "conscience" (1 Cor 8:12; 10:25). This identification is rather arbitrary. Taking into account these factors makes it unlikely that the "minority consensus" offers the most probable scenario.

70. Lagrange, *Saint Paul,* 323.

71. Kaesemann, *Romans,* 366.

72. Wilckens keeps together the issues of food and days for his interpretation (*Roemer,* 115). This does not help his efforts.

Chapter 8: The Sabbath in the Letter to the Colossians

1. Dunn, "Colossian Philosophy," 181.

2. On this see Herold Weiss, "The Law in the Epistle to the Colossians," *CBQ* 34 (1972): 294–314.

3. See, e.g., James Tabor, *Things Unutterable: Paul's Ascent to Paradise in Its Greco-Roman, Judaic and Early Christian Contexts* (Lanham, Md.: University Press of America, 1986), 57–111.

4. This is not accepted by Dunn, *Colossians,* 165. It is recognized by Peter Pokorny, *Der Brief des Paulus an die Kolosser,* THKNT 10 (Berlin: Evangelische Verlagsanstalt, 1987), 139.

5. Luhrmann, "Tage," 428–45; see Paul Giem, "Sabbaton in Col. 2:16," *AUSS* 19 (1988): 195–210, for the background of the calendric string.

6. Eduard Schweizer, *The Letter to the Colossians* (Minneapolis, Minn.: Fortress Press, 1982), 128.

7. Troy Martin, *By Philosophy and Empty Deceit: Colossians as a Response to a Cynic Critique,* JSNTSup 51 (Sheffield: Sheffield Academic Press, 1996).

8. Troy Martin, "But Let Everyone Discern the Body of Christ (Colossians 2:17)," *JBL* 114 (1995): 249–55.

9. Rordorf explains that these feasts "were like *silhouettes* cast by that which was to come; now, however, the reality has come, the 'substance' which cast these shadows" (*Sunday,* 101). Dunn translates, "these things are a shadow of what was to come" (*Colossians,* 171). The original does not allow this reading.

10. Martin thinks that the items described in 2:18 are also being defended by the author, but in this he is unconvincing (*Philosophy,* 137–39). He fails to realize that the expression "wishing in" (θέλων ἐν) is a Hebraism, and not a brachylogy. He argues correctly, however, that the practices listed in 2:16 are being defended by the author, and are not the teaching of the other teachers. His attempt to characterize the other teachers as Cynics fails also because it depends on the construction of a peculiar ideal Cynic who happens to match the issues in Colossians.

11. J.-N. Aletti, *Saint Paul épître aux Colossiens* (Paris: Gabalda, 1993), 194.

12. Gunter Bornkamm, "Die Haeresie des Kolosserbriefes," in *Das Ende des Gesetzes: Paulusstudien,* BEvT 16 (Munich: Kaiser, 1958), 147.

13. The connection to Plato's cave is explicit in Rordorf, *Sunday,* 101n. 4.

14. See Weiss, "Law," 298–325.

15. Most notably, Dunn, *Colossians,* 34.

16. A notable exemption is Schweizer, *Colossians,* 110.

17. The formula is also used by Josephus, *A.J.* 3.294. Josephus, however, has "day of gladness, new moon, and feasts."

18. Philo, *Migr.* 89.

19. Philo, *Migr.* 93.

20. Wayne A. Meeks characterizes the author of Colossians as one who was "tipping more and more in the direction of adopting the commonsense universe of popular morality" (*The Origins of Christian Morality* [New Haven: Yale University Press, 1993], 64). I see him also firmly within traditional Jewish piety.

21. In the middle of the second century, Marcion argued for the abolition of the Old Testament as scripture, claimng Pauline authority for the move.

22. As John Calvin grudgingly, yet candidly, admits, "We still keep some observance of days" (*The Epistles of Paul the Apostle to the Galatians, Ephesians, Philippians and Colossians* [Grand Rapids, Mich.: Eerdmans, 1965], 337).

23. E. Schweizer also finds a connection between the authors of Matthew and Colossians, but he suggests that the Sabbath in Colossians "may have been influenced by gentile customs" ("Christianity of the Circumcised and Judaism of the Uncircumcised: The Background of Matthew and Colossians," in *Jews, Greeks and Christians: Religious Cultures in Late Antiquity,* ed. R. Hamerton-Kelly and R. Scroggs [Leiden: Brill, 1976], 245–60). This is a rather gratuitous suggestion.

24. Luhrmann traces a development from one to the other (*Galater,* 104–5), but his reconstruction is not convincing. He fails to take into account the differences in vocabulary, and that the Torah plays no role in the Colossian controversy.

25. Segal, *Paul,* 236.

26. See Dennis R. MacDonald, *The Legend and the Apostle: The Battle for Paul in Story and Canon* (Philadelphia: Westminster, 1983), 54–77.

27. For an early reconstruction of this process, see John Knox, *Marcion and the New Testament* (Chicago: University of Chicago Press, 1942).

Chapter 9: God's Sabbath in the Epistle to the Hebrews

1. J. C. McCullough, "Some Recent Developments in Research on the Epistle to the Hebrews," *IBS* 2 (1980): 141–65; 3 (1981): 228–54. See p. 142.

2. E. Kaesemann, *Das wandernde Gottesvolk: Eine Untersuchung zum Hebra-erbrief,* FRLANT 55 (Goettingen: Vandenhoeck and Ruprecht, 1939), 75. His argument is accepted by Gerd Theissen, *Untersuchungen zum Hebraerbrief,* SNT 2 (Guetersloh: Mohn, 1969), 127.

3. James W. Thompson, *The Beginnings of Christian Philosophy: The Epistle to the Hebrews,* CBQMS 13 (Washington: Catholic Biblical Association, 1982), 92–93.

4. Otfried Hofius, *Katapausis: Die Vorstellung vom endzeitlichen Ruheort im Hebraerbrief,* WUNT 11 (Tuebingen: Mohr [Siebeck], 1970), 53–54.

5. George W. Buchanan, *To the Hebrews,* AB 36 (Garden City, N.Y.: Doubleday, 1972), 9, 63–65.

6. Attridge, *Hebrews,* 128.

7. Theissen, *Untersuchungen,* 127.

8. On the other hand, to deny that the author of Hebrews had philosophical interests goes too far in the opposite direction. See L. D. Hurst, "Eschatology and 'Platonism' in the Epistle to the Hebrews," SBLSP (Atlanta: Scholars Press, 1984), 41–74. Barrett finds Hebrews closer to Barnabas than to Philo and suggests that the author "may well have read Plato" ("Eschatology," 393). Attridge considers that the author of the epistle had "at least [a] superficial rhetorician's acquaintance with contemporary philosophy" (*Hebrews,* 26).

9. See, e.g., *1 En.* 39:7; *T. Dan* 5:12; *4 Ezra* 7:98.

10. See Barrett, "Eschatology," 372.

11. Ibid. He boldly asserts, "The doctrine of the Sabbath rest in Hebrews is neither Hellenistic nor Midrashic but Christian." This claim, it would seem, depends on rather reductionist definitions of the terms.

12. Attridge, *Hebrews,* 28.

13. It is important to retain "hope" as the central concept in this assertion, and not to reduce the word to an adjective (hopeful boast) as most translations do.

14. von Rad, "There Remains," 94–102.

15. R. Reid, "The Use of the Old Testament in the Epistle to the Hebrews," (Th.D. diss., Union Theological Seminary, New York, 1964), 82.

16. M. Jastrow defines it as "an analogy between two laws established on the basis of verbal congruities in the texts" (*A Dictionary of the Targumim, the Talmud Babli and Yerushalmi, and the Midrashic Literature* [New York: Putnam, 1886–1900], 1:232b).

17. F. F. Bruce, *The Epistle to the Hebrews,* rev. ed., NIBCNT (Grand Rapids, Mich.: Eerdmans, 1990), 97–98.

18. Attridge says "indicative" and gives parallels (*Hebrews,* 116), but the only parallel for μήποτε ἔσται is Mark 14:2.

19. Bruce, *Hebrews,* 99.

20. Thompson, *Christian Philosophy,* 94.

21. O. Bauernfeind, "καταπαύω κατάπαυσισ," *TDNT,* 3:628.

22. Hofius correctly identifies several details of the midrash in Hebrews as dependent on the story in Numbers, rather than on Psalm 95 (*Katapausis,* 131).

23. 1 Chr 22:9, 18; 23:25; 2 Chr 14:6–7; 15:15; 20:30; cf. Josh 21:44; 22:4; 23:1.

24. von Rad, "There Remains," 100–102.

25. See Thompson, *Christian Philosophy,* 91.

26. See chapter 1 above.

27. S. Kristemaker denies the use of a *gezera shawa,* and argues that the text is to be explained in terms of liturgical usage (*The Psalm Citations in the Epistle to the Hebrews* [Amsterdam: Soes, 1961], 36). This line is adopted by Bruce, as mentioned in note 17. The use of a *gezera shawa,* however, cannot be denied.

28. In the LXX, Ps 94:11 reads κατάπαυσισ and Gen 2:2 has the cognate verb καταπαύω; in the Hebrew text, Ps 95:11 has the noun מנוחה, derived from the root נוח, and Gen 2:2 reads שׁבת.

29. Contra Bruce who states that the biographical details in chapter 11 illustrate how the present generation, already experiencing the Sabbath rest which is theirs as a heritage, may live by faith (*Hebrews,* 110).

30. E. Lohse makes the point that the word is a *hapax legomenon* in the NT, is not found in the LXX at all, and is found elsewhere in Greek literature only in Plutarch, *De superstitione* 3.2.166a. Plutarch gives the term a negative connotation, but his bias cannot be ignored ("σαββατισμόσ," *TDNT,* 7:34–35).

31. Buchanan translates the word as "namely" (*Hebrews,* 71), but since the anarthrous participle cannot be attributive, it must be translated as an adversative.

32. See H. Koester, "ὑπόστασισ," *TDNT,* 8:572–89.

33. Ibid., 575.

34. Ibid., 587.

35. In his rather interesting analysis of the divine rest motif in Hebrews, Khiok-Khng Yeo suggests that the author is appealing to the audience's acquaintance with the notion of the divine *otiositas* (*What Has Jerusalem to Do with Beijing? Biblical Interpretation from a Chinese Perspective* [Harrisburg, Pa.: Trinity Press International, 1998], 91). In a footnote he recognizes that this is "speculation" on his part (91, n. 111). I consider it much safer to use concepts explicitly used by the author to illumine his understanding of the divine rest.

36. Attridge, *Hebrews,* 128, n. 76. This footnote is a grudging concession on Attridge's part. In the body of his commentary he does not take sufficiently into account the futuristic eschatology of Hebrews.

37. Barrett, "Eschatology," 371.

38. See Rudolf Bultmann, "The Problem of Ethics in the Writings of Paul,"

in *The Old and New Man in the Letters of Paul* (Richmond: John Knox Press, 1967), 7–32.

39. It is well recognized that the Letter of Barnabas is pseudonymous; therefore its author is identified as Pseudo-Barnabas.

40. Barrett, "Eschatology," 387–89.

41. In Hebrews it is said that the law made nothing perfect (7:19). Therefore, when what could make perfect came, that which could not became obsolete and ready to vanish away (8:13).

42. Albert Hermans has argued that the synonymous use of "Sabbath" and "eighth day" as designations of the eschatological new age, which recurs in Egyptian Gnosticism, are not to be taken to mean that Pseudo-Barnabas is a chiliast even if it leaves in tension two contrasting eschatological systems, one with seven and the other with eight days ("Le Pseudo-Barnabé est-il millenariste?" *ETL* 35 [1959]: 849–876). His argument, however, cannot be sustained against the explicit millenarian allegorization of the creation week in the text. It is true, however, as Hermans argues, that Pseudo-Barnabas does not intend to give to the eighth day the qualities of the Sabbath, or to make the observance of the eighth day the fulfillment of the commandment.

43. Pseudo-Barnabas creates confusion by stating that both the arrival of the seventh and of the eighth millennium makes it possible for humans to restfully sanctify the Sabbath. Clearly neither one of these exists now, but when he introduces the eighth he describes it as "that which I have made," using the perfect tense in Greek. But the coming of the Son in the seventh has not yet taken place. The most plausible explanation has been suggested by L. W. Barnard, *Studies in the Apostolic Fathers and Their Background* (New York: Schocken Books, 1966), 78. The epistle is connected to the celebration of Easter, and counting days from Palm Sunday on the eighth day, which the author points out "we indeed celebrate with gladness" (15:9), is Easter Sunday. In this way, proleptically, on Easter Sunday God has already made the eighth day (millennium).

Bibliography

Aletti, Jean-Noël. *Saint Paul épître aux Colossiens.* Paris: Gabalda, 1993.

Andreasen, Niels-Eric. *The Old Testament Sabbath: A Tradition-Historical Investigation.* Cambridge, Mass.: Scholars Press, 1972.

Anderson, A. T. "Mount Gerizim: Navel of the World." *Biblical Archaeology* 43 (1980): 217–21.

The Apostolic Fathers. Translated by Kirsopp Lake. 2 vols. Loeb Classical Library, 1952.

Arrian. *Anabasis.* Translated by E. Iliff Robson. Loeb Classical Library, 1929.

Artemidorus, *Oneirocritica: The Interpretation of Dreams.* Translation and commentary by Robert J. White. Noyes Classical Studies. Park Ridge, N.J.: Noyes Press, 1975.

Attridge, Harold W. *The Epistle to the Hebrews: A Commentary.* Hermeneia. Minneapolis, Minn.: Fortress Press, 1989.

———. *The Interpretation of Biblical History in the* Antiquitates Judaicae *of Flavius Josephus.* Harvard Dissertations in Religion 7. Missoula, Mont.: Scholars Press, 1976.

———. "Historiography." In *Jewish Writings of the Second Temple Period: Apocripha, Pseudoepigrapha, Qumran, Sectarian Writings, Philo, Josephus,* edited by M. E. Stone, 157–84. Compendia rerum Indaicarum ad Novum Testamentum 2. Philadelphia: Fortress Press, 1984.

———. "Thematic Development and Source Elaboration in John 7:1–36." *Catholic Biblical Quarterly* 42 (1980): 160–79.

Augustine. *City of God.* Translated by G. E. McCracken et al. 7 vols. Loeb Classical Library, 1957–72.

Augustine. *Confessions.* Translated by W. Watts. 2 vols. Loeb Classical Library, 1946.

Baarda, Tjitze. "'If you do not Sabbatize the Sabbath . . .' The Sabbath as God, or World in Gnostic Understanding [Ev. Thom. Log. 27]." In *Knowledge of God in the Graeco-Roman World,* edited by R. van den Broek, T. Baarda, and J. Mansfeld, 178–201. Etudes préliminaires aux religions orientales dans l'empire romain 112. Leiden: Brill, 1988.

Bacchiocchi, Samuele. *From Sabbath to Sunday: A Historical Investigation of the Rise of Sunday Observance in Early Christianity.* Rome: Pontifical Gregorian University Press, 1977.

Banks, Robert. *Jesus and the Law in the Synoptic Tradition.* Society of New Testament Studies Monograph Series 28. Cambridge: Cambridge University Press, 1975.

Barnard, L. W. *Studies in the Apostolic Fathers and Their Background.* New York: Schocken Books, 1966.

Barrett, C. K. *The Epistle to the Romans.* Harper New Testament Commentary. New York: Harper, 1957.

————. "The Eschatology of the Epistle to the Hebrews." In *The Background of the New Testament and Its Eschatology,* edited by W. D. Davies and D. Daube, 369–95. Cambridge: Cambridge Univeristy Press, 1956.

————. *The Gospel according to St. John.* London: SPCK, 1960.

————. *Jesus and the Gospel Tradition.* Philadelphia: Fortress Press, 1968.

————, ed. *The New Testament Background: Selected Documents.* San Francisco: Harper and Row, 1989.

Bartolomé, Juan J. *El evangelio y su verdad: La justificaci—n por la fe y su vivencia en comœn.* Rome: Pontifical Biblical Insitute, 1988.

Bassler, Jouette. *Divine Impartiality: Paul and a Theological Axiom.* Society of Biblical Literature Dissertation Series 59. Atlanta: Scholars Press, 1982.

Baumgarten, J. "The Qumran Shabbat Shirot and Rabbinic Merkhabah Traditions." *Revue de Qumran* 13 (1988): 199–213.

Beall, T. S. *Josephus' Description of the Essenes Illustrated by the Dead Sea Scrolls.* Society of New Testament Studies Monograph Series 58. Cambridge: Cambridge University Press, 1988.

Beare, F. W. *Earliest Records of Jesus.* Oxford: Blackwell, 1962.

Belkin, Samuel. *Philo and the Oral Law: The Philonic Interpretation of Biblical Law in Relation to the Palestinian Halakah.* Cambridge: Harvard University Press, 1940.

Ben-Hayyim, Z. *The Literary and Oral Traditions in Hebrew and Aramaic among the Samaritans.* 3 vols. Jerusalem: Magnus, 1957–77.

Betz, Hans Dieter. *Galatians.* Hermeneia. Minneapolis, Minn.: Fortress Press, 1979.

Bietenhardt, H. "Sabbatvorschriften von Qumran im Lichte des rabbinischen Rechts und der Evangelien." In *Qumran Probleme: Vortrage des Leipziger Symposium ueber Qumran Probleme von 9 bis 14 Oktober 1961,* edited by H. Bardke, 56–60. Berlin: Akademie Verlage, 1963.

Blinzler, Josef. "Lexicalisches zu dem Terminus *stoicheia tou kosmou* bei Paulus." In *Studiorum Paulinorum Congressus Internationalis Catholicus 1961.* Analecta Biblica 17–18. Rome: Pontifical Biblical Institute, 1963.

Blosser, David. "The Sabbath Year Cycle in Josephus." *Hebrew Union College Annual* 52 (1981): 129–39.

Boccaccini, Gabriele. *Middle Judaism: Jewish Thought, 300 B.C.E. to 200 C.E.* Minneapolis, Minn.: Fortress Press, 1991.

Boid, Iain R. M. *Principles of Samaritan Halachah.* Studies in Judaism in Late Antiquity 38. Leiden: Brill, 1989.

Borg, Marcus J. *Conflict, Holiness, and Politics in the Teaching of Jesus.* Studies in the Bible and Early Christianity, 5. New York: Edwin Mellen Press, 1984.

Borgen, Peder. *Bread from Heaven: An Exegetical Study of the Concept of Manna in the Gospel of John and the Writings of Philo.* Novum Testamentum Supplements 10. Leiden: Brill, 1965.

———. *Philo, John and Paul: New Perspectives on Judaism and Early Christianity.* Brown Judaic Studies 131. Atlanta: Scholars Press, 1987.

Bornkamm, Gunter. "Die Haeresie des Kolosserbriefes." In *Das Ende des Gesetzes: Paulusstudien,* 139–56. Beitrage zur evangelischen Theologie 16. Munich: Kaiser, 1958.

Bowman, John. *Samaritan Documents Relating to Their History, Religion and Life.* Pittsburgh: Pickwick Press, 1977.

Braun, Herbert. *Jesus of Nazareth: The Man and His Times.* Translated by E. R. Kalin. Philadelphia: Fortress Press, 1979.

Briant, P. *Rois, tributs, et paysans.* Annales de l'Universite de Besançon. Paris: Les Belles Lettres, 1982.

Broadie, Alexander. *A Samaritan Philosophy: A Study of the Hellenistic Cultural Ethos of the Memar Marqah.* Studia post-Biblica 31. Leiden: Brill, 1981.

Brown, Francis, S. R. Driver, and Charles Briggs. *A Hebrew and English Lexicon of the Old Testament.* Oxford: Clarendon Press, 1907.

Brown, P. "The Sabbath and the Week in Thomas 27." *Novum Testamentum* 34 (1992): 193.

Brown, Raymond E. *The Community of the Beloved Disciple.* New York: Paulist Press, 1979.

———. *The Gospel according to John.* 2 vols. Anchor Bible 29. New York: Doubleday, 1966.

Brown, Raymond E., and John Meier. *Antioch and Rome.* New York: Paulist Press, 1983.

Bruce, F. F. *The Epistle to the Hebrews.* Rev. ed. New International Biblical Commentary on the New Testament. Grand Rapids, Mich.: Eerdmans, 1990.

Brunt, John C. "Paul's Attitude toward and Treatment of Problems Involving Dietary Practice: A Case Study in Pauline Ethics." Ph.D. diss., Emory University, 1978.

Buchanan, George W. *To the Hebrews.* Anchor Bible 36. Garden City: Doubleday, 1972.

Budge, E. A. *The Book of the Dead.* Seacacus: University Books, 1960.

Bultmann, Rudolf. "Adam and Christ in Romans 5." In *The Old and New Man in the Letters of Paul.* Translated by K. R. Crim, 145–65. Richmond: John Knox Press, 1967.

———. *The Gospel of John: A Commentary.* Translated by G. R. Beasley-Murray. Philadelphia: Westminster, 1971.

———. *History of the Synoptic Tradition.* Translated by John Marsh. Oxford: Blackwell, 1963.

———. "The Problem of Ethics in the Writings of Paul." In *The Old and New Man in the Letters of Paul.* Translated by K. R. Crim, 7–32. Richmond: John Knox, 1967.

Burns, J. F. "The Use of Time in the Fourth Gospel." *New Testament Studies* 13 (1966–67): 285–90.

Byrne, Brendan. *Romans.* Sacra Pagina 6. Collegeville: Liturgical Press, 1996.

Calvin, John. *The Epistles of Paul the Apostle to the Galatians, Ephesians, Philippians, and Colossians.* Grand Rapids, Mich.: Eerdmans, 1965.

Capps, Donald. "Parabolic Events in Augustine's Confessions." *Theology Today* 40 (1983): 260–72.

Carson, Donald A., ed. *From Sabbath to Lord's Day: A Biblical and Theological Investigation.* Grand Rapids, Mich.: Zondervan, 1982.

Cleomedes. *Théorie élémentaire: De motu circulari corporum caelestium.* Texte présenté, truduit et commenté par Richard Goulet. Histoire des doctrines de l'Antiquité classique 3. Paris: J. Vrim, 1980.

Coggins, R. J. "The Samaritans in Josephus." In *Josephus, Judaism and Christianity,* edited by L. H. Feldman, and G. Hata, 257–73. Detroit: Wayne State University Press, 1987.

Cohen, Jeffrey. M. *A Samaritan Chronicle: A Source-Critical Analysis of the Life and Times of the Great Samaritan Reformer Baba Rabbah.* Studia post-Biblica 30. Leiden: Brill, 1981.

Cohen, Shaye J. D. *Josephus in Galilee and Rome: His Vita and Development as a Historian.* Columbia Studies in the Classical Tradition 8. Leiden: Brill, 1979.

Corsani, Bruno. *Lettera ai Galati.* Rome: Pontifical Biblical Institute, 1990.

Cosgrove, Charles. "The Law and the Spirit: An Investigation into the Theology of Galatians." Ph.D. diss., Princeton University, 1985.

Cranfield, C. E. B. *A Critical and Exegetical Commentary on the Epistle to the Romans.* 6th ed. 2 vols. Edinburgh: T and T Clark, 1977.

———. *The Gospel according to Mark.* Cambridge: Cambridge University Press, 1959.

Cross, Frank M. "Aspects of Samaritan and Hellenistic History in Late Persian and Hellenistic Times." *Harvard Theological Review* 59 (1966): 201–11.

———. "Papyri of the Fourth Century B.C. from Daliyeh." In *New Directions in Biblical Archaeology,* edited by D. N. Freedman, and J. Greenfield. 45–69. Garden City: Doubleday, 1969.

Crown, Alan D. "The Samaritan Diaspora to the End of the Byzantine Era." *Australian Journal of Biblical Archaeology* 2 (1974–75): 107–23.

————, ed. *The Samaritans.* Tuebingen: Mohr, 1989.

Cullmann, Oscar. *Early Christian Worship.* London: SCM Press, 1953.

Culpepper, R. Alan. *Anatomy of the Fourth Gospel.* Philadelphia: Fortress Press, 1983.

Danker, Frederick W., ed. *Greek-English Lexicon of the New Testament and Other Early Christian Literature.* 3d ed. Chicago: University of Chicago Press, 2000.

Davies, Philip R. "Calendrical Change and Qumran Origins: An Assessment of VanderKam's Theory." *Catholic Biblical Quarterly* 45 (1983): 80–89.

Davies, Stevan. "The Christology and Protology of the 'Gospel of Thomas.'" *Journal of Biblical Literature* 111 (1992): 663–82.

Dederen, Raoul. "On Esteeming One Day Better Than Another." *Andrews University Seminary Studies* 9 (1971): 21–31.

DeMaris, Richard E. *The Colossian Controversy: Wisdom in Dispute at Colossae.* Journal for the Study of the New Testament Supplement Series 96. Sheffield: Sheffield Academic Press, 1994.

Demsky, A. "When the Priests Trumpeted the Onset of the Sabbath." *Biblical Archaeology Review* 24, no. 6 (Nov.–Dec. 1986): 50–52.

Dexinger, F. "Limits of Tolerance in Judaism: The Samaritan Example." In *Jewish and Christian Self-Definition,* edited by Edward P. Sanders, vol. 2, 88–114. London: SMC Press, 1981.

Dodd, C. H. *The Epistle to the Romans.* London: Hodder and Stoughton, 1932.

Doering, Lutz. *Schabbat: Sabbathalacha und -praxis im antiken Judentum und Urchristentum.* Texte und Studien zum antiken Judentum 78. Tuebingen: Mohr Siebeck, 1999.

Douglas, Mary. *How Institutions Think.* Syracuse: Syracuse University Press, 1986.

Droge, A., and J. Tabor. *A Noble Death: Suicide and Martyrdom among Christians and Jews in Antiquity.* New York: Harper Collins, 1992.

Duke, P. D. *Irony in the Fourth Gospel.* Atlanta: John Knox, 1985.

Dunn, James D. G. "The Colossian Philosophy: A Confident Jewish Apology." *Biblica* 76 (1995): 153–63.

————. *The Epistles to the Colossians and to Philemon.* New International Biblical Commentary on the New Testament. Grand Rapids, Mich.: Eerdmans, 1996.

————. *The Epistle to the Galatians.* Peabody, Mass.: Hendrickson, 1993.

————. *Romans 9–16.* Word Bible Commentary 3. Waco, Tex.: Word, 1988.

Dupont, Jacques. "Appel aux faibles et aux forts dans la communauté romaine (Rom 14,1–15,13)." In *Studiorum Paulinorum Congressus Internationalis Catholicus 1961.* vol. 1. Analecta Biblica 17–18. Rome: Pontifical Biblical Institute, 1963.

Dupont-Sommer, Andre. "L'ostracon aramèen du Sabbat." *Semitica* 2 (1949): 29–39.

Ebeling, Gerhardt. *Die Wahrheit des Evangeliums: eine Lesenhilfe zum Galaterbrief.* Tuebingen: Mohr, 1981.

Eliade, Mircea. *Cosmos and History: The Myth of Eternal Return.* New York: Harper Torchbooks/Bollingen Library, 1954.

Egger, Rita. *Josephus Flavius und die Samaritaner.* Novum Testamentum et Orbis Anticuus 4. Goettingen: Vandenhoeck und Ruprecht, 1986.

Eusebius. *The Ecclesiastical History.* Translated by Kirsopp Lake and J. E. L Oulton. 2 vols. London: Heinemann, 1926–38.

Feldman, Louis. "Palestinian and Diaspora Judaism in the First Century." In *Christianity and Rabbinic Judaism: A Parallel History of Their Origins and Early Development,* edited by Hershel Shanks, 1–40. Washington: Biblical Archaeology Society, 1992.

Ferraro, G. "Il senso di *heos arti* nel texto di Giovanni 5.17." *Rivista biblica italiana* 20 (Suppl., 1972): 529–45.

Fishbane, Michael. *Biblical Interpretation in Ancient Israel.* Oxford: Clarendon Press, 1985.

Flusser, David. *Jesus.* New York: Herder and Herder, 1969.

Fossum, Jarl. "Sects and Movements." In *The Samaritans,* edited by A. D. Corwn, 293–389. Tuebingen: Mohr, 1989.

Fredriksen, Paula. *From Jesus to Christ: The Origins of the New Testament Images of Jesus.* New Haven: Yale University Press, 1988.

Friedlander, M. *Die Religiosen Bewegungen innerhalb des Judentums im Zeitalter Jesu.* Berlin: Reiner, 1905. Reprint, Stuttgart: Magnus, 1980.

Friedman, Theodore. "The Sabbath: Anticipation of Redemption." *Judaism* 16 (1967): 443–52.

Frontinus. *Stratagems and The Aqueducts of Rome.* Translated by C. E. Bennett, revised by M. B. McElwain. Loeb Classical Library, 1980.

Funk, Robert W., R. W. Hoover, and the Jesus Seminar. *The Five Gospels: The Search for the Authentic Words of Jesus.* New York: Macmillan, 1993.

Furnish, Victor P. *The Love Commandment in the New Testament.* Nashville: Abingdon, 1972.

Gaster, Moses. *The Samaritans: Their History, Doctrines and Literature.* Oxford: Oxford University Press, 1925.

Giem, Paul. "Sabbaton in Col 2:16." *Andrews University Seminary Studies* 19 (1988): 195–210.

Gilat, Yitzhak D. "On Fasting on the Sabbath." *Tarbiz* 52 (1982): 1–15.

Ginsburg, Elliot K. *The Sabbath in the Classical Kabbalah.* Albany: State University of New York Press, 1989.

Ginzberg, Louis. *The Legends of the Jews.* 4 vols. Philadelphia: Jewish Publication Society of America, 1956.

Goldenberg, Robert. "The Jewish Sabbath in the Roman World up to the Time of Constantine the Great." In *Aufstieg und Niedergang der roemischen Welt: Geschichte und Kultur Roms im Spiegel der neueren Forschung.* Part 2, *Principat,* 19.1. Edited by H. Temporini and W. Hasse. New York: de Gruyter, 1989.

Goodenough, Erwin R. *An Introduction to Philo Judaeus.* New Haven: Yale University Press, 1940.

———. *By Light Light: The Mystic Gospel of Hellenistic Judaism.* New Haven: Yale University Press, 1935.

Grabbe, Lester L. "Synagogues in Pre-70 Palestine." *Journal of Theological Studies* 39 (1988): 101–10.

Grant, Michael. *The Jews in the Roman World.* New York: Scribner, 1973.

Green, A. "Sabbath as Temple: Some Thoughts on Space and Time in Judaism." In *Go and Study: Essays and Studies in Honor of A. Jospe,* edited by S. Fishman and R. Jospe, 67–91. Chicago: University of Chicago Press, 1983.

Grenfell, Bernard P., and Arthur S. Hunt, eds. *The Oxyrhynchus Papyri.* 65 vols. London: Clarendon Press, 1898–.

Gutmann, Joseph. *Ancient Synagogues: The State of Research.* Missoula, Mont.: Scholars Press, 1981.

Haenchen, Ernst. "Johanneische Probleme." *Zeitschrift fur Theologie und Kirche* 56 (1959): 1–54.

———. *Der Weg Jesu: Eine Erklaerung des Markusevangelium und der kanonischen Parallelen.* Berlin: Toepelmann, 1966.

Harrington, Daniel. *The Gospel of Matthew.* Sacra Pagina 1. Collegeville: Liturgical Press, 1991.

Harvey, Anthony E. *Jesus and the Constraints of History.* Philadelphia: Fortress Press, 1985.

Heinevetter, H.-J. *Das Hohelied als programmatische Komposition.* Bonner Biblische Beitraege 69. Frankfurt: Athenaeum, 1988.

Helfgott, Samson. "The Sabbath in the Classical Writers." DHL diss., Yeshiva University, 1974.

Hermans, Albert. "Le Pseudo-Barnabé est-il millenariste?" *Ephemerides theologicae lovanienses* 35 (1959): 849–76.

Herr, M. "The Problem of War on the Sabbath in the Second Temple and the Talmudic Periods." *Tarbiz* 30 (1960–61): 242–56.

Heschel, Abraham. *The Sabbath: Its Meaning for Modern Man.* New York: Farrar, Straus and Young, 1951.

Hoenig, Sidney. *The Great Sanhedrin: A Study of the Origin, Development, Composition, and Function of the Bet ha-Gadol during the Second Jewish Commonwealth.* Philadelphia: Dropsie College for Hebrew and Cognate Learning, 1953.

Hofius, Otfried. *Katapausis: Die Vorstellung vom endzeitlichen Ruheort im Hebraerbrief.* Wissenschaftliche Untersuchungen zum Neuen Testament 11. Tuebingen: Mohr, 1970.

Hooker, Morna D. *The Son of Man in Mark.* London: SPCK, 1967.

Horace. *Satires.* Translated by H. R. Fairclough. Loeb Classical Library, 1942.

Hoskyns, C. E. *The Fourth Gospel.* 2d ed. London: Faber and Faber, 1947.

Houle, J. "The Mystical Journey and the Garden Archetype in the Confessions of St. Augustine." *Studies in Formative Spirituality* 9 (1988): 63–77.

Howard, George. *Paul: Crisis in Galatia.* New Testament Studies Supplement Series 35. Cambridge: Cambridge University Press, 1979.

Hruby, K. "Le sabbat et sa célébration d'après les sources juives anciennes." *L'Orient Syrien* 8 (1963): 72–79.

Hultgren, Arland. *Jesus and His Adversaries.* Minneapolis, Minn.: Augsburg Press, 1979.

Hurst, L. D. "Eschatology and 'Platonism' in the Epistle to the Hebrews." *Society of Biblical Literature Seminar Papers.* Atlanta: Scholars Press, 1984.

Isser, Stanley J. *The Dositheans: A Samaritan Sect in Late Antiquity.* Studies in Judaism in Late Antiquity 17. Leiden: Brill, 1976.

James, M. R. *The Apocryphal New Testament.* Oxford: Clarendon Press, 1924.

Jastrow, Marcus. *A Dictionary of the Targumim, the Talmud Babli and Yerushalmi, and the Midrashic Literature.* 2 vols. New York: Putnam, 1886–1900.

Jeremias, Joachim. *Unknown Sayings of Jesus.* London: SPCK, 1958.

Jewett, Robert. "The Agitators and the Galatian Congregation." *New Testament Studies* 17 (1971): 198–212.

———. *Christian Tolerance: Paul's Message to the Modern Church.* Philadelphia: Westminster, 1982.

———. "The Law and the Coexistence of Jews and Gentiles in Romans." *Interpretation* 39 (1985): 341–56.

Johns, Alger F. "The Military Strategy of Sabbath Attacks on the Jews." *Vetus Testamentum* 13 (1963): 482–86.

Johnston, Robert M. "Patriarchs, Rabbis and Sabbath." *Andrews University Seminary Studies* 12 (1974): 94–102.

———. "The Rabbinic Sabbath." In *The Sabbath in Scripture and History*, edited by Kenneth A. Strand, 70–91. Washington: Review and Herald Publishing Association, 1982.

Josephus. Translated by H. St. J. Thackeray, R. Marcus, and L. H. Feldman. 9 vols. Loeb Classical Library, 1926–65.

Juster, Jean. *"Les juifs dans l' empire romain: leur condition juridique, économique et sociale.* 2 vols. Paris: P. Geuthner, 1914.

Justinus Cornelius Nepos and Eutropius. Translated by J. S. Watson. London: George Bell and Sons, 1902.

Juvenal. *Satires.* Translated by G. G. Ramsay. Loeb Classical Library, 1950.

Karris, Robert J. "Romans 14,1–15,13 and the Occasion of Romans." In *The Romans Debate,* edited by K. F. Donfried, 75–99. Minneapolis, Minn.: Fortress Press, 1977.

Kaesemann, Ernst. *Commentary on Romans.* Translated and edited by G. W. Bromiley. Grand Rapids, Mich.: Eerdmans, 1980.

———. *Das wandernde Gottesvolk: Eine Untersuchung zum Hebraerbrief.* Forschungen zur Religion und Literatur des Alten und Neuen Testaments 55. Goettingen: Vandenhoeck and Ruprecht, 1939.

Kee, Howard C. *The Community of the New Age.* Philadelphia: Westminster Press, 1977.

Keel, O. *Das Hohelied.* Zurich: Theologischer Verlag, 1986.

Kelber, Werner. *Mark's Story of Jesus.* Philadelphia: Fortress Press, 1979.

Kimbrough, S. T. Jr. "The Concept of Sabbath at Qumran." *Revue biblique* 5 (1966): 483–502.

Kippenberg, Hans G. *Garizim und Synagogue: Traditionsgeschichtliche Untersuchungen zur samaritanschen Religion der arameische Periode.* Religionsgeschichtliche Versuche und Vorarbeiten 30. Berlin: de Gruyter, 1971.

Kittel, G., and G. Friedrich, eds. *Theological Dictionary of the New Testament.* Translated by G. W. Bromiley. 10 vols. Grand Rapids, Mich.: Eerdmans, 1964–76.

Knox, John. *Marcion and the New Testament.* Chicago: University of Chicago Press, 1942.

Koester, Helmut. *Introduction to the New Testament.* 2 vols. New York: de Gruyter, 1982.

Kraabel, A. Thomas. "New Evidence of the Samaritan Diaspora Has Been Found at Delos." *Biblical Archaeology* 47 (1984): 44–46.

Kristemaker, S. *The Psalm Citations in the Epistle to the Hebrews.* Amsterdam: Soes, 1961.

Lagrange, Marie-Josephe. *L'évangile selon Saint Luc.* Paris: Gabalda, 1948.

———. *Saint Paul épître aux galatas.* Paris: Gabalda, 1950.

Lambert, W. G., and A. R. Millard. *Atra-Hasis: The Babylonian Story of the Flood.* Oxford: Clarendon Press, 1969.

Landy, Francis. *Paradoxes of Paradise: Identity and Difference in the Song of Songs.* Sheffield: Almond Press, 1982.

Lauterback, Jacob Z. *Mekilta de-Rabbi Ishmael.* 3 vols. Schiff Library of Jewish Classics. Philadelphia: Jewish Publication Society of America, 1933–35.

———. "The Sabbath in Jewish Ritual and Folklore." In *Rabbinic Essays,* 437–70. Cincinnati: Hebrew Union College Press, 1951. Reprint, New York: KTAV, 1973.

Leenhardt, Franz J. *The Epistle to the Romans: A Commentary.* Translated by Harold Knight. London: Lutterworth, 1961.

Leon, H. J. *The Jews of Ancient Rome.* Philadelphia: Jewish Publication Society of America, 1960.

Levine, Lee I., ed. *Ancient Synagogues Revealed.* Jerusalem: Israel Exploration Society, 1981.

Lightfoot, R. H. *St. John's Gospel.* Oxford: Oxford University Press, 1956.

Lindars, Barnabas. *The Gospel of John.* London: Oliphants, 1972.

Lohmeyer, Ernst. *Das Evangelium des Markus.* 2d ed. Goettingen: Vandenhoeck and Ruprecht, 1963.

Lohse, Eduard. *Colossians and Philemon.* Translated by W. R. Poehlmann and R. J. Karris. Hermeneia. Philadelphia: Fortress Press, 1971.

———. "Jesu Worte ueber den Sabbat." In *Judentum, Urchristentum, Kirche,* edited by W. Eltester, 79–89. Beiheft zur Zeitschrift fur die neutestamentliche Wissenschaft und die Kunde der alteren Kirche 26. Berlin: Toepelmann, 1964.

Longenecker, Richard N. *Galatians.* Word Biblical Commentary 41. Waco, Tex.: Word, 1990.

Lowy S. "Some Aspects of Normative and Sectarian Interpretations of the Scriptures: The Contribution of the Judean Scrolls toward Systematization." *The Annals of Leeds University Oriental Society* 6 (1966–68): 98–1163.

Luhrmann, Dieter. *Der Brief an die Galater.* Zuricher Bibelkommentare. Zurich: Theologischer Verlag, 1978.

———. "Tage, Monate, Jahreszeiten, Jahre (Gal 4,10)." In *Werden und Wirken des Alten Testaments,* edited by R. Albertz. 428–45. Goettingen: Vandenhoeck and Ruprecht, 1980.

Luther, Martin. *Der Brief an die Roemer.* D. Martin Luther Werke 56. Weimar, 1938.

Maccoby, Hyman. *Early Rabbinic Writings.* Cambridge: Cambridge University Press, 1988.

MacDonald, Dennis R. *The Legend and the Apostle: The Battle for Paul in Story and Canon.* Philadelphia: Westminster Press, 1983.

Macdonald, John, ed. *Memar Marqah: The Teaching of Marqah.* 2 vols. Beihefte zur Zeitschrift fur die alttestamentliche Wissenschaft 84. Berlin: Toepelmann, 1963.

———. *The Samaritan Chronicle II: From Joshua to Nebuchadnezzar.* Beihefte zur Zeitschrift fur die alttestamentliche Wissenschaft 107. Berlin: Toepelmann, 1969.

———. *The Theology of the Samaritans.* London: SCM Press, 1964.

MacGregor, H. C., and A. Q. Morton. *The Structure of the Fourth Gospel.* London: Oliver and Boyd, 1961.

Marjanen, A. "Is Thomas a Gnostic Gospel?" In *Thomas at the Crossroads: Studies of the New Testament and Its World,* edited by R. Uro, 107–39. Edinburgh: T and T Clark, 1998.

Martial. *Epigrams.* Translated by D. R. Shackleton Bailey. 3 vols. Cambridge: Harvard University Press, 1993.

Martin, Troy. "Apostasy to Paganism: The Rhetorical Stasis of the Galatian Controversy." *Journal of Biblical Literature* 114 (1995): 437–61.

———. "But Let Everyone Discern the Body of Christ (Colossians 2:17)." *Journal of Biblical Literature* 114 (1995): 249–55.

———. *By Philosophy and Empty Deceit: Colossians as a Response to a Cynic Critique.* Journal for the Study of the New Testament Supplement Series 51. Sheffield: Sheffield Academic Press, 1996.

———. "Pagan and Judeo-Christian Time-Keeping Schemes in Gal. 4,10 and Col. 2,16." *New Testament Studies* 42 (1996): 105–19.

Martyn, J. Louis. "Christ, the Elements of the Cosmos, and the Law in Galatians." In *The Social World of the First Christians,* edited by L. M. White and O. L. Yarbrough, 20–45. Minneapolis, Minn.: Fortress Press, 1995.

———. *Galatians: A New Translation with Introduction and Commentary.* Anchor Bible 33A. New York: Doubleday, 1998.

———. *History and Theology in the Fourth Gospel.* New York: Harper, 1968.

Matera, Frank J. *Galatians.* Sacra Pagina 9. Wilmington: Glazier, 1992.

Maurer, C. "Steckt hinter Joh 5.17, ein Uebersetzungsfehler?" *Wort und Dienst* 5 (1957): 130–40.

McCullough, J. C. "Some Recent Developments in Research on the Epistle to the Hebrews." *Irish Biblical Studies* 2 (1980): 141–65; 3 (1981): 228–54.

McKay, Heather A. *Sabbath and Synagogue: The Question of Sabbath Worship in Ancient Judaism.* Etudes préliminaires aux religions orientales 122. Leiden: Brill, 1994.

McKinnon, James. "The Exclusion of Musical Instruments from the Ancient Synagogue." *Proceedings of the Royal Musical Association* 106 (1979–80): 77–87.

———. "On the Question of Psalmody in the Ancient Synagogue." *Early Music History* 6 (1986): 159–91.

Meeks, Wayne A. "Judgment and the Brother: Romans 14,1–15,13." In *Tradition and Interpretation in the New Testament: Essays in Honor of E. Earle Ellis,* edited by G. E. Hawthorne with O. Betz. 290–300. Grand Rapids, Mich.: Eerdmans, 1987.

———. "The Man from Heaven in Johannine Sectarianism." *Journal of Biblical Literature* 91 (1972): 44–72.

———. *The Origins of Christian Morality.* New Haven: Yale University Press, 1993.

Meleager. *The Greek Anthology.* Translated by W. R. Paton. 2 vols. Loeb Classical Library, 1916.

Mendelson, Alan. *Philo's Jewish Identity.* Brown Judaic Studies 61. Atlanta: Scholars Press, 1988.

———. *Secular Education in Philo of Alexandria.* Hebrew Union College Monographs 7. Cincinnati: Hebrew Union College Press, 1982.

Michael, J. H. "The Jewish Sabbath in the Latin Classical Writers." *American Journal of Semitic Languages and Literature* 40 (1924): 117–24.

Miles, Margaret R. "Infancy, Parenting and Nourishment in Augustine's Confessions." *Journal of the American Academy of Religion* 50 (1982): 349–64.

Moehring, Horst. "Arithmology as an Exegetical Tool in the Writings of Philo of Alexandria." *Society of Biblical Literature Seminar Papers* 13, no. 1 (1978): 191–227.

Montgomery, James A. *The Samaritans, The Earliest Jewish Sect: Their History, Theology and Literature.* Philadelphia: J. C. Winston Press, 1907. Reprint, New York: KTAV, 1968.

Moo, Douglas J. *The Epistle to the Romans.* New International Biblical Commentary on the New Testament. Grand Rapids, Mich.: Eerdmans, 1996.

Moore, George Foote. *Judaism in the First Centuries of the Christian Era: The Age of the Tannaim.* 2 vols. Cambridge: Harvard University Press, 1927.

Moule, H. C. G. *The Epistle of St. Paul to the Romans.* 9th ed. London: Hodder and Stoughton, 1893.

Nemoy, Leon. "Al Quirquisani's Account of the Jewish Sects and Christianity." A translation of "Book of Lights and Watch-Towers." *Hebrew Union College Annual* 7 (1930): 317–97.

Neubauer, Adolf. *La géographie du Talmud.* Paris, 1868. Reprint, Hildesheim: G. Olms, 1967.

Newsom, Carol. *Songs of the Sabbath Sacrifices: A Critical Edition*. Atlanta: Scholars Press, 1985.

Neyrey, Jerome. *Paul in Other Words: A Cultural Reading of His Letters*. Louisville, Ky.: John Knox Press, 1990.

Nikiprovetzky, Valentin. "Problèmes du 'Récit de la création' chez Philon d'Alexandrie." *Revue des études juives* 124 (1965): 271–306.

Nineham, Dennis E. *The Gospel of St. Mark*. Baltimore, Md.: Penguin, 1963.

North, Robert J. "Maccabean Sabbath Years." *Biblica* 34 (1953): 501–15.

O'Day, Gail R. *Revelation in the Fourth Gospel: Narrative Mode and Theological Claim*. Philadelphia: Fortress Press, 1986.

Origen. *On First Principles*. Translated by G. W. Butterworth. Gloucester, Mass.: P. Smith, 1973.

Ovid. *The Art of Love*. Translated by J. H. Mosley. Loeb Classical Library, 1962.

Pagels, Elaine. "Exegesis of Genesis 1 in the Gospels of Thomas and John." *Journal of Biblical Literature* 118 (1999): 477–96.

Patterson, Stephen. "The Gospel of Thomas within the Development of Early Christianity." Ph.D. diss., Claremont Graduate School, 1988.

Pearson, Birger A. *Gnosticism, Judaism and Egyptian Christianity*. Minneapolis, Minn.: Fortress Press, 1990.

———. "Pre-Valentinian Gnosticism in Alexandria." In *The Future of Early Christianity: Essays in Honor of Helmut Koester,* edited by Birger A. Pearson with A. Thomas Kraabel, George W. E. Nickelsburg, Norman R. Petersen, 455–66. Minneapolis, Minn.: Fortress Press, 1991.

Persius. *Satires*. Translated by G. G. Ramsay. Loeb Classical Library, 1950.

Petronius. *Satyricon*. Translated by Michael Heseltine. Loeb Classical Library, 1939.

Philo. Translated by F. H. Colson, G. H. Whitaker, and R. Marcus. 12 vols. Loeb Classical Library, 1929–61.

Pliny, The Elder. *The Natural History*. Translated by H. Rackham and D. E. Eichholz. 2 vols. Loeb Classical Library, 1958–62.

Plutarch. *Moralia*. Translated by F. C. Babbitt. 2 vols. Loeb Classical Library, 1928.

Pokorny, Petr. *Der Brief des Paulus an die Kolosser*. Theologischer Handkommentar zum Neuen Testament 10. Berlin: Evangelische Verlagsanstalt, 1987.

Porten, Bezalel. "The Religion of the Jews of Elephantine in Light of the Hermopolis Papyri." *Journal of Near Eastern Studies* 28 (1969): 116–21.

Purvis, James D. "The Samaritan Problem: A Case Study in Jewish Sectarianism in the Roman Era." In *Traditions in Transformation: Turning Points in Biblical Faith,* edited by B. Halpern and J. D. Levenson. 323–50. Winona Lake: Eisenbaums, 1981.

Quispel, Giles. "Ezekiel 1:26 in Jewish Mysticism and Gnosis," *Vigiliae christianae* 34 (1980): 1–13

———. "Der gnostische *Anthropos* und die juedische Tradition." *Eranos-Jahrbuch* 22 (1953): 195–234.

Rad, Gerhard von. "There Remains a Rest for the People of God: An Investigation of a Biblical Conception." In *The Problem of the Hexateuch and Other Essays.* Translated by E. W. Trueman Dicken, 94–102. New York: McGraw-Hill, 1966.

Radin, Max. *The Jews among the Greeks and Romans.* Philadelphia: Jewish Publication Society of America, 1915.

Rajak, Tessa. "Jewish Rights in the Greek Cities under Roman Rule." In *Judaism and Its Graeco-Roman Context.* Edited by W. S. Green. Vol. 5, *Approaches to Ancient Judaism.* South Florida Studies in the History of Judaism. Atlanta: Scholars Press, 1985.

Rauer, Max. *Die 'Schwachen' im Korinth und Rom nach den Paulusbriefen.* Biblische Studien 21. Freiburg: Herder, 1923.

Reasoner, Mark. *The Strong and the Weak: Romans 14.1–15.13 in Context.* Society for New Testament Studies Monograph Series 103. Cambridge: Cambridge University Press, 1999.

Reid, Richard. "The Use of the Old Testament in the Epistle to the Hebrews." Th.D. diss., Union Theological Seminary, New York, 1964.

Richard, Earl. *The Gnostic Gospel of Thomas: A Lost, Secret Vision of Jesus.* Yamauchi Lectures in Religion. New Orleans: Loyola University, 1993.

Riesenfeld, Harald. "Sabbat et jour du Seigneur." In *New Testament Essays in Memory of T. W. Manson,* edited by A. J. B. Higgins, 210–17. Manchester: Manchester University Press, 1959.

Robbins, F. E. "Arithmetic in Philo Judaeus." *Classical Philology* 26 (1931): 345–61.

Robinson, John A. T. *Wrestling with Romans.* London: SCM Press, 1979.

Roloff, Jurgen. *Das Kerygma und der irdische Jesu: Historische Motive in den Jesus-Erzaehlungen der Evangelien.* Goettingen: Vandenhoeck and Ruprecht, 1970.

Rordorf, Willi. *Sunday: The History of the Day of Rest and Worship in the Earliest Centuries of the Christian Church.* Translated by A. A. K. Graham. Philadelphia: Westminster Press, 1968.

Rosenthal, Franz, ed. *An Aramaic Handbook: Porta Linguarum Orientalium.* Wiesbaden: Harossowitz, 1967.

Runia, David T. *Philo of Alexandria and the* Timaeus *of Plato.* Leiden: Brill, 1986.

Safrai, Shemuel. "The Temple." In *The Jewsih People in the First Century: Historical Geography, Political History, Social, Cultural and Religious Life and*

Institutions, edited by Safrai and M. Stern in cooperation with D. Flusser and W. C. van Unnik. Vol. 2. Compendia rerum Iudaicarum ad Novum Testamentum, section I. Assen: van Gorcum, 1974–76.

Sanday, W., and A. C. Headlam. *A Critical and Exegetical Commentary on the Epistle to the Romans.* Edinburgh: T. and T. Clark, 1895.

Sanders, Edward P. *Judaism: Practice and Belief, 63 BCE–66 CE* Philadelphia: Trinity Press International, 1992.

———. *Jewish Law from Jesus to the Mishnah.* Philadelphia: Fortress Press, 1990.

———. *Paul.* Oxford: Oxford University Press, 1991.

Sanders, James A. "From Isaiah 61 to Luke 4." In *Christianity, Judaism and Other Greco-Roman Cults,* edited by Jacob Neusner. Vol. 1. Studies in Judaism in Late Antiquity 12. Leiden: Brill, 1975.

Saulnier, Christiane. "Lois romaines sur les juifs selon Flavius Josèphe." *Revue biblique* 88 (1981): 161–98.

Schiffman, Lawrence. "Merkavah Speculation at Qumran: The 4qSerekh Shirot ᶜOlat ha-Shabbat." In *Mystics, Philosophers and Politicians: Essays in Jewish Intellectual History in Honor of Alexander Altmann,* edited by J. Reinharz and D. Swetchinski, 15–47. Durham, N.C.: Duke University Press, 1982.

Schlier, Heinrich. *Der Brief an die Galater.* Kritisch-exegetischer Kommentar ueber das Neue Testament 7. Goettingen: Vandenhoeck and Ruprecht, 1949.

———. *Der Roemerbrief.* Herders theologischer Kommentar zum Neuen Testament 6. Freiburg: Herder, 1977.

Schnackenburg, Rudolf. *The Gospel according to St. John.* Translated by K. Smyth. 3 vols. New York: Herder and Herder, 1968–82.

Schulz, S. *Die Stunde der Botschaft: Einfuehrung in die Theologie der vier Evangelisten.* Hamburg: Furche, 1967.

Schurer, Emil, G. Vermes, and F. Millar. *The History of the Jewish People in the Age of Jesus Christ.* Edinburgh: T. and T. Clark, 1973.

Schwartz, D. R. "Philonic Anonyms of the Roman and the Nazi Periods: Two Suggestions." *Studia Philonica* 1 (1989): 63–69.

Schweizer, Eduard. "Christianity of the Circumcised and Judaism of the Uncircumcised: The Background of Matthew and Colossians." In *Jews, Greeks and Christians: Religious Cultures in Late Antiquity,* edited by R. Hamerton-Kelly and R. Scraggs, 245–60. Studies in Judaism in Late Antiquity 21. Leiden: Brill, 1976.

———. *Good News according to Mark.* Richmond: John Knox Press, 1970.

———. *The Letter to the Colossians.* Minneapolis, Minn.: Fortress Press, 1982.

———. "Slaves of the Elements and Worshipers of Angels: Gal 4:3 and Col 2:8,18,20." *Journal of Biblical Literature* 107 (1988): 455–68.

Segal, Alan F. *Paul the Convert: The Apostolate and Apostacy of Paul the Pharisee.* New Haven: Yale University Press, 1990.

Seneca. *Moral Essays.* Translated by John W. Basore. 3 vols. Loeb Classical Library, 1928, 1935, 1951.

Smith, J. A. "The Ancient Synagogue, The Early Church and Singing." *Music and Letters* 65 (1984): 1–16.

———. "First Century Christian Singing and Its Relationship to Contemporary Jewish Religious Songs." *Music and Letters* 75 (1994): 1–15.

Spitta, Friedrich. *Das Johannes-Evangelium als Quelle der Geschichte Jesus.* Goettingen: Vandenhoeck and Ruprecht, 1910.

Staehle, K. *Die Zahlenmystik bei Philon von Alexandreia.* Leipzig: Tuebner, 1931.

Stauffer, E. "Neue Wege der Jesusforschung." In *Gottes ist der Orient,* 161–86. Berlin: Evangelische Verlagsanstalt, 1959.

Strachan, R. H. *The Fourth Gospel: Its Significance and Environment.* 3d ed. London: SCM Press, 1941.

Suchocki, M. "The Symbolic Structure of Augustine's Confessions." *Journal of the American Academy of Religion* 50 (1982): 365–78.

Suetonius, *The Lives of the Caesars.* Translated by J. C. Rolfe. 2 vols. Loeb Classical Library. Rev. ed., 1997.

Sylva, Dennis. "Nicodemus and his Spices (John 19.39)." *New Testament Studies* 34 (1988): 148–51.

Tabor, James. *Things Unutterable: Paul's Ascent to Paradise in Its Greco-Roman, Judaic, and Early Christian Contexts.* Lanham: University Press of America, 1986.

Tacitus. *The Histories.* Translated by Clifford H. Moore. 2 vols. Cambridge: Harvard University Press, 1937.

Talmon, Shemaryahu. *The World of Qumran from Within.* Jerusalem: Magnes Press, 1989.

———. "The Community of the Renewed Covenant: Between Judaism and Christianity." In *The Community of the Renewed Covenant: The Notre Dame Symposium on the Dead Sea Scrolls.* Edited by Eugene Ulrich and James VanderKam, 1–23. Notre Dame: Notre Dame University Press, 1994.

Tarazi, Paul N. *Galatians: A Commentary.* Crestwood, N.Y.: St. Vladimir's Seminary Press, 1994.

Taylor, Vincent. *The Gospel according to Mark.* London: Macmillan, 1959.

Tcherikover, Victor A., ed. *Corpus Papyrorum Judaicarum.* 3 vols. Cambridge: Cambridge University Press, 1957–64.

Terian, Abraham. "A Philonic Fragment on the Decad." In *Nourished with Peace: Studies in Hellenistic Judaism in Memory of Samuel Sandmel,* edited by F. E.

Greenspahn, E. Hilgert, and B. L. Mack, 173–82. Chico, Calif.: Scholars Press, 1984.

Thackeray, Henry St. John. *Josephus: The Man and the Historian.* 1929. Reprint, New York: KTAV, 1967.

Theissen, Gerd. *The Miracle Stories of the Early Christian Tradition.* Translated by Francis McDonagh. Philadelphia: Fortress Press, 1983.

———. *The Religion of the Earliest Churches: Creating a Symbolic World.* Translated by John Bowden. Minneapolis, Minn.: Fortress Press, 1999.

———. *Untersuchungen zum Hebraerbrief.* Studien zum Neuen Testament 2. Guetersloh: Mohn, 1969.

Thiering, Barbara. "The Biblical Source of Qumran Ascetism." *Journal of Biblical Literature* 93 (1974): 429–44.

Thompson, James W. *The Beginnings of Christian Philosophy: The Epistle to the Hebrews.* Catholic Biblical Quarterly Monograph Series 13. Washington: Catholic Biblical Association, 1982.

Thompson, Michael. *Clothed with Christ: The Example and Teaching of Jesus in Rome 12.1–15.13.* Journal for the Study of the New Testament: Supplement Series 59. Sheffield: Sheffield Academic Press, 1991.

Tomson, Peter J. *Paul and the Jewish Law: Halakha in the Letters of the Apostle to the Gentiles.* Compendia rerum iudaicarum ad Novum Testamentum 3. Minneapolis, Minn.: Fortress Press, 1990.

VanderKam, James. *Calendars in the Dead Sea Scrolls: Measuring Time.* New York: Routledge, 1998.

———. "2 Maccabees 6, 7a and Calendrical Change in Jerusalem." *Journal for the Study of Judaism* 12 (1981): 52–74.

Vermes, Geza. *Jesus the Jew.* New York: Macmillan, 1973.

Vielhauer, Philipp. "Gesetzesdienst und Stoicheiadienst im Galaterbrief." In *Oikodome: Aufsaetze zum Neuen Testament,* edited by G. Klein, 183–95. Theologische Buecherei 65. Munich: Kaiser Verlag, 1979.

Vilmar, Eduardus. *Abu ᶜl-Fath b. Abi ᶜl-Hasan' aṣ-Sâmiri, Annales samaritani quos fidem codicum manuscriptorum Berolinensium, Bodlejani, Parisini, edidit et prolegomenis insturxit Eduardus Vilmar.* Gotha: F. A. Perthes, 1865.

Wacholder, Ben Zion. "The Calendar of Sabbath Cycles during the Second Temple and the Early Rabbinic Period." *Hebrew Union College Annual* 44 (1973): 153–96.

———. "The Calendar of Sabbath Years during the Second Temple Era: A Response." *Hebrew Union College Annual* 54 (1983): 123–33.

Walter, Nikolaus. *Der Toraausleger Aristobulus.* Texte und Untersuchungen 86. Berlin: de Gruyter, 1964.

Watson, Francis. *Paul, Judaism and the Gentiles: A Sociological Approach.* Society for New Testament Studies Monograph Series 56. Cambridge: Cambridge University Press, 1986.

Wedel, G. *Kitâb aṭ-Ṭabbâh des Samaritaners Abu ᶜl-Hasan aṣ-Sûri. Kritische Edition und kommentierte Uebersetzung des ersten Teils.* Ph.D. diss., Berlin, 1987.

Weiss, Herold. "Footwashing in the Johannine Community." *Novum Testamentum* 21 (1979): 298–325.

———. "The Law in the Letter to the Colossians." *Catholic Biblical Quarterly* 34 (1972): 294–314.

———. "Paul and the Judging of Days." *Zeitschrift fur die neutestamentliche Wissenschaft und die Kunde der alteren Kirche* 86 (1995): 137–53.

———. *Paul of Tarsus: His Gospel and Life.* Rev. ed. Berrien Springs: Andrews University Press, 1989.

———. "Philo on the Sabbath." In *Heirs of the Septruaging: Philo, Hellenistic Judaism and Early Christianity,* edited by D. Runia, D. Hay, and D. Winston, 83–105. Studia Philonica Annual 3. Atlanta: Scholars Press, 1991.

———. "The Sabbath among the Samaritans." *Journal for the Study of Judaism* 25 (1994): 252–73.

———. "The Sabbath in the Fourth Gospel." *Journal of Biblical Literature* 110 (1991): 311–21.

———. "The Sabbath in the Pauline Corpus." In *Wisdom and Logos: Studies in Jewish Thought in Honor of David Winston,* edited by D. Runia and G. Sterling, 287–315. Studia Philonica Annual 9. Atlanta: Scholars Press, 1997.

———. "The Sabbath in the Synoptic Gospels." *Journal for the Study of the New Testament* 38 (1990): 13–27. Reprint, in *New Testament Backgrounds: A Sheffield Reader,* edited by Craig A. Evans and Stanley E. Porter, 109–23. Sheffield: Sheffield Academic Press, 1997.

———. "The Sabbath in the Writings of Josephus." *Journal for the Study of Judaism* 29 (1998): 363–90.

———. "*Sabbatismos* in the Epistle to the Hebrews." *Catholic Biblical Quarterly* 58 (1996): 674–89.

White, L. Michael. *Building God's House in the Roman World: Architectural Adaptation among Pagans, Jews, and Christians.* Baltimore, Md.: Johns Hopkins University Press, 1990.

Wilckens, U. *Der Brief an die Roemer.* 3 vols. Evangelisch-Katholischer Kommentar zum Neuen Testament 6. Zurich: Benzinger, 1978.

Williams, Michael. *Rethinking Gnosticism: An Argument for Dismantling a Dubious Category.* Princeton: Princeton University Press, 1996.

Williamson, Ronald. *Jews in the Hellenistic World: Philo.* Cambridge: Cambridge University Press, 1989.

Willis, Wendell L. *Idol Meat at Corinth: The Pauline Argument in 1 Cor 8 and*

10. Society of Biblical Literature Dissertation Series 68. Atlanta: Scholars Press, 1985.

Wink, Walter. *Naming the Powers.* Philadelphia: Fortress Press, 1984.

Witkamp, L. T. "The Use of Tradition in John 5:1–18." *Journal for the Study of the New Testament* 25 (1985): 19–47.

Wojciechowski, M. "La source de Jean 13.1–20." *Novum Testamentum* 34 (1988): 135–41.

Wolfson, Harry A. *Philo: Foundations of Religious Philosophy in Judaism, Christianity and Islam.* 2 vols. Cambridge: Harvard University Press, 1947.

Xenophon. *Oeconomicus.* Translated by E. C. Marchant. Loeb Classical Library, 1938.

Yang, Yong-Eui. *Jesus and the Sabbath in Matthew's Gospel.* Journal for the Study of the New Testament Supplement Series 139. Sheffield: Sheffield Academic Press, 1997.

Yeo, Khiok-Khng. *What Has Jerusalem to Do with Beijing? Biblical Interpretation from a Chinese Perspective.* Harrisburg: Trinity Press International, 1998.

Zeitlin, Solomon. "The Takkanot of Erubim. A Study in the Development of the Halakah." *Jewish Quarterly Review* 41 (1951–52): 351–61.

Ziesler, J. A. *The Epistle to the Galatians.* London: Epworth, 1992.

———. *Paul's Letter to the Romans.* Philadelphia: Fortress Press, 1989.

Index of Biblical References

Index of Ancient Texts

Index of Names and Subjects

Lagrange, M.-J., 125, 127, 130
Levi, Rabbi. *See* Rabbi Levi
Lindars, Barnabas, 99
Logos, 58
Lohse, Eduard, 32, 87, 96, 97, 102
Longenecker, Richard N., 114, 115
Luhrmann, Dieter, 119, 120
Luther, Martin, 125

Maccoby, Hyman, 87
Maimonides, 29
manna, 36, 45, 46, 56, 165, 193n. 40
Marcion, 142
Marqah, 58
Martin, Troy, 114, 134, 135
Martyn, J. Louis, 99, 117
martyrdom, 72, 73, 168
Matera, Frank F., 114
Mattathias, 73
McCullough, J.C., 147
Meeks, Wayne A., 122, 128
Meier, Rabbi. *See* Rabbi Meier
Mekilta, Shabbat, 15
Mendelson, Alan, 32, 35
merkabah, 133
Metilius, 79
midrash, 28
millennium. *See* cosmic week schemas
Mishnah, 2, 13, 23, 25, 29, 167
Mithridates, 76
Montgomery, James A., 52
Moses, excellence of, 12, 160, 169, 199n. 24
Moses/Jesus contrast, 149
Moule, H. C. G., 125
Mount Gerizim, 2, 52
muktzeh, 20

Neo-Pythagoreanism, 133, 134
Nicholas of Damascus, 67, 76, 79
Nicodemus, 109
numerology, 41–45, 60

Origen, 17, 53

parousia, 141, 171, 173, 179
Paul: advice to Romans, 129; the Jew, 119; traditional portrait of, 146
pax romana, 85
perennial Sabbath, 30, 104, 107, 126, 161, 174, 176
perfection, 119, 139, 140, 142, 144–45, 172,
permissible activity, 23, 164
Philo, 2, 12, 15, 24, 30, 51, 59, 60, 70, 106, 119, 141, 147, 148, 164, 165, 168, 169, 173; birthday of the world, 45, 50; on contemplation, 47; on equality, 48; evidential sign of creation, 45; on forbidden activity, 34; on freedom, 37; on man gathering wood, 35, 55; on Motherless and Virgin, 45, 46, 47, 165; on peace and learning, 44, 50; on the symbolists, 33, 49, 141, 164, 165; on the significance of number seven, 41–45; on the use of servants, 36–37; relation of observance to meaning, 33–34, 49; like relation of body to soul, 37–38, 49, 166; on universality, 45, 50
platonism, 138, 147
pleroma, 139, 140, 147
Pliny the Elder, 83
plucking of grain, 91, 94